A Photo Index of the
Principal Participants in
Forging the Alliance

4. Ernest Bevin

5. Georges Bidault

6. Charles E. Bohlen

7. Henri Bonnet

12. Lewis W. Douglas

13. John Foster Dulles

14. Anthony Eden

15. General
Dwight D. Eisenhower

20. W. Averell Harriman

21. Sir Nicholas Henderson

22. Lord Ismay

23. Sir Gladwyn Jebb

28. John J. McCloy

29. General George Marshall

30. Jan Masaryk

31. Vyacheslav Molotov

36. Lester Pearson

37. President
Franklin D. Roosevelt

38. Dean Rusk

39. Robert Schuman

1. Dean G. Acheson

2. Konrad Adenauer

3. Clement Attlee

8. David K. E. Bruce

9. Winston Churchill

10. General Lucius Clay

11. Tom Connally

16. James V. Forrestal

17. Sir Oliver Franks

18. General Charles de Gaulle

19. General Alfred M. Gruenther

24. George F. Kennan

25. Halvard Lange

26. Louis St. Laurent

27. Robert A. Lovett

32. Jean Monnet

33. Field Marshal
Viscount Montgomery

34. Paul H. Nitze

35. René Pleven

40. Paul-Henri Spaak

41. Joseph Stalin

42. Harry S. Truman

43. Arthur H. Vandenberg

Forging the Alliance

Books by Don Cook

Forging the Alliance:
NATO, 1945–1950

Charles de Gaulle: A Biography
(1984)

Ten Men and History
(1981)

The War Lords: Eisenhower
(Essays edited by Field Marshal Lord Carver)
(1976)

Floodtide in Europe
(1965)

Forging the Alliance
NATO, 1945–1950

DON COOK

ARBOR HOUSE/WILLIAM MORROW
New York

The author wishes to express grateful appreciation
for constant professional assistance and support
from the Publications Department of the North Atlantic
Treaty Organization Information Directorate, and to
numerous old NATO hands, past and present, for
sharing recollections, guidance, and advice in the
research and preparation of this book.

Library of Congress Cataloging-in-Publication Data

Cook, Don, 1920–
    Forging the alliance.

    Bibliography: p.
    Includes index.
    1. North Atlantic Treaty Organization – History.
    2. Europe – History – 1945–   . 3. World politics –
    1945–1955   I. Title.
    UA646.3.C62   1989   355′.031′091821   88-34226
    ISBN 1-55710-043-8

Contents

ACKNOWLEDGMENTS TO END PAPER PHOTO INDEX

Photograph numbers 1, 14, 39 are reprinted by kind permission of Photographie Shape; 2, 4, 5, 8, 9, 10, 11, 13, 15, 16, 18, 19, 20, 21, 22, 23,

25, 29, 30, 33, 34, 35, 36, 37, 40, 42, of NATO; 3, 6, 11, 12, 17, 24, 27, 28, 38, 41, 43 of Popperfoto; 7 and 32 of Hulton Picture Company, and 31 of Camera Press, London.

Author's Note

From 1945 to 1950 a fundamental transformation took place in the traditional foreign policy of the United States – the most profound and important change in American history. For 150 years, from the days of the Founding Fathers to the end of the Second World War, that policy had rested firmly on George Washington's famous farewell admonition to his countrymen in 1796 to attend to their own affairs and avoid entangling alliances or involvement in the conflicts of Europe. Despite or even because of wars that twice took American soldiers across the Atlantic, Washington's watchword and warning were still in 1945 almost as sacred in American politics and foreign policy as the Constitution itself.

But in a maelstrom of events, diplomacy and politics in the most crowded and decisive peacetime years of this century, the United States was propelled, pushed and pulled step by step into abandonment of this traditional, historic isolationist inhibition. The process culminated in the signing of the North Atlantic Treaty on April 4, 1949, and the assignment of an American Supreme Allied Commander to Europe at the end of 1950. America joined permanently in an entangling military and political alliance with the nations of Western Europe.

Yet when the North Atlantic Treaty was unveiled after a year of secret diplomacy, it was almost a nonevent. Against the blur of so much fast-moving history, its negotiation and signing may well have seemed simple, logical and obvious steps for the United States to have taken in shouldering its postwar responsibilities of realpolitik. From the Truman Doctrine to the Marshall Plan to the NATO Treaty may now look like some seamless progression, some up escalator of history. But that was not at all the way it was or the way it happened.

In 1945, 1946 and 1947, neither President Harry S Truman, General George C. Marshall, James F. Byrnes, Dean Acheson, Senator Arthur H. Vandenberg nor anyone else in high government and political circles in the United States had the slightest thought or intention of taking America into a European alliance. The NATO treaty was far from any American initiative. The initiative and the constant diplomatic driving force behind the treaty came from Britain's great postwar foreign secretary, Ernest Bevin. Within the State Department and the Truman administration there were strong doubts and divisions for months about the wisdom or the necessity of an alliance with Europe, and above all about whether the United States Senate could ever be persuaded to give its consent to such an abandonment of history and transformation of American foreign policy.

The politics of negotiating with senators on an acceptable treaty text was as difficult as the diplomacy of negotiating with the European Allies, and the two had to go hand in hand. Everything was veiled in almost total secrecy at the time, but this allowed the diplomats to move forward carefully behind the scenes, below the surface, while postwar events in Europe – in particular the Berlin blockade – steadily propelled political and public acceptance in the United States of the wisdom and necessity of an entangling alliance to keep the peace.

For Ernest Bevin and the British, the North Atlantic Treaty was no less a major historic achievement and transformation of foreign policy – for it firmly committed the United States to a world role that Great Britain could no longer go on fulfilling, the role of an active and powerful arbiter of peace and freedom in Europe in particular and the world in general, the role that Britain had exercised and America had shielded behind for two centuries.

The events that brought about the birth of NATO in 1949 have long since faded, but NATO continues as the longest-standing alliance in all history. It is as fundamental to the foreign policies of its sixteen member states as democracy itself. It has kept the peace in Europe and provided a stable anchor for the rest of the world. It has enabled Europe to revive, grow and prosper in economic health beyond the wildest dreams of 1949.

Today, when the Soviet Union is going through its greatest period of change since the death of Lenin, NATO's purposes and its *raison d'être* of stability and peace remain as valid as they were when the treaty was signed in parlous times four decades ago.

L'Etang la Ville
France
1988

ONE

Victory and Illusions

Generals are often said to spend their time preparing to fight the previous war. So it was that President Franklin D. Roosevelt prepared with sustained and single-minded determination and great political skill during the Second World War to achieve the kind of peace that had eluded Woodrow Wilson in 1919 after World War I.

Once again it was to be a peace of idealism, not realpolitik. In place of Wilson's "world made safe for Democracy," and Fourteen Points, it would now be a world of the Atlantic Charter and the Four Freedoms – Freedom from Fear, Freedom from Want, Freedom of Speech and Freedom of Religion. In place of the old League of Nations with its empty palace on the shores of the Lake of Geneva, moribund in its brief life to a large degree because the United States had turned its back on Wilson's idealism and refused to join, there would now be a new United Nations Organization – in the words of the Tennyson ode, "the Parliament of Man, the Federation of the World."

In place of spheres of influence and the old European military politics of balance of power, precariously waiting to be tipped into conflict, peace this time would be based on universal harmony and understanding, all nations working together and the Great Powers united in a Security Council to squelch any would-be wrongdoers threatening war.

In place of nineteenth-century imperialism and colonialism there would be independence and freedom for subject states, trusteeships and tutelage under the United Nations for people aspiring to self-government around the globe. A world of free trade would replace the protectionism of the interwar years of economic depression. Instead of world finance dominated by private bankers of London and Wall Street, an International Monetary Fund would stabilize currencies and supervise free movement of money across foreign exchanges.

Under Roosevelt's drive in this postwar One World of peace and order, a World Bank would be created to lend capital on favorable terms and stimulate economic development in poorer lands, free of any political taint. International organizations were to multiply and flourish to look after food and agriculture, regulate civil aviation, direct economic and social cooperation, set rules and standards for health and labor, stimulate education, science and cultural activities around the world. Never in history had so much concentrated and detailed planning and wide diplomatic and political effort gone into preparing for peace while fighting a war, almost entirely on American initiative.

"The world of the 20th Century must be to a significant degree an American Century," proclaimed the publisher Henry R. Luce in a famous editorial in his *Life* magazine, which captured and idealized the mood of America as victory neared in 1945. For Henry A. Wallace, the ardent New Deal liberal who had been Roosevelt's third-term vice-president, it was simpler. He preferred to call it "The Century of the Common Man," and his war aim was "to make sure that everybody in the world has the privilege of drinking a quart of milk a day."

In missionary idealism, America's vision at the time of victory seemed limitless. Its cities and factories were booming, untouched by war. Its military power was spread around the globe. America's belief in its own virtues and idealism was unclouded and supreme. America, it seemed, had the means and the material to do with the world almost whatever it wished. Roosevelt's Wilsonian blueprint for world order and an idealistic peace was perfectly in tune with America's victory spirit. The diplomatic preparations had virtually been completed and the structure was ready to be put in place when the President died on April 12, 1945.

But victory and illusions have always gone hand in hand in history, whenever, wherever and for whatever purposes or causes wars have been fought. The peace that Roosevelt sought to create was built on illusions. In the beginning, there was the illusion of Great Power harmony that had been precariously sustained throughout the war from one conference to the next, all the way to Potsdam. It was an illusion to believe that having been forced into an unnatural alliance with the Soviet Union to fight a common German enemy, the United States and Great Britain could or would go on sharing with the Great Power of Communism the same ideals and objectives of peace. Given such a fundamental ideological schism in the world, it was an illusion to expect a new United Nations Organization to take over and succeed in managing peace where the League of Nations had failed.

Roosevelt had ignored almost entirely the fundamental problem of *security*, the foundation on which peace has always rested. He had concentrated on building structures and institutions to run a world in which goodwill and understanding would reign supreme. Roosevelt's expectation was that after a couple of years of military occupation of a defeated and dismembered Germany, the Great Powers would work out a peace treaty so the troops could go home, with something of the old European order restored in a more peaceful and stable form. Great Power accord was supposed to substitute for European security, and this was the most dangerous illusion of all.

Of course, America on its own enjoyed greater security at the end of the war than at any other time in its history. Its own navy was now all-powerful in command of vast expanses of the Atlantic and the Pacific, and the nation was the sole possessor of the terrifying new power of the atomic bomb. Nazi Germany had been wiped off the map, Japan had collapsed, the major nations of the world seemed dedicated to Roosevelt's concept of peace, and the last great war had probably been fought. Yet it was illusory and unwise to disregard the security problems of others, and place all bets on a nebulous world organization not yet formed.

For the reality was that a power vacuum had opened up in Europe under the guise of peace. German power had of course been obliterated. In its place, the Red Army had reached the Elbe River and had settled down in massive force across the heart of Europe. Facing the Russians were only the limited forces of a war-exhausted Great Britain, a handful of French divisions dependent on the United States for almost everything but manpower, and an American Army that began to melt away rapidly after May of 1945, redeployed for action in the Far East and otherwise restlessly anxious to get home now that the war in Europe was over. From the North Cape of Norway to the toe of the Italian boot, there was destruction everywhere, and nowhere was there anything that could be described as power. Governments-in-exile, after years of German occupation, had returned to the old capitals of Paris, Brussels, Oslo, The Hague, Copenhagen, Athens and were struggling simply to demonstrate that they could again govern. There was no government at all in Germany. In Rome a fragile administration was propped up by Allied occupation while the country debated what to do about its monarchy. In Vienna a handful of Social Democrats home from exile were trying bravely to re-create Austria. Just as the old balance of power in Europe could always be tipped or tilted, so this new power vacuum had to be filled. This was the simple realpolitik that both Churchill and Stalin understood.

Roosevelt was dead a month before the war in Europe ended, and the time of illusion did not last long. But what policies and actions would replace the illusions on which peace had been predicated and so much had been built? How would the reality of a Soviet threat be perceived and faced; how was the power vacuum to be filled and a balance restored? How would security be achieved to enable the United Nations peace to be kept? It would take four long and turbulent years for the United States to forge a new historic role in the security of Europe through the North Atlantic Treaty.

With the Red Army on the Elbe and victory won, the Soviet Union saw the twentieth century not as an American Century but a Communist Century. If Stalin lacked the atomic bomb or the material and economic means with which to spread Communist power, he had overwhelming, disciplined military might at his disposal and the sinister tentacles of his machinery of government reaching out from the Kremlin. To this was added the political power of the Communist parties throughout Europe, emerging from wartime underground fighting with their organizations and numbers greatly strengthened and Communist prestige higher in the old Western democracies than it had ever been. Stalin's postwar aim, as Lenin's had been in 1918, was not world order but world revolution. He was not about to submit Communist power to any restraints or vetoes piously handed down by some nebulous world body heavily weighted on the side of Western democracy and dominated by the United States. The power game would not be played by rules of restraint in a United Nations arena.

Of the Soviet attitude toward Roosevelt's concept of organizing for peace, George F. Kennan, then chargé d'affaires at the American Embassy in Moscow, told the State Department in September 1944, while preparatory work was in progress in Washington at the Dumbarton Oaks Conference on the draft of a United Nations Charter:

> Western conceptions of future collective security and international collaboration seem naïve and unreal to the Moscow eye. But if talking in unreal terms is the price of victory, why not? If the Western World needs Russian assurances of future collaboration as a condition of military support, why not? Once satisfied of the establishment of her power in Eastern and Central Europe, Russia would presumably not find too much difficulty in going through whatever motions are required for conformity with these strange western schemes for collaboration and preservation of peace. What dangers would such collaboration bring to a country already holding in its hands the tangible guarantees of its own security, while prestige would demand that Russia not be missing from any councils of world power.

So Stalin cynically played along with "these strange western schemes for collaboration and preservation of peace." Why not? With the war still on, he held the diplomatic advantage, and what had he to lose? Roosevelt could not allow his Wilsonian dream of the postwar world to go down the drain in the hour of victory. Nor could he risk a major breach of the alliance as the armies closed in on Hitler from the east and the west. Hence his reluctance at Yalta, and right up to his death, to go to the breaking point as Churchill was prepared to go with Stalin over Poland and its right to a democratic government. Hence his acceptance at Yalta of Stalin's demand for additional seats in the still-to-be-born United Nations Organization for the pseudo-republics of the Ukraine and Byelorussia. (Originally Stalin wanted separate seats and votes for all sixteen of his "socialist republics"!) While Roosevelt diligently solicited, negotiated and compromised to involve the Soviet Union in peace-keeping machinery that it would ignore and sabotage, Stalin continued in single-minded pursuit to use the wartime alliance to expand and consolidate his Communist empire.

Yet it was much more the *attitude* that Roosevelt adopted toward the Soviet Union as the war neared its end, rather than any of the specific decisions taken at Yalta, that continued to shape and drag at United States foreign policy in the early postwar years. Decisions in the end are usually a reflection of attitude rather than the kind of cold clinical judgments that political leaders and statesmen are supposed to show in the face of perceived realities. It usually takes longer to change an attitude than it does decisions.

As an example, the President had conceived somewhere along the line that he could get more out of Stalin by dealing with him alone, and that he should keep his distance from Churchill and not appear to be "ganging up" on the Soviet Union.

But this belief in his own powers of persuasion and compromise, in "babying Uncle Joe along," the techniques of charm and political manipulation that had made Roosevelt such an extraordinary success in American politics turned out to be his weakness in the power game, not his strength. In the opinion of Charles E. Bohlen, the Soviet specialist who interpreted for Roosevelt at Teheran and Yalta, the idea of distancing himself from Churchill "was a basic error stemming from Roosevelt's lack of understanding of the Bolsheviks, who expected and realized that Britain and the United States were bound to be much closer in their thinking than either could conceivably be with the Soviet Union. In his rather transparent attempt to dissociate himself from Churchill, the President was not fooling anybody, and probably aroused secret amusement in Stalin."

While maneuvering and compromising at Yalta to build his peacekeeping machinery, Roosevelt displayed an almost total indifference to problems of postwar Western security in Europe. He arrived rather grudgingly prepared to allocate the French an occupation zone in defeated Germany, but he still opposed allowing France a seat on the proposed Allied Control Council that would rule the dismembered German state, and Stalin agreed with him. In their tête-à-tête conversation alone before the meetings began, Roosevelt said that "he would tell the Marshal something indiscreet that he would not wish to say in front of the Prime Minister, namely that the British for two years have had the idea of artificially building up France into a strong power which would have some 200,000 troops on the eastern border of France to hold the line for a period required to assemble a strong British army – the British were a peculiar people and wished to have their cake and eat it too."

Having thus mocked his closest ally and more or less dismissed France as having no relevance to postwar European security, Roosevelt went on to tell both Stalin and Churchill at the conference table that he "did not believe that American troops would stay in Europe much more than two years. . . . He felt that he could obtain support in Congress and through-out the country for any reasonable measures designed to safeguard the future peace, but he did not believe that this would extend to the maintenance of an appreciable American force in Europe." Later the President amended this rather dangerous giveaway somewhat by adding that he had "current American attitudes in mind," and that if an international organization were set up along the lines of the Dumbarton Oaks proposals, then the American people "were much more likely to take part in world activity."

Stalin, in short, would not have to worry very much or for very long about a strong presence of American power on the continent of Europe!

In the face of this disheartening candor on the part of the President of the United States, it is little wonder that Churchill and his foreign secretary, Anthony Eden, fought back hard at Yalta to get Roosevelt to swallow his manifest dislike of General Charles de Gaulle, and finally obtain acceptance that France would play a full and equal role with the other three Great Powers in the occupation and administration of defeated Germany – "our nearest neighbor to Germany and the only ally of any strength on which Britain could count," in Churchill's summation. Eden had minuted more colorfully to the prime minister before Yalta: "We should not be left alone to share the cage with the bear."

Realpolitik was certainly on the minds of the British at Yalta. But it scarcely seemed to occur to Roosevelt as he sat with Stalin and Churchill that he might be attempting to build peace on a power vacuum, that there could be a new threat to the security and stability of Europe right at that table, that the security of Europe would affect the security of the United States as well, that America could not walk away and go home in a couple of years and leave peace-keeping in the hands of a United Nations Organization not yet even established.

And so the frail and fading President sailed home from Yalta, to declare in his last public speech to the American Congress, sitting in his wheelchair in the well of the House of Representatives on March 1, 1945:

> The Crimea Conference ought to spell the end of the system of unilateral action, the exclusive alliances, the spheres of influence, the balances of power and all the expedients that have been tried for centuries – and have always failed.

Far from an end, the Crimea Conference was the beginning of a new round of dangerous power plays in the heart of devastated Europe. But Roosevelt clung to his illusions to the very end. In the last message that he drafted to Churchill from Warm Springs only hours before he died, the President said:

> I would minimize the general Soviet problem as much as possible, because these problems in one form or another seem to arise every day and most of them straighten out. We must be firm, however, and our course thus far is correct.

He was responding to a Churchill cable sent on April 6, 1945, in which the prime minister asked whether "the brutality of Russian messages does not foreshadow some deep change of policy for which they are preparing," and urged that *"we should join hands with the Russian armies as far to the east as possible, and if circumstances allow enter Berlin."* (Italics added)

Churchill's message had concluded, in marked contrast to Roosevelt's attitude:

> I deem it of the highest importance that a firm and blunt stand should be taken at this juncture by our two countries in order that the air may be cleared and that they realize that there is a point beyond which we will not tolerate insult. I believe that this is the best chance of saving the future. If they are ever convinced that we are afraid of them and can be bullied into submission, then indeed I should despair of our future relations with them, and much else.

Roosevelt was in possession of the same facts as Churchill, as their voluminous and fascinating correspondence across six years of war amply shows. He was fully informed and aware of issues and complexities that were boiling up. But when it came to attitude, and the increasingly menacing tone of Soviet actions and dealings with Stalin in the closing stages of the war, Churchill was an activist ready for confrontation while Roosevelt was a politician who preferred patience to see things through to the next problem.

The President's overriding concern was that nothing be allowed to hinder or throw off course the creation of the new United Nations Organization to preside over peace. To achieve this crowning of Allied victory, Roosevelt certainly had the American people and world opinion solidly behind him. After six years of devastation and some thirty-two million human casualties, the world yearned for peace and order and an act of statesmanship and political leadership that would erase the failure of the League of Nations in the 1930s and give new hope to the second half of the century. Roosevelt had to succeed where Woodrow Wilson had failed. He was bending everything in politics and diplomacy to this great objective, and this meant ignoring or minimizing the onrushing difficulties and fundamental clash of ideology with the Soviet Union.

In any case, whatever the urging of Churchill, whatever the realities of the deterioration of Great Power relations, it had become impossible in the final months of the war and the early months of peace to face up to a showdown with Stalin over Poland or anything else. There was very wide popular support and sympathy for the Soviet Union in the United States and Britain, and the realities of what had begun to happen in the "liberated" lands of Eastern Europe did not filter through wartime censorship very much, or register very deeply in the awareness of people whose sole preoccupation was when the war would be over. Much that was going on was automatically excused in the face of all that the Russians had manifestly suffered at the hands of the Nazis, and the vast Soviet contribution to Allied victory. For the rest, it was part of the price of war. The great majority of people in the West *wanted* to believe in the illusion of Great Power harmony, and *wanted* their governments to have good relations with the Soviet Union to make peace work.

This produced an attitude and a state of mind in the West that Kennan sharply summarized in another lengthy dispatch to the State Department from Moscow in May 1945, shortly after VE Day:

It is entirely agreeable to Moscow that Americans should be indulged in a series of illusions which lead them to put pressures on their government to accomplish the impossible and to go always one step further in pursuit of the illusive favor of the Soviet Government. Getting along with the Russians is political capital of prime importance in both of the Anglo-Saxon countries, and no English or American politician can pass up any halfway adequate opportunity for claiming that he has been successful in gaining Russian confidence and committing the Russians to a more moderate course of action. If things at any time get hot, all the Russians have to do is allow another personal meeting with Western leaders, and thus make a fresh start with all forgotten.

This indeed was the pattern of relations with the Soviet Union that Harry S Truman inherited from Roosevelt, and tried to make work for two more years until by 1947 it had become so ragged and frayed that it was impossible to go on with the illusion any longer.

But in the meantime as the war neared an end, Roosevelt's great domestic apprehension was the latent strength of American isolationism, the forces that had wrecked Woodrow Wilson's peace in 1920. Roosevelt had shown this concern at Yalta when he told Stalin and Churchill that he did not believe American troops could be kept in Europe for more than two years or so. He knew that the cry to "bring the boys home" would swamp any suggestions he might make that America might need to go on shouldering overseas responsibilities to keep the United Nations peace. After all, in his third-term election campaign in 1940 he had pledged "again and again and again" that American boys would not be sent to fight in a foreign war, and the isolationists never allowed that ringing phrase to be forgotten. Now Roosevelt had to be wary of giving the isolationist rump any excuse to leap up and charge him all over again with "trying to involve us in another war." So he sought constantly to damp down problems and eruptions that might cloud the vision of a peaceful and democratic postwar world, the illusion that all would be well if America would now do its duty and join the United Nations, an illusion that the United States could then more or less retire to the sidelines and guide and influence solutions to the world's troubles from a safe and secure distance, the illusion that America's new interventionism could be limited to United Nations debate and speechmaking, not any exercise of military power.

It was good politics, but it was not realpolitik. Probably it was the best that Roosevelt could do under the political circumstances and given the tenor of the times, which his own aspirations had largely created. But it did not augur well for the security of Europe and the West.

The year of victory was a poor year in Anglo-American relations, a difficult year, often a sour year. The nearer the two Allies got to the end of the war, the less the alliance seemed to count any longer, at least in Washington. At working levels, the wartime momentum of military cooperation quickly began to slow down, except for the vital area of intelligence sharing. At higher levels there were growing divergencies on questions of military strategy in the closing days of the war, along with political-diplomatic differences over how to deal with the Soviet Union. The two governments were increasingly at odds, often to the point of open clashes, over plans and policies, aims and preparations for the postwar world, particularly in the economic field. Things never quite got out of hand or boiled over into any major breach or falling-out, largely because of the rather bitter forbearance of the British, who could not risk a broken partnership no matter how difficult things became. Under Churchill they had long accepted with relative good grace (but much skillful and dogged argument) the role of secondary partner after the United States entered the war, and in victory they were under no illusions about the danger of "being left alone to share the cage with the bear."

The British knew full well, better than the Americans, that they could no longer hold a European balance of power. The primary aim of British postwar policy, therefore, had to be to ensure that American power was not withdrawn from Europe. America would have to take up in Europe a role that Britain had played for nearly two centuries. The need, the necessity for the United States to maintain a postwar military commitment to Europe may seem simple and obvious now, but in 1945 it was far from clear or certain what America would do. America had won the war and the prevailing mood was to go home. Neo-isolationism was strong in America, and plenty of anti-British feeling was being stoked up again. All the British could do was sit tight and hope that a new sense of reality about the state of the world would soon prevail across the Atlantic.

The fact was that there had never been any true "special relationship" between the two countries until the beginning of that extraordinary secret correspondence in 1939 between Roosevelt and Churchill, which will long remain one of the great quarries of history of this century. But the previous 150 years had been marked not by any intimacy or much identity of interests, but by wars, disagreements, antipathy, confrontation, distrust and mistrust and just plain bad blood. Of course, most of this history was behind the two nations by the time the United States entered World War I. But residual feelings persisted and it took a long time for America to forget that it had once been a colony and Britain to forget that it was no longer a colonial ruler.

In the Depression years, in American schoolrooms before the war, I can well remember the maps on the walls of the geography classes that displayed the British Commonwealth and Empire printed in pink around the world – and it was vast, all controlled by that little island way up in the corner. The subliminal effect for American students was to set them to wondering whether all those pink areas might not be yearning for independence from Britain the way the United States had. And indeed, Franklin Roosevelt, in tune with American history and his own liberalism, had made one of his war aims an end to imperialism, independence for colonies. He was more restrained about this in his dealings with Churchill than he was with the French and General de Gaulle, but the goal was never far below the surface in his thinking and attitude. It was unfortunate that in this he also found himself closer to Stalin than to Churchill. Of course the prime minister brushed all this aside with his famous declaration: "I have not become the King's First Minister in order to preside over the liquidation of the British Empire." And in fact, the Roosevelt attitude put the United States in a pretty contradictory position with its ally, a position Americans failed to grasp. It was summarized by Charles E. Bohlen:

Here is an extraordinary twist of history. The American President morally opposed British imperialism, yet counted on the power of Great Britain – essentially powerful as the leader of a great Empire – as an equal democratic partner in the postwar world. I do not believe that Roosevelt thought of his anti-colonial attitude as a factor in Britain's decline. In fact, one of the most astounding features of the war and immediate postwar period was that literally no one in the American government foresaw the extent and rapidity of the decline of British power.

As the war progressed, the Roosevelt-Churchill correspondence lost none of its pace and volume, but from about the middle of 1943 Roosevelt can be seen to distance himself increasingly from the advice of his self-styled "Loyal Lieutenant," going his own way and leaving the prime minister to adjust and tag along. In the early stages of the war, the British view of Grand Strategy generally prevailed, in such matters as the decision to land in North Africa instead of attempting a cross-Channel attack in 1942. After that, not only did American power become dominant, but also American strategic direction and decision-making. In particular, Churchill's efforts to pursue a "soft underbelly" strategy and fight from Italy into the Balkans and up through Trieste to Austria and Central Europe were brushed aside in favor of the Normany landings in June of 1944.

In all of these arguments with Churchill, the Americans became increasingly dismissive of the old imperialist for trying to sell not a military strategy to win the war but a political strategy to preserve British interests in restoring the map of Europe. In a sense, of course, this was correct. But, the British would say, what's so wrong with a political strategy while fighting a war? That's what wars in Europe have always been about. That's why the British had fought on the Continent for 250 years, ever since the time of Marlborough, Churchill's great ancestor. Peace, Churchill well knew, would be shaped and determined by where the armies were when the fighting ended. But in American and West Point doctrine, the sole aim of strategy is rapid defeat of the enemy, not the aftermath of peace.

Historically, of course, Churchill was right. It would have been better to shake hands with the Russians as far to the east as possible. But that was not the way the Americans saw it in 1945. Churchill and the British, viewed through that prism of suspicion, were regarded as not only primarily concerned with "British interests," but in the process ready to risk an open clash with the Russians on the eve of European victory when America still counted on Soviet help to end the war with Japan.

This prism view was heightened, moreover, by the political atmosphere that developed in Western Europe as exiled governments moved from

London back to their home capitals, and domestic politics revived. Most of these governments were on the conservative side, and monarchist. But now the Communist parties everywhere began coming out from the wartime underground to take up the cudgels and bid for political power. The British were not embarrassed to use their political and military strength to stand by their democratic friends – even if this meant that they were also labeled as reactionaries and rightists, ready to support outdated prewar politicians against the aspirations of liberated Europe for a new dawn of social justice under the left.

In late 1944, soon after the liberation of Brussels, British troops were deployed on the streets around Parliament and other government buildings to protect the Belgian government against left-wing activists clashing with the police. An anti-British chorus was in full cry in the United States at this same time over the situation in Greece, where British troops were engaged in street battles not against the retreating Germans but against the Greek underground forces of ELAS, the Greek Communist party, seeking to seize power before the returned government-in-exile could establish control. Churchill and Eden flew to Athens at Christmas, with fighting still going on, to set up a cease-fire that saved the country from a Communist takeover. The best that Roosevelt could offer was a message to Churchill that said:

> As anxious as I am to be of the greatest help to you in this trying situation, there are limitations imposed in part by the traditional policies of the United States and in part by the mounting adverse reaction of public opinion in this country. I don't need to tell you how much I dislike this state of affairs as between you and me. My one hope is to see it rectified. . . .

This was not much help to the British. Ironically, the United States then had to plunge decisively into this same Greek imbroglio barely two years later, when Britain informed Washington that it could no longer go on holding the fort in Athens in the second round of civil war with the Communists.

As the war ended, Washington and London were increasingly at odds over postwar political and economic policies. At a conference held in Chicago late in 1944 to negotiate a new international agreement on civil aviation for postwar "freedom of the skies," they came close to an open break. With the British fighting hard for a more restrictive agreement than the Americans were prepared to accept, Roosevelt bluntly messaged Churchill:

> Our people have gone as far to meet yours as I can let them go. If the conference should end either in no agreement or in an agreement which the American people would regard as preventing the development and use of the great air routes, the repercussions would seriously affect many other things. We are doing our best to meet your lend-lease needs. We will face Congress on that subject in a few weeks, and it will not be in a generous mood if the people feel that the United Kingdom has not agreed to a generally beneficial air agreement. They will wonder about the chances of our two countries, let alone any others, working to keep the peace if we cannot even get together on an aviation agreement.

It did not take any reading between the lines for Churchill to see the threat and arm-twisting in this one. The American drive for the American Century was gaining momentum, and it was increasingly on a collision course against two centuries of British interests around the world.

At the Bretton Woods Conference to organize the postwar International Monetary Fund, a long battle was fought over rules that would force Britain to make the pound sterling a convertible currency when the war ended, and gradually dismantle the sterling-area currency bloc. On the trade front, Secretary of State Cordell Hull was an ardent free trader who believed that protectionism had been one of the causes of the war, and had made the elimination of British imperial-preference tariffs as much of a U.S. war aim as the breakup of the enemy German I. G. Farben chemical cartel. Seen defensively from London, these American postwar objectives constituted a direct attack on the war-decimated British economy and the power and influence of the British Empire. When the Labour government then took power in July of 1945, it held up ratification of the Bretton Woods agreement for many months, until in the end it was forced to give it parliamentary approval as part of the price England had to pay to obtain a major $4.4 billion postwar loan from the United States.

In this corroding transatlantic atmosphere, Roosevelt's death brought an abrupt end to the most special feature of the "special relationship." But history would not stand still, and soon Churchill was messaging President Harry S Truman with his concerns about Soviet behavior and the need to push the Allied armies to the east as far and as fast as possible. He did have one last success.

Just before VE Day he cabled Truman in almost frantic terms to urge that immediate orders be given for an Allied advance in Italy on the Adriatic port city of Trieste, to get there before the Yugoslav Army under Marshal Tito. Truman was quick to respond, sensing the importance of the city, but initially he hedged in a way that Churchill felt would be too restrictive to the operation.

After another rapid exchange, this was cleared up – but with a final injunction from Truman at the behest of his own military: "I wish to avoid having American forces used to fight Yugoslav forces or being used in combat in the Balkan political arena." So on Churchill's orders to Field Marshal Sir Harold Alexander, the Supreme Allied Commander in the Italian theatre, British forces, together with the New Zealand Division, headed rapidly for Trieste on their own, with a real risk of a clash with Tito's Communist troops when they got there. But they arrived first and in force, and it is thanks to Churchill's action that Trieste remains an Italian city today.

Truman, of course, reassured the world at the outset that he was dedicated to carrying forward Roosevelt's postwar policies. But his no-nonsense, down-to-earth, feisty nature did not allow for illusions for very long. However, with arrangements under way for a last "Big Three" conference in the Berlin suburb of Potsdam, he declined Churchill's overtures for a separate early meeting and stuck to the Roosevelt line of taking distance from the British so as not to "gang up" on Stalin. Instead, he sent Roosevelt's devoted aide, Harry Hopkins, on a last mission to Moscow, and to balance this he decided to send Joseph E. Davies, a former U.S. ambassador to Moscow, to London to see Churchill and ostensibly to explain the views and thinking of the new President. As an exercise in Anglo-American understanding, it was a disaster.

Joe Davies was probably the silliest ambassador America ever sent to Moscow, an ardent Russophile even while living in the Soviet Union during the Great Terror from 1936 to 1938, a man whose naïveté about Stalin and the Soviet system ranked with those of two other famous prewar pilgrims to the capital of Communism, George Bernard Shaw and Lady Nancy Astor. Now, in 1945 at Downing Street, when Churchill sought to deploy his warnings about what the Soviet Union was up to in the guise of peace, Davies records that he lectured the prime minister as follows:

> I said that frankly, as I had listened to him inveigh so violently against the threat of Soviet domination and the spread of Communism in Europe, and disclose such a lack of confidence in the professions of good faith in the Soviet leadership, I had wondered whether he, the Prime Minister, was now willing to declare to the world that he and Britain had made a mistake in not supporting Hitler, for as I understood him, he was now expressing the doctrine which Hitler and Goebbels had been proclaiming and reiterating for the past four years in an effort to break up Allied unity and "divide and conquer." Exactly the same conditions which he described and the same deductions were drawn from them as he now appeared to assert.

Davies then submitted a formal report to Truman: "The Prime Minister is a very great man, but there is no doubt that he is first, last and all the time a great Englishman – I could not escape the impression that he was basically more concerned over preserving England's position in Europe than in preserving peace."

When this reached the White House, Admiral William D. Leahy, chief of staff to Roosevelt and then Truman, passed it along to the new President with the approving comment: "This is consistent with our staff estimate of Churchill's attitude throughout the war." Churchill, not inclined to descend to stupid argument, merely messaged the President with concealed irony: "I had an agreeable talk with Mr. Davies which he will report to you when he returns."

Fortunately for history, Davies was of no importance. But unfortunately, in May of 1945 he *did* typify a certain state of mind in America and an attitude toward Britain that the British could scarcely ignore. Politics makes strange bedfellows, and at this period the American liberal left and isolationist right were in bizarre agreement that it was the British who were posing the real postwar problems for America.

When President Truman reached Potsdam in July of 1945 and held a first meeting with Churchill and then Stalin, he was face to face with reality rather than theory or illusions about what Great Power relations were all about. He was still going to do his best in the Roosevelt mode to find agreement with the Soviet Union. But he was still Harry Truman. The Potsdam agenda was stark indeed. Among the unresolvable issues were the question of Poland's new borders, Soviet demands for German reparations, the setting up of a German occupation administration, how to proceed on peace treaties, and new, surprising demands from Stalin for a Soviet military base on Turkish territory in the Straits of the Dardanelles and Soviet trusteeship over the former Italian colony of Tripolitania (now Libya) in North Africa at the center of the Mediterranean coast. The overall thrust of all these Potsdam arguments was clear. The Soviet Union was not going to be content merely with all that it had acquired in Europe where the victorious Red Army was now sitting, but was reaching out in the tradition of czarist imperialism to acquire more. The Cold War was already beginning.

It was at Potsdam that Churchill first used the phrase "iron curtain" (although the American minutes of the meeting noted him saying "iron fence"). He complained to Stalin that an "iron curtain" had come down around British representatives on the Allied Control Commission in Soviet-occupied Romania, to which Stalin simply snapped back: "All fairy tales."

Truman's firm and straightforward handling of his role in these largely abortive discussions impressed Churchill and the British. A new reality seemed to be taking hold in place of Roosevelt's more accommodating and compromising style. Then, on July 25, 1945, ballots were counted in the first British general election since 1936, and the British stunned themselves and the world by voting the great Churchill out of office.

The last page of the wartime "special relationship" was now closed. On Saturday, July 28, a new British prime minister arrived back in Potsdam – Clement R. Attlee, leader of the Labour party, accompanied by the new foreign secretary, Ernest Bevin, a massive, hulking, dominant figure whose life had been the British trade-union movement. The only thing the British seem to do in a hurry is change governments. But Attlee and Bevin were experienced men who had served with distinction in

Churchill's coalition War Cabinet, and both were fully aware of Britain's problems and the international scene.

The initial chemistry between the new British leaders and the Americans was not very good. To be sure, Churchill and Eden were a difficult act to follow, and Attlee and Bevin were not the easiest of men for the Americans to size up and understand. Attlee was taciturn and uncommunicative. Bevin, who now did most of the talking for the British, was combative, roughhewn, forceful and blunt in the colloquial accents of a British workingman – none of the Eden diplomatic polish in his speech. It was difficult to see in Attlee the well-hidden qualities of a strong and effective prime minister, and difficult to see in Bevin the qualities of wide-ranging intellect, diplomatic intuition, negotiating skills and common sense that made him the outstanding foreign secretary of this century.

Moreover, Bevin wasted no time plunging in at Potsdam to oppose the Soviet Union over a boundary settlement for Poland in what Secretary of State James F. Byrnes described as "a manner so aggressive that both the President and I wondered how we would get along with this new foreign secretary." Bevin also clashed with Byrnes over a tentative deal the Americans had worked out with the Russians on the complex and highly charged question of German reparations for the Soviet Union from the Western occupation zones. Byrnes had set this up without the British, while Churchill was absent from Potsdam awaiting the election count in London. It was not a smooth start with Attlee and Bevin.

Although Byrnes later came to voice "high regard" for Bevin, and probably meant it, Bevin in fact formed a distrust of Byrnes at the outset and this never basically improved. As a trade unionist, loyalty was a touchstone for Bevin, but he expected loyalty in return. In the words of Bevin's biographer, the historian Alan Bullock, "Byrnes had left the impression of being devious and quite prepared to do a deal with the Russians without taking the British into consultation, if the opportunity offered." Bullock goes on to say that after the Potsdam meeting "the British were left uneasily wondering whether, if a European settlement proved too hard to reach, the Americans might lose patience, and pull out as they had after 1918, leaving the British to make the best terms they could with the Russians." If this seems a little extreme, it nevertheless was real enough for Bevin at the time, and there was little that was reassuring in the general state of Anglo-American relations and Byrnes's tactics of lone diplomatic maneuvering in the ensuing months.

Moreover, a worse blow for Britain fell barely two weeks after the Potsdam Conference, when President Truman on his return to Washington abruptly canceled the entire program of wartime Lend-Lease without any warning or consultation with the British or anyone else.

Truman acknowledged in later years that his action had been a great mistake. At the time he told a news conference that "Congress defined Lend-Lease as a weapon of war, and after we ceased to be at war it is no longer necessary." In fact, he acted with undue haste, primarily out of fear of an isolationist backlash in Congress. But Japan had not yet surrendered and there would have been ample justification to continue military assistance to Britain, fighting with America in the Far East, and other Allies to meet unfinished war tasks of disarming the enemy, shipping prisoners of war back home, coping with occupation of enemy territory and policing and stabilizing conditions of peace. Lend-Lease could have been a useful instrument of American power in the transition to peace.

The Lend-Lease cutoff was a disaster for Britain – "an economic Dunkirk" in the words of the country's most prestigious economist, Lord Keynes. The Labour government immediately dispatched Keynes to Washington to explain the economic crisis the country was facing, and hopefully seek an interest-free loan with a target figure of $6 billion, an enormous sum in those times. But Keynes found the Washington atmosphere discouragingly cool. An interest-free loan was out of the question, and he was told that even getting approval out of Congress for a modest loan at low interest would be difficult. A Gallup poll showed 60 percent of Americans interviewed to be opposed to any help for Britain at all.

Moreover, anti-British feeling was now compounded by the Palestine situation, as the British fought to hold back Jewish immigration to the Zionist homeland – then indisputably Arab territory administered by Britain under an old League of Nations mandate. Stories and pictures of the Royal Navy intercepting cargo boats crammed with pathetic Jewish immigrants, remnants of the Nazi Holocaust, and British soldiers rounding up Jews as they managed to wade ashore on the Palestine beaches, did little to enhance Britain's image in the United States, whatever the wider dimensions of the Palestine problem.

In this atmosphere, the loan negotiations lasted from September to December 1945. In the words of Will Clayton, one of America's most successful cotton merchants, who was in charge of economic policy at the State Department at the time, the Truman administration set out to load the terms of the loan "with all the conditions the traffic would bear," and at one point the British nearly packed up and went home. For the Americans, it was a chance finally to force all those objectives of convertible currency and free trade, an end to the sterling area and imperial preferences, trade quotas and exchange controls and all the other economic measures the British had been using to keep afloat.

The chairman of Sears Roebuck wrote approvingly to Clayton: "If you succeed in doing away with the Empire Preferences and opening up the Empire to United States commerce, it may well be that we can afford to pay a couple of billion dollars for the privilege."

In the end Britain had to agree to a loan of $4.4 billion for fifty years at 2 percent interest, and will be repaying Washington almost to the end of this century. The hard choice was to swallow the harsh terms and borrow money or cut food rations. But when the agreement came up for a vote in Parliament, *The Economist*, hardly anti-American or extreme in its views, commented bitterly:

> It is aggravating to find that our reward for losing a quarter of our national wealth in the common cause is to pay tribute for half a century to those who have been enriched by the war. . . . Beggars cannot be choosers. But they can by long tradition put a curse on the ambitions of the rich.

In September after the surrender of Japan, Truman notified the British that it was time to wind up the various Anglo-American combined boards, which had been so effective in coordinating joint resources of shipping, food, raw materials, blockade polices for the two nations in the war effort. On the military side, there was a reprieve for the Combined Chiefs of Staff Committee, pending negotiations for peace treaties.

As for atomic development and the nuclear bomb, British scientists had played a major role in developing the bomb and the assumption in London had been that wartime cooperation would continue. Instead they found a growing reticence in the United States about sharing classified information, and then the shutout became complete when Congress passed the McMahon Act in 1946, closing off any further sharing of atomic information with anyone. Britain had no choice but to go it alone in the expensive process of developing her own nuclear bomb with the know-how she had contributed to the joint wartime effort with America.

Not only was the intimacy of the Roosevelt-Churchill correspondence long gone. More than that, a sense of common purpose between the two great English-speaking democracies had also faded. On the American side, Britain was increasingly taken for granted and no longer seemed to be much needed. Certainly little thought or consideration was then being given in Washington to the parlous state of the British economy, the decline of British power, and what this was going to mean for the power balance of European security, what could or should be done to maintain or sustain the wartime alliance in order to assure peace.

At the end of 1945, after six hectic months in office, Ernest Bevin circulated to his fellow Cabinet ministers a bleak summation of how the postwar world now seemed to him to be developing:

> Instead of world cooperation we are rapidly drifting into spheres of influence, or what can better be described as three great Monroes. The United States have long held, with our support, to the Monroe Doctrine for the Western Hemisphere, and there is no doubt now, notwithstanding all the protestations, that they are attempting to extend this principle financially and economically to the Far East to include China and Japan, while the Russians seem to me to have made up their minds that their sphere is going to be from Lübeck on the Baltic to Port Arthur in the Far East.
>
> Britain therefore stands between the two, with the western world all divided up. The Continental side of this western empire would also be influenced and to a very large extent dominated by the colossal military power of Russia, and by her political power which she can bring to bear through the Communist parties in the various countries.
>
> It seems to me vital not to deceive people by leading them to believe that a United Nations Organization is going to protect them from future wars, while we know in fact that nothing of the kind is happening. There are two mighty countries in the world which, by the very nature of things, are following the present policy which is certain to see them line up against

each other. We in Great Britain who have had the brunt of two great wars will be left to take sides with either one or the other.

Of course, there was no doubt in Ernest Bevin's mind which side Britain would be on, but that was not the problem. If the world was splitting up into rival spheres of influence and the United Nations Organization already proving that it could not protect peoples from future wars, then how could security be achieved, how could peace be maintained? That was the problem. These were the vital questions yet to be asked and answered in Washington.

Twice before in this century, Britain and Europe had waited for the arrival of American power to turn the tide against aggression – from 1914 to 1917 during the First World War and from 1939 to 1941 during the Second World War. Now, with the Red Army on the Elbe and the communization of Eastern Europe well under way, Western Europe could not survive a third time while waiting for help from across the Atlantic. Yet how, in 1945, could the United States be brought once again to commit its power to the security of Europe, not in war but to maintain peace?

Securing such an American commitment had to be Ernest Bevin's primary task as foreign secretary, whatever the waning state of Anglo-American relations. Britain was the only power able to speak and act and deal with the United States on behalf of Europe in 1945. Elsewhere power had ceased to exist. France was reviving but dialogue between the United States and General de Gaulle was nonexistent. There was intrinsically a "special relationship" between the two great English-speaking democracies, whatever the ups and downs. There remained the indestructible relationship of common heritage and common values and traditions, a common cause in peace and security. But finding a new way to bring America to join in a new commitment to the security of Europe, to rebuild or renew the wartime alliance, seemed to Bevin and the British almost like starting from scratch all over again in 1945.

TWO

1946: Byrnes Tries for Peace

James F. Byrnes almost became President of the United States instead of Harry S Truman. In July 1944, when the Democratic party convention gathered in Chicago, Byrnes seemed to be the odds-on favorite to replace Vice-President Henry A. Wallace as President Roosevelt's running mate for a fourth term. Byrnes thought he would have Roosevelt's backing, and he did have the President's encouragement – not surprisingly, since he was then serving as director of war mobilization in the White House, practically running the home front while the President concentrated on running the war. Before heading for Chicago, Byrnes had even asked Truman if he would make the speech placing him in nomination, and the senator from Missouri readily agreed.

But in four short days in Chicago the world turned upside down for Byrnes and Truman. Roosevelt deliberately waffled over a vice-presidential choice, adroitly sprinkling words of inconclusive praise for several potential contenders without clearly backing anybody. Then at the convention it quickly became clear that Byrnes, a conservative from South Carolina, was unacceptable to the liberal wing of the party and its power brokers – the labor leaders and city bosses from Boston, New York, Jersey City, Chicago, and most important of all, Robert Hannegan, chairman of the Democratic National Committee and party boss of Truman's home state of Missouri. In the smoke-filled-room tradition of old-fashioned American politics, the bosses decided that Harry Truman was their choice. Truman neither sought the nomination nor played any part in this maneuvering, trying to stay loyal to Byrnes. When Roosevelt then gave his final blessing by telephone, Truman's reaction was: "Oh, shit! Why didn't he tell me in the first place?" Byrnes bitterly withdrew. Truman won on a second ballot over Wallace, and nine months later, on Roosevelt's death, became President of the United States.

Truman and Byrnes had been good friends in the Senate in the 1930s when Byrnes was majority leader, steering Roosevelt's New Deal legislation through Congress. When Roosevelt's death abruptly brought Truman into the White House, almost the first man he turned to was Byrnes. Truman was then sixty-one and Byrnes was five years older. Byrnes had accompanied Roosevelt to the Yalta Conference, but partly out of bitterness at having missed out on the vice-presidency, he had resigned as director of war mobilization only one week before Roosevelt died. A plane was sent immediately to bring him to Washington from his home in Spartanburg, South Carolina. Then, on the funeral train bearing the President's coffin to Hyde Park, Truman asked Byrnes to become his secretary of state. Byrnes readily agreed, but for the time being all was kept secret. Edward R. Stettinius would continue in office until work was completed on the United Nations Charter at the San Francisco Conference, due to open at the end of April. Byrnes became secretary of state on July 3, 1945, and four days later he sailed with Truman aboard the U.S.S. *Augusta* for Europe and the Potsdam Conference.

Byrnes held office for a chaotic and crowded seventeen months. For more than half that entire time he was away from Washington – at one period during 1946 for six months almost continuously while he conducted negotiations in Paris and New York on peace treaties for Bulgaria, Romania, Hungary and Italy. Although Charles E. Bohlen, who served as one of his close advisers, felt that Byrnes was "an underrated Secretary of State," his tenure was not a very happy time for President Truman, the State Department or America's principal European allies, Britain and France.

From the outset, Byrnes was very much a loner in the way he chose to conduct foreign policy. He played his cards very close to his chest, and consulted practically nobody (including the President) outside his own little inner circle – Bohlen on Soviet affairs; H. Freeman Matthews, another able career Foreign Service officer, who was assistant secretary for European affairs; and finally Benjamin V. Cohen, an experienced and agile New Deal lawyer close to Byrnes, who joined the State Department as counselor. Most of the time during Byrnes's tenure, therefore, the running of the department and the main task of advising and consulting the President fell on Dean Acheson, who had tried to return to his law practice when the war was over but was persuaded by Byrnes to stay on as undersecretary of state. Of Byrnes's relations with the President, Acheson subsequently wrote:

> Mr. Byrnes maintained toward Mr. Truman – at least so the President thought – the attitude of the leader of the Senate to a freshman senator. The whole unhappy episode impressed me deeply with the reciprocal nature of the President-Secretary of State relationship. If the President cannot be his own Secretary of State, it is equally true that the Secretary cannot be his own President. However much freedom he may properly be given for operation and maneuver, he cannot be given ultimate Presidential responsibility. To discharge that, the President must be kept fully informed far enough in advance of the need for decision to make choice possible.

Moreover, while Byrnes was on the road in single-minded pursuit of the peace treaties, almost every week seemed to produce a new postwar overseas development to test the inadequacy of Washington's governmental machinery under a new and untried President feeling his way in the exercise of power. In those days there was no National Security Council, no unified Department of Defense, no Central Intelligence Agency. There was not even a Policy Planning Staff in the State Department. It was not until the second half of 1947 that all of these institutions were created.

In the meantime, interdepartmental consultations on foreign policy were handled by an ad hoc State-War-Navy Coordinating Committee, with Acheson and Navy Secretary James V. Forrestal as the prime movers. (There was no separate U.S. Air Force at that time – it was still part of the Army.) At the White House, Admiral William D. Leahy, as chief of staff to the President, functioned more or less as a forerunner of today's White House national security adviser. But Leahy had no staff machinery outside his own office, and certainly no statutory coordinating responsibility for government decision-making.

Perhaps the most serious weakness in the Washington machinery was an almost complete absence of any effective coordination of *political* intelligence for the government decision-making process. The operations of the wartime Office of Strategic Services had of course been geared, directed and controlled entirely for military intelligence in fighting the war. The gathering, coordination and above all the assessment of political intelligence was an entirely different matter, requiring different operations and a far different approach. Acheson made a major effort in 1946 to create a strong political intelligence unit within the State Department, but he was thwarted first by bureaucratic infighting and in the end by Byrnes himself, who decided against all logic to leave the intelligence work of the department dispersed among its geographical divisions. The State Department thereby lost its fleeting chance to establish the same paramountcy over political intelligence that the British Foreign Office has long exercised and continues to exercise in London. Truman next established by executive order a Central Intelligence Group, which was supposed to function as a stepchild of the State, War and Navy departments. Finally, with the creation of a unified Department of Defense in mid-1947 also came the Central Intelligence Agency, independent of all other departments of the government.

All in all, this was not a government that was prepared or equipped in 1945 and 1946 to undertake any strategic foreign-policy planning or rethinking of the nation's postwar role and responsibilities in the world. Fortunately, the men were better than the machinery. But in the meantime, broad foreign-policy strategy – such as it was – remained as sketched out by Roosevelt. Although illusions about the Soviet Union were fading fast, it nevertheless was still the first goal of American policy to seek Great Power understanding and accord to maintain peace in the world. The United States still did not want to appear to be "ganging up" with the British or anyone else against the Soviet Union. It still hoped that a process of peace-treaty negotiations, as laid down at the Potsdam Conference, would eventually produce a unified demilitarized Germany in the heart of a peaceful Europe. Byrnes set out to give it a try.

Although foreign affairs was scarcely Jimmy Byrnes's specialty, he had a quick intelligence and an agile mind, a lawyer's training and courtroom experience, a politician's debating skills and a parliamentarian's tactical keenness and procedural expertise. He was an able man, more than a match against Vyacheslav M. Molotov and Andrei Vishinsky in the endless hours of turgid argument and pigheaded maneuvering that constituted the negotiations in the months ahead. Byrnes got on well enough with people in a superficial political manner. But he approached the process of negotiating the peace treaties more or less as if he were maneuvering a piece of New Deal legislation through the Senate. He was a relentless tactician, wheeling and dealing to pick up votes. But this caused considerable unease for the British and French because Byrnes was constantly springing tactical surprises, and they never could be quite sure that he wasn't engaged in some giveaway maneuver behind their backs. Indeed, sometimes he was.

Twenty-eight days after returning to the United States from the Potsdam Conference, Byrnes boarded the liner *Queen Elizabeth* to sail for London on September 5, 1945, to attend a first meeting of the Council of Foreign Ministers that had been established at Potsdam to direct the peace process. Participating would be the five permanent members of the soon-to-be-established United Nations Security Council: the United States, the Soviet Union, Britain, France, China. The first task in London, supposedly, would be consideration of peace treaties beginning with Italy, and then Bulgaria, Hungary, Romania, Finland, Austria and Germany, for subsequent submission to a peace conference, or conferences, of the powers that had declared war against the Axis.

But the conference plunged at once into endless procedural wrangles instigated by the Soviet Union either to block progress or make progress only at the price of prior agreement on exaggerated Soviet claims. You want a peace treaty with Italy? First we must agree on Italian reparations for the Soviet Union, divide up the Italian Navy, hand over the Italian colony of Tripolitania to Soviet trusteeship and give the city of Trieste to the Yugoslavs. You want treaties with Bulgaria, Romania and Hungary? First the Western powers must recognize the puppet governments established in those capitals under the liberating Red Army. You want to talk about peace with Germany and Austria? Not until we have settled peace with the other countries first. So it went round and round in circles. Then suddenly when the conference had been under way more than two weeks,

Molotov astounded everybody by abruptly demanding that France and China be excluded from any further participation because they had not been present at Potsdam and should never have been invited in the first place. This was a slap in the face for General Charles de Gaulle, who had gone to Moscow in November of 1944 while the war was still on to negotiate a much-publicized Treaty of Friendship with Stalin. Georges Bidault, the French foreign minister, was furious at this Molotov insult, but to walk out would of course only give the Russians what they wanted, so he kept his seat.

Molotov had brought the conference proceedings effectively to a dead end. Next he confronted Byrnes with a sudden demand that an Allied Control Council be established forthwith in Japan to give the Soviet Union a voice in the occupation, similar to the Control Council already set up in Germany. Byrnes quickly replied that the United States was not about to cede veto power to anybody over General of the Army Douglas MacArthur, but he would think about Molotov's proposal. It was now a question of how to end the conference. Molotov refused to agree to any communiqué that would even acknowledge the presence of France and China. But it was then the turn of the Chinese foreign minister, Dr. Wang Shih-chieh, to take the chair in rotation. Byrnes, the smooth tactician, arranged with Dr. Wang that after a predictable rerun of one of Molotov's diatribes, he simply adjourn the council without calling another meeting. Molotov was taken completely by surprise. So ended the first stab at Great Power postwar peacemaking.

Byrnes left for Washington believing that the main stumbling block had been the refusal of the United States and Britain to recognize the puppet governments installed by the Soviets in Budapest, Bucharest and Sofia. He saw it, in short, as a tactical, not a strategic, problem. In November, elections in Hungary produced a glimmer of democratic hope when the Smallholders Party outpolled the Communists – the last time that was permitted to happen. When a new government was installed, it was promptly recognized by the United States and Britain in the hope of nudging the peace-treaty process forward.

Bevin, on the other hand, judged that deadlock lay in the Soviet demand over Tripolitania, which he was utterly determined to continue to resist and refuse. Molotov had complained, "Russia has no place in the

Mediterranean for her merchant ships and the expansion of her trade and you don't want to give us even a corner of the Mediterranean." Bevin's reply later in the House of Commons was:

> Not having taken one inch of territory or asked for it, one cannot help being a little suspicious if a Great Power wants to come right across, shall I say, the throat of the British Commonwealth, which has fought this war and done no harm to anybody. One is driven to ask oneself the motive. That is not unreasonable. I think we next have to get down to stopping this demand for transfer of territory, and within reason make adjustments here and there.

Bevin and Byrnes had moved a little closer together in common opposition to Molotov's tactics at the first London meeting. But Bevin did not feel that Byrnes was solidly behind him on the Tripolitania issue, and did not grasp the *strategic* importance of this as well as the Soviet demand for a base on Turkish territory to control the Straits of the Dardanelles. On top of that was the continued Soviet refusal to withdraw the Red Army from Iran now that the war was over. Bevin was not as quick or facile as Byrnes in debate with Molotov, but this only deepened his apprehension that Byrnes might give away something strategic, thinking that it was only tactical. In fact, James Forrestal's diaries record that at a State Department conference on the Italian peace treaty, in the spring of 1946, "Ben Cohen advocated giving Russia the Tripolitania trusteeship and permitting her to fortify the Dardanelles." Fortunately other advice prevailed.

Meanwhile, in early November 1945, Byrnes began pressuring the British to cede base facilities to the United States on a list of no less than thirty-five islands or island groups, most of them in the Pacific, some involving long sovereignty disputes between the United States and Britain going back to the days of nineteenth-century imperialism. Bevin deliberately adopted a dilatory attitude, and took the unusual step of passing the American communication to Winston Churchill for comment. British governments do not usually consult much with their opposition, but Bevin and Churchill had worked closely with great mutual respect in the wartime coalition. Churchill's response was illuminating.

He addressed Bevin as "Dear Ernest" and said that in his opinion the great objective of British policy should be to intertwine the affairs of the Commonwealth and the United States to such an extent that any idea of conflict between them would be unthinkable. The more "strategic points" that could be held in joint occupation with the Americans, the better, Churchill continued. Joint occupation, he said, was the key that could then strengthen the case for retaining the wartime Combined Chiefs of Staff Committee, which at that time had not yet been disbanded, and strengthen cooperation between British and American military forces.

Here, then, was the first discernible point of departure for Bevin and the British to begin slowly trying to rebuild an alliance relationship with the United States, against all that had been happening since the end of World War II. It was not much of a starting point, but Bevin did what he could with this opportunity to open a basic discussion with Washington. He replied to Byrnes asking that the Americans consider the idea of joint bases in the various islands under a mutual-assistance arrangement that would be in accordance with Article 48 of the United Nations Charter. He said he would have to consult the Dominions, and asked that Australia and New Zealand be brought into the discussions. Were the Americans, he asked, making any similar approaches to the Dutch or the French about their Pacific island possessions? Finally he wanted to know how much the air bases that the Americans wanted would be used for military purposes, and how much for civil aviation.

All of this posed much wider problems and arrangements than the Americans had bargained for. Discussions then went on between Bevin and Byrnes for nearly a year, until a limited agreement was quietly reached in the second half of 1946. But at least by that time the need for interdependent security arrangements was becoming a lot more clear in Washington.

Far from any ganging up on the Soviet Union, the Western powers scarcely had any common approach or common priorities or a common view of postwar diplomatic and political strategy at all. Such coordination as there was on policy was largely in ad hoc consultations as problems arose at conference tables – certainly no consistent effort at advance

planning or concerted diplomatic strategy and tactics. Bevin was preoccupied with the security of the British Empire worldwide, and in
particular the Middle East, where Britain had long held sway. Bidault and
the French focused almost exclusively on the great enemy, Germany, and
as a result they were more often in the Soviet camp to support measures to
keep Germany weak and divided than they were with the United States
and Britain to revive the German economy so the country would no longer
be an economic drain. Byrnes focused almost exclusively on trying to
clean up the peace treaties as quickly as possible, with American forces in
Germany being steadily run down to a postwar low in 1948 of approximately 140,000 men. For Stalin, this division in the Western camp was a
pure bonus – "divide and conquer" handed to him free on a platter.

In this situation at the end of November 1945, Byrnes made the most
controversial lone move of his brief career as secretary of state. Acting
completely on his own, without consulting the President, Acheson,
Bohlen or anybody in the State Department, let alone Bevin and the
British, he sent off a telegram to Molotov proposing another meeting of
foreign ministers – but this time the Big Three only. France would be
excluded. Byrnes recalled to Molotov that at Yalta it had been agreed that
foreign ministers should meet about every three months, and they had met
in San Francisco in May, at Potsdam in July and London in September –
so why not a December meeting in Moscow. Molotov, like a cat swallow-
ing a canary, "beamed with pleasure" according to Ambassador Averell
Harriman, who delivered the message.

Not Ernest Bevin, who was furious when he learned of Byrnes's move.
The Foreign Office got the news via its embassy in Moscow, when
Harriman informed Ambassador Sir Archibald Clark-Kerr of his instructions. Apart from being incensed at the distrustful way in which Byrnes
had acted, Bevin was completely against seeking a meeting with the
Russians because he reasoned that Molotov had been taken aback at the
fashion in which the Western Allies broke off the London talks, and the
best tactic would be to sit tight and leave it to Moscow to take the initiative
to meet again.

Bevin was also irritated at the cavalier fashion in which Byrnes was
leaving the French out in the cold – in effect, conceding the French
exclusion from Big Power discussions that Molotov had demanded in

London. Moreover, the move came at a delicate time, when General
Charles de Gaulle was throwing out hints that he might at last be willing to
consider some treaty arrangements with Britain.

Despite two world wars, there never had been any treaty of alliance
between France and Britain.* Churchill had proposed such a pact to de
Gaulle during a visit to Paris while the war was still on, around Armistice
Day in November 1944. But at that time de Gaulle was secretly preparing
to go to Moscow (he did not even tell Churchill of his plan) to seek a
friendship treaty with Stalin and the Soviet Union first, and he was in one
of his thoroughly anti-Anglo-Saxon moods anyway. So he brushed
Churchill's suggestion aside, saying that the time was not ripe, and first
they would have to agree on their policies toward postwar Germany. De
Gaulle did have some reason for hostility. At that time there was still no
Great Power agreement even to give France an occupation zone in
Germany. When Bevin then took over at the Foreign Office, he decided
early on that an Anglo-French alliance would have to be the starting point
for any postwar security system for Europe. But in the light of de Gaulle's
tetchiness and rebuff to Churchill, he had to be careful and wait for an
opening.

Weighing up all these factors, Bevin was in no mood to be hijacked into
Byrnes's Moscow meeting. But he was urged by his ambassadors in both
Washington and Moscow that if he refused to go this would strengthen an
impression that Britain was dragging its feet in seeking good relations with
the Soviet Union. Harriman put it more brutally to his embassy staff in
Moscow: "The Labour Government can ill afford an independent
foreign policy in spite of Bevin's distaste for Byrnes and his high-handed
measures. Having mortgaged her future to pay for the war, England is so
weak she must follow our leadership. She will do anything we insist upon
and she won't go out on a limb alone."

So Bevin headed for Moscow – convinced it was a mistake, certain that
nothing substantial would come of it, and knowing that in going to another
Big Power meeting without the French he was also quashing the chance of
doing any business on a treaty with General de Gaulle. Indeed, it was a full
year before Bevin found the moment to move with the French.

*The *Entente Cordiale* of 1904 was only a declaration of friendship, issued at the
conclusion of a state visit to Paris by King Edward VII.

Meanwhile, Byrnes encountered a logistical problem because of his snub of the French. Flying from Washington in a propeller-driven DC-4, he had to land in Paris, but arranged to transfer immediately to a smaller DC-3, which then took off at once in a driving rain for Frankfurt, where he could count on hospitality from General Lucius D. Clay, the U.S. occupation commander. Flying on to Moscow involved a hair-raising search for an airport in a driving snowstorm before the American plane, with a Soviet navigator, finally made it safely to ground at the wrong field.

George Kennan, Harriman's Number Two at the American Embassy, gave a vivid word-picture of the opening meeting:

> Bevin looked highly disgusted with the whole procedure. It was easy to see by his face that he found himself in a position he did not like and was well aware that nothing good could come out of the meeting. Molotov sat leaning forward over the table, a Russian cigarette dangling from his mouth, the look of a passionate poker-player who knows that he has a royal flush and is about to call the last of his opponents. He was the only one clearly enjoying every minute of the proceedings.

Both Harriman and Kennan were almost as irritated as Bevin over Byrnes's Moscow performance. He did not even show Harriman some of the papers he was working from, and he sharply rebuffed both Harriman and Bohlen when each of them proposed drafting telegrams to President Truman to report on the discussions. He snapped at Harriman that he wasn't going to send any telegrams and when Harriman pressed him that it was customary to keep the President informed, Byrnes replied adamantly: "The President has given me complete authority. I can't trust the White House to prevent leaks." Harriman found it "preposterous for any Secretary of State to show such disregard for the President's position." Harry Truman certainly found it preposterous – or even worse.

The meetings began on December 16, and although Byrnes wanted to be home by Christmas, Harriman warned him that if he tried to fix a deadline he might find Molotov using this to gain some advantage over him. At least Byrnes took this advice and the meetings went on until 3:30 A.M. on December 27. The results were as meager as Bevin had anticipated. There was an inconclusive discussion about the American proposals for sharing of atomic knowledge while retaining a monopoly over the atomic bomb. Byrnes got nowhere with Stalin over withdrawing Soviet troops from Iran. But Byrnes did agree to set up an Allied Council in Tokyo to "consult" with General MacArthur on occupation policy. It would have American, Soviet, Chinese and British Commonwealth members, but MacArthur would not be subject to any veto and would have final say. The Russians accepted this.

Stalin then promised some window-dressing changes in the composition of the puppet governments he had installed in Bulgaria and Romania, in return for a promise of recognition by the United States and Britain when this was done. The new appointees eventually disappeared in the Cold War terror that followed. But with this concession in the bag, Stalin agreed to unblock the London deadlock over convening a peace conference.

Byrnes recounts:

> Stalin asked me to convey acceptance of this to Mr. Bevin. I agreed to inform the British Foreign Secretary, and added jokingly that even though we were supposed to have a bloc with Britain I had not informed Bevin about my proposal to Mr. Molotov for this meeting in Moscow as soon as I should have. The Generalissimo smiled and replied that this obviously was only a cloak to hide the reality of the bloc.

Stalin clearly assumed that relations between the Anglo-Saxons were closer and more intimate than they really were under Byrnes. Neither Harriman nor Bohlen thought much of Stalin's "concessions," but Byrnes wrote that he headed home "a far happier man than the one who had returned from London only fifteen weeks earlier." He could not have been very happy at the reception awaiting him from President Truman.

Truman, Acheson, Admiral Leahy and the White House staff were by now fuming at the total absence of any firsthand reports from the secretary of state. Moreover, when Byrnes finally did cable that the meeting had been successful and was over, he requested Acheson to arrange air time so he could make an immediate "report to the nation" the evening of his return. "It was my unhappy duty to ruffle the President's temper still further," Acheson says, and Truman at once told Acheson to have Byrnes report to him first, and delay his planned speech until the day after his return. Truman then sailed down the Potomac on the presidential yacht

Williamsburg, leaving instructions for Byrnes to follow as soon as his plane landed.

Even though Byrnes said in his memoirs that the encounter was "cordial," everyone else who was aboard the *Williamsburg* recounted otherwise. Truman himself, who was known to exaggerate in recollection, said in his memoirs that behind closed doors in his stateroom he told Byrnes that he did not like being left in the dark, that he "would not tolerate a repetition of such conduct," and that he had concluded that the secretary of state "had taken it upon himself to move the foreign policy of the United States in a direction to which I could not and would not agree."

When accounts of the *Williamsburg* meeting came out in later years, Byrnes said that if he had been told anything like that by the President he would have resigned. At any rate, whatever the details, there is no doubt as to Truman's irritation and indignation, and it was the beginning of the end for Byrnes. Years later a letter written in Truman's own hand came to light in the Truman Archives, dated January 5, 1946 – six days after the *Williamsburg* confrontation – and addressed to "Hon. Jas. F. Byrnes." The letter clearly was never delivered to Byrnes, for in any case by this time the peripatetic secretary of state was already on his way back to London for the first meeting of the General Assembly of the new United Nations.

The letter was apparently a reflective attempt by Truman to define his thoughts after the Byrnes incident, and is therefore of importance in marking a decisive change of mood with regard to the Soviet Union that was by now taking hold in Washington. After first stating "I do not intend to turn over the complete authority of the President nor to forgo the President's prerogatives to make the final decision," and then declaring that he would not agree to the recognition of the Romanian and Bulgarian governments as Byrnes had arranged with Stalin "unless they are radically changed," Truman wrote:

> There isn't a doubt in my mind that Russia intends an invasion of Turkey and the seizure of the Black Sea straits to the Mediterranean. Unless Russia is faced with an iron fist and strong language, another war is in the making. Only one language do they understand – "How many divisions have you?" I do not think we should play compromise any longer.
>
> I am tired of babying the Soviets.

From this point on, the focus of American policy began to shift steadily away from the pursuit of a Rooseveltian peace of Great Power understanding to the central problem of recognizing and dealing with a Soviet threat to international security. The President was "tired of babying the Soviets," and although Byrnes could scarcely be accused of being "soft on Communism," his determined search for agreements with the Soviet Union, as well as the style of his diplomacy, simply left an uneasy impression that he was prepared to give away much more than he ever actually did. In particular, he began coming under increasing fire from his old colleagues in the Senate. The redoubtable Senator Arthur H. Vandenberg of Michigan was in the process of consolidating his conversion from prewar isolationism to that of postwar statesman, and the focal point of all this, of course, was how to face the Soviet challenge. Midterm elections were in the offing in 1946, and after thirteen years of Roosevelt's rule, the Republicans were preparing to bear down on the Democrats and Truman with everything they could muster. Both Truman and Byrnes were determined that bipartisan foreign policy had to be an overriding American political priority to avoid the kind of retreat into isolationism that took place after World War I. Byrnes was above all a politician, and so, after the abortive peace efforts of 1945, he, too, began to toughen up to keep in line with the President, Senator Vandenberg and even his Western allies.

Joseph Stalin then helped clarify things for the administration with his first major postwar policy speech on February 9, 1946, which marked with brutal clarity an end of any pretense of continued collaboration or cooperation with the West to keep the peace. It was a sharp turn to what would soon be called the Cold War.

Announcing the goals of the first postwar Five-Year Plan, Stalin declared in classical Leninist ideological terms that the causes of World War II lay in the demands and contradictions of capitalist-imperialist monopoly, and that with these same forces still in control outside the Soviet Union, "no peaceful international order is possible." He went on to proclaim that the Soviet Union "must be capable of guarding against all kinds of eventualities," and the Five-Year Plan would therefore give absolute priority to rearmament, treble the production of iron and steel and double the production of coal, oil and energy sources, while consumer goods must wait. The columnist Walter Lippmann wrote immediately that "now that Stalin is making military power his first objective, we are forced to make a corresponding decision."

But Henry A. Wallace, still the commerce secretary in Truman's Cabinet, a holdover from the Roosevelt days, clinging determinedly to Roosevelt's ideas of peace and One World, wrote in his diary:

> I think this is accounted for in some measure by the fact that it is obvious to Stalin that our military is getting ready for war with Russia; that they are setting up bases all the way from Greenland, Iceland, northern Canada and Alaska to Okinawa with Russia in mind. I think that Stalin obviously knows what these bases mean and also knows the attitude of many of our people through the press. We are challenging him, and his speech is taking up the challenge.

This was a theme and a conviction on Wallace's part that led to his abrupt firing by Truman six months later, when he said it all in a major speech at Madison Square Garden while Byrnes was at a crucial stage of the peace-treaty negotiations in Paris. It was a theme that would be repeatedly worked over, analyzed, endorsed and praised by American revisionist historians in their brief heyday in the 1960s. But in the meantime, Truman had to deal with the reality of what was happening, not some airy theories about political cause and effect.

When Byrnes arrived in London in early January 1946 to attend the first General Assembly and Security Council meetings of the new United Nations, the Iranian government had decided to lodge formally with the fledgling world body a complaint against the Soviet Union for its failure to withdraw its troops from Iranian territory now that the war was over. There was some apprehension on the part of the Western powers over the risk of plunging the UN into an East-West confrontation in the first hours of its existence. But the Iranian government certainly was within its rights under the charter to which it and the Soviet government had both adhered. So the first clash was on.

American, British and Soviet troops had gone into Iran in 1942 after the overthrow of a pro-Nazi shah to establish and secure a supply line for the movement of American equipment for the Russians from the Persian Gulf to the Caspian Sea. At the Teheran Conference in December 1943,

Roosevelt, Churchill and Stalin all pledged that these forces would be withdrawn after the war, and eventually the date of March 2, 1946, was fixed. But in November 1945, well after the end of the war, the Communist Tudeh party, armed by the Soviets, staged a separatist uprising in the northern Iranian province of Azerbaijan, bordering on the Soviet Union. The new shah (eventually overthrown in 1979 by the Ayatollah Khomeini) attempted to send his troops into the province to quell the disturbances, but they were halted by the Red Army. This "threat to stability on the Soviet borders" then became Stalin's excuse for refusing to withdraw his troops as the deadline approached.

In Washington, as the Security Council of the United Nations gingerly took up the crisis, Navy Secretary Forrestal proposed that a task force be sent to the Mediterranean, and this was immediately supported by Byrnes. As a first step, it was decided to dispatch the battleship U.S.S. *Missouri* to Istanbul on a much-publicized voyage to return home the body of the Turkish ambassador to Washington, who had died at his post some months earlier.

This was the first reinforcement of United States forces in the European theater – the first postwar American show of force – since the drawdown of troops and naval units had begun soon after VE Day in May 1945. Whether by coincidence or not, as the *Missouri* prepared to sail for the Mediterranean, an agreement was announced between Moscow and Teheran in late March to establish a joint oil company to exploit petroleum reserves in Azerbaijan Province, after which Russian troops would be withdrawn. There was some apprehension in Washington and London that the province would be passing to Soviet control in a different form. But at the end of May the Red Army troops finally left. Then, suddenly, the Iranian Parliament voted to repudiate the oil agreement, and the Tudeh party in Azerbaijan again began agitating for a separate state. By the end of the summer of 1946 tension was rising over a possible new Soviet intervention.

Meanwhile Soviet pressure had been stepped up against Turkey. In June Moscow asked for bilateral talks on the future of the Straits of the Dardanelles. Stalin had far from given up the demand he had first put forward in Potsdam a year earlier. The Turks were dilatory in responding, and in early August the Russians delivered a peremptory demand to

Ankara to organize "a joint defense of the Straits" with control resting henceforth exclusively with the powers bordering on the Black Sea.

Two days after this note to the Turks, on August 9, 1946, Yugoslav fighter planes forced down an unarmed U.S. Army transport plane as it crossed the Italian province of Venezia Giulia near the city of Trieste at the head of the Adriatic Sea. Ten days later this was followed by the actual shooting down of another U.S. transport in the same area.

Byrnes, in Paris at the time for the peace conference, immediately summoned the Yugoslav foreign minister, who was also on hand, and demanded an apology, compensation and an end to such actions. Yugoslavia was trying to back up its claims for Trieste with force. Truman was heading for a first military confrontation of the Cold War.

On the President's instructions, Acheson convened the State-War-Navy Coordinating Committee to consider a United States response to this triple threat in Trieste, Turkey and Iran. On August 15 the Cabinet officers met with Truman at the White House. They were unanimous that the actions "should be resisted at all costs" and a formal note sent to the Russians "that by its studied restraint should impress them that we mean every word of it." They proposed that air reinforcements be sent to northern Italy and naval reinforcements to the eastern Mediterranean where the *Missouri* was still cruising after its visit to Istanbul.

Truman fully and quickly concurred with all these recommendations, and was even more emphatic and decisive than some of his advisers. At one point, General Eisenhower, then Army Chief of Staff, leaned over to Acheson to ask in a whisper if they were making it clear to the President that this could lead to war. Truman overheard and quickly launched into a brisk off-the-cuff lecture on the strategic importance of the eastern Mediterranean and the extent to which America must be prepared to go to keep it free of Soviet domination. But the fact is that the Cabinet officers had given no detailed consideration to the available military forces that might be needed to back up their proposals if the confrontation deepened into a war crisis. Forrestal's proposal back in February to establish a Navy task force in the Mediterranean had not been implemented for the unhappy reason that the Navy did not have the ships and the manpower. Forrestal was all for a tough stance by the President, but an entry in his diaries one week later, on August 22, reveals the dismal picture as the United States threw down the gauntlet to Stalin for the first time:

> The Fleet is stripped down as a result of our rapid demobilization to a dangerously low point of efficiency, although it is beginning to climb again in this respect slightly since July, which was the nadir of our effectiveness. We have a large number of vessels in the active fleet which cannot go to sea because of lack of competent personnel. When we wanted to move the command ship *Catoctin* on maneuvers, the Admiral had to get personnel from all the other ships in Norfolk in order to be able to proceed. Even then the ship had a minor accident.
>
> The Army's available strength for application in Europe is estimated at 460 fighters and about 90 bombers with possibly 175 really trained first-line pilots. [The Air Force at that time was still part of the Army]. I talked to Acheson and told him I was apprehensive about our capabilities, and that it seemed to me it was incumbent upon us to make an evaluation of what we had to back up these notes [to the Russians].

Acheson concurred, with a formal request to the Joint Chiefs of Staff for a review of available resources. At least by this time, the new supercarrier *Franklin D. Roosevelt* had also reached European waters. The JCS, apparently acting on their own but no doubt with Forrestal's concurrence, then invited service representatives at the British Embassy from the Royal Navy and the British Army to a meeting at the Pentagon on August 30 for "a general discussion of what this country and Britain had available with which to meet an emergency, should it arise." So, after a year of drifting apart, events had forced a first step toward a resumption of Anglo-American military liaison and planning, from which the North Atlantic Treaty Organization would eventually emerge. But Forrestal recorded of that first meeting:

> It developed that no very definite plans had been evolved because no one had raised the question. Admiral Leahy kept insisting that there should be specific and definite answers, particularly in the way of clear and precise planning for movements in Europe and for support. The British agreed that they would send over their top planners for the Army, Navy and Air Force, but were most apprehensive about security, and felt it should be on an informal basis. To this the JSC agreed.

The Forrestal diary note added bleakly that "the most important problem would be how to get General McNarney's people [the U.S. occupation forces] out of Germany, and how to support British and Americans in the Trieste area. . . ." West Germany, in other words, could not be defended against the Russians.

Nevertheless, with Truman's show of determination, Tito got the message and hostile air action against United States planes in Venezia Giulia halted. The Turks, with American backing, told the Soviets that they were ready to discuss a revision of the old Montreux Convention on passage through the Straits with all its signatory powers, but they refused any Soviet joint control. That, effectively, was the end of the Soviet demand, though not necessarily the end of Russian ambitions. The shah of Iran moved his troops into Azerbaijan in October to a wild welcome. The Soviets did not respond and the Tudeh separatist movement collapsed.

A first American demonstration of strength, however precarious it really was, had worked.

Meanwhile, the full-dress Paris Peace Conference of all the powers that had declared war on the Axis formally convened at last on July 29, 1946, to take final decisions on treaties with Italy, Bulgaria, Romania and Hungary. A treaty with Finland was also on the agenda, but the United States took no part in this because it had not declared war on Finland. This left the country at the tender mercy of the Soviet Union, and the price of Finnish independence was harsh and high. The tedious battle of the peace treaties ground on until October 15 and then shifted to New York for a final round of negotiations on the fringes of the second United Nations General Assembly. By the end, Byrnes calculated that out of 562 days in office, he had spent 350 away from the State Department at international conferences.

Throughout the long peace-treaty process, the central problem of the future of Germany remained in abeyance. The Western powers raised the German question repeatedly with Molotov, but about the only thing he was prepared to discuss was his demand for reparations from the Western occupation zones. Nothing, he insisted, could be done about a German peace treaty until the other treaties were cleared up – not even the setting up of an experts group to begin preliminary work. Given Molotov's track record in diplomatic delaying tactics, it was increasingly clear to the Western powers that they might never get to a German peace treaty at all. Meanwhile the German economic situation was steadily worsening, and the Soviet occupation zone in East Germany was closed off as tightly as the Soviet Union itself. The Western powers could not allow the German situation to drift on this way indefinitely.

On July 11, 1946, Byrnes took the first major step to break out of the German deadlock and stalemate. In Paris he announced that the United States was ready to merge its occupation zone with any or all of the other three zones as a means of furthering German recovery in order for it to meet the reparations burden and become self-sufficient once again. Next day, Bevin announced that Britain would accept, and merge its northern occupation zone, including the vital Ruhr industrial valley, with the U.S. zone in the south. Instructions were sent to the U.S. and British occupation commanders in Berlin to work out the details.

The French, however, continued to keep their zone to themselves. They were wedded to a separatist policy toward Germany, and were determined at that time to hold the Saarland for themselves in one form or another of annexation. They had the additional political problem of a strong and active Communist party to contend with. The Moscow propaganda machine quickly opened up with denunciations of the United States and Britain for preparing a revival of German militarism. But the creation of a Western Bizonia began to breathe a little life into German recovery.

Next Byrnes left the Paris peace talks to journey to Stuttgart to deliver a turning-point speech on German policy on September 6. He declared that it was time for the Germans to be given back responsibility for running their own local affairs, and that this should be followed by "early establishment of a provisional government" to draft a federal constitution for the whole country under the authority of the occupying powers. Byrnes of course called for four-power cooperation in all of this for all of Germany. But, as with the merger of the occupation zones, he made it clear that the United States was ready to move ahead in West Germany, without the Soviet Union. He was opening another door for Germany, and he added an important pledge:

Security forces will probably have to remain in Germany for a long period. I want no misunderstanding. We will not shirk our duty. We are not withdrawing. We are staying here, and will furnish our proportionate share of the security forces.

Thus, twenty months after the Yalta Conference, Byrnes erased Roosevelt's remark to Stalin and Churchill that America would probably keep troops in Germany only for "a couple of years." To the Germans, and to the Soviet Union, it was a message that the United States would stand firm.

Meanwhile, in mid-September, Field Marshal Viscount Montgomery, postwar Chief of the Imperial General Staff, arrived in Washington on a "goodwill visit" that in fact provided the cover for a follow-up on the Pentagon meeting between the British and the American Chiefs of Staff. On September 16, General Eisenhower arranged a well-photographed Potomac River cruise on the yacht *Sequoia* for Monty and the American Chiefs, in Monty's words "to avoid suspicion and preserve secrecy." Truman had given his blessing in advance, and they agreed to begin joint Anglo-American secret staff talks as soon as possible to coordinate strategic planning against the possibility of war. The hiatus in Anglo-American cooperation was beginning to fade in Washington and in Germany, and the wartime alliance was slowly getting back into business.

In Paris on his return from Stuttgart, Byrnes again took up with Bevin the American request, now nearly a year old, for base rights on scattered possessions in the Pacific and elsewhere. He now proposed that the two nations instigate a "common user policy" for reciprocal sharing of each other's ports and air bases, including the British Commonwealth, as had been suggested by Churchill. Bevin referred this to London, and the British Chiefs of Staff gave their ready endorsement. When he and Byrnes next discussed it, they agreed that it would be best to avoid any formal written action. Instead it was simply decided to revive the wartime practice of making port facilities automatically available to each other's naval vessels, and at the same time to increase reciprocal naval visits, and allow the process to grow from there.

On October 1, 1946, Navy Secretary Forrestal was able to announce that a new U.S. Naval Command was being established in the Mediterranean on a permanent basis. The carrier *Franklin D. Roosevelt* would remain on station as the nucleus of a new task force, later to become the Mediterranean Sixth Fleet. By the end of the year, the *Roosevelt* had been joined by three cruisers and eight destroyers. Along with the revival of Anglo-American military cooperation, the power buildup had also now begun.

As soon as the peace treaties with all but Germany and Austria were concluded in New York in mid-December, Byrnes asked Truman to accept his resignation. He had told the President nine months before that his doctors had discovered a mild heart condition and when the treaties were concluded he would have to slow down. Truman secretly contacted General George C. Marshall, at the time on his mission to China trying to avert civil war, about taking over the State Department. Marshall had responded that he would serve "in whatever capacity you wish." The President now asked Marshall to return to Washington.

Once again, General Marshall would be the right man in the right place at the right time of history.

THREE

The Long Telegram
and the Iron Curtain Speech

Less than one year after the end of the war, the visionary One World of Great Power harmony and peace that Roosevelt planned and worked for had inexorably and remorselessly divided into two worlds. At the same time, a parallel political debate increasingly divided the party leaders, opinion formers and intellectuals of the Western democracies.

What was going wrong with the postwar world? What was causing – who was causing – this new "Cold War," as it soon was labeled? Why was the world already apparently lurching toward another war? Were governments devoid of reason and common sense? In Britain, the extreme left of the Labour party ceaselessly yapped and sniped at Ernest Bevin for conducting a "warmongering" anti-Soviet Conservative foreign policy. The governments of France and Italy, seeking to defend their national interests, had to fight publicly in the streets with Communists battling on behalf of the Soviet Union and supported by upwards of 25 percent of the voters. In the United States, the Cold War split the Democratic party wide open when Henry A. Wallace walked out in opposition to Truman's policies and formed the Progressive party of left-liberals in 1947.

A cause-and-effect debate over who was fanning the Cold War became a dominant factor in American politics in 1946. This has continued ever since in one way or another with a more or less permanent American political debate over how to deal with the Soviet Union. Revisionist historians have contended that the Cold War began because America overreacted to an exaggerated idea of a Communist threat in 1945–1946, and, by resorting to a military buildup culminating in the North Atlantic

Treaty, only fed Stalin's paranoia about encirclement and Soviet security.

It would be possible to argue, for example, that the United States, in its own interests, should have made a postwar loan to the Soviet Union or should not have been so tough in resisting Soviet claims for German reparations from the Western zones. It could be argued that America sent ships needlessly to the Mediterranean, should have been more forthcoming about sharing nuclear information, or was overly provocative in the anti-Communist rhetoric of the Truman Doctrine. But the most ardent believer in all of this could scarcely argue, let alone prove, that if the United States *had* acted with such moderation to seek a path of understanding with the Soviet Union it would have had any effect at all on postwar Soviet policy. Whether the United States was friendly or hostile, Stalin's policies had their own roots and followed a logic of Russian history, in which Soviet Communism and modern military power simply added a new and terrifying dimension to traditional aims of czarist expansionism going back three centuries. Ideology had changed, but historic policies had not. As to the origins of the Cold War, in the words of the American historian Adam Ulan:

> The simplest and most banal explanation is not necessarily wrong. The Soviet Union was bent upon expanding her sphere of power and influence, but without incurring the risk of war.

This was a confrontation with Russian expansionism – not a matter of marginal postwar difficulties and disagreements and territorial disputes to be sorted out by diplomatic compromise. In the United States there was probably less intrinsic awareness of the basic historic dimension of Soviet policy than there was in Europe for a very simple reason. Every country in Europe had been caught up in past history in wars or diplomatic struggles with Russian expansion as it ebbed and flowed, from Peter the Great to Catherine the Great, through the Napoleonic Wars, the peace of the Congress of Vienna, the Crimean War, the Afghan Wars, the Russo-Japanese War, and two world wars across a mere thirty years of this century.

Czarist territorial expansion into Eastern Europe during the nineteenth century had been virtually expunged in the First World War after the

Bolsheviks came to power in 1917 and took Russia out of the war, paying the high price of the Treaty of Brest-Litovsk with imperial Germany. After that, the Second World War carried the Germans into Russia on a far greater scale and depth than Napoleon had achieved. To restore czarist gains and secure Russia's frontiers at the expense of Eastern Europe once again was Stalin's minimum objective, and Communism had little to do with that except in terms of method. The United States became a new power on the European stage, ill prepared to cope with the forces of history behind the players. It was history as well as ideology that produced the Cold War.

Yet much had been foreseen more than a century before by Alexis de Tocqueville who wrote in 1835 in a famous passage in his classic *Democracy in America*:

> There are at the present time two great nations in the world which started from different points, but seem to tend towards the same end. I allude to the Russians and the Americans. Both of them have grown up unnoticed; and while the attention of mankind was directed elsewhere they have suddenly placed themselves in the front rank among nations, and the world learned of their existence and their greatness at almost the same time.
>
> All other nations seem to have nearly reached their natural limits, and they have only to maintain their power; but these are still in the act of growth. The American struggles against the obstacles that nature opposes to him; the adversaries of the Russians are men. The former combats the wilderness and savage life; the latter civilization with all its arms. The conquests of the Americans are therefore gained by the plowshares; those of the Russians by the sword. The Anglo-American relies upon personal interests to accomplish his ends and gives free scope to the unguided strength and common sense of the people. The Russian centers all the authority of society in a single arm. The principal instrument of the former is freedom; of the latter, servitude; yet each of them seems marked out by the will of heaven to sway the destinies of half of the globe.

In 1835 Alexis de Tocqueville could almost be said to have anticipated the Cold War. In 1946 the two voices that had the most impact in defining and delineating what was now happening in the world, as opposed to what the world had been led to expect, were those of Winston Churchill and George F. Kennan. From the considerable outpouring of public speeches and analytical writings of that postwar period, the contributions of Churchill and Kennan stand out for clarity, and for political and historic impact, still to be read with a sense of immediacy put into perspective, a crystallization of illusion into reality.

In fact, what can be seen as the three basic "declarations of the Cold War" all emerged in four short weeks from early February 1946. On February 9, Stalin delivered his first major postwar speech on the new Soviet Five-Year Plan, in which he laid it down that rearmament would take absolute priority over consumer needs, because "no peaceful international order is possible" between the Communist camp and the world of capitalism-imperialism, and the Soviet Union must prepare to defend itself against encroachment and threat.

In Moscow on February 22, George Kennan, chargé d'affaires at the American Embassy, with well over a decade of intensive experience in Soviet affairs, sat down to write at almost breakneck speed an eight-thousand-word *cri de coeur* to the State Department, which became famous as the Long Telegram, in which he set out to examine the techniques of Soviet diplomacy and the historic objectives and context of Soviet foreign policy – as Kennan later put it, "to try to make them understand the nature of the phenomenon with which we in the Moscow Embassy were daily confronted and which our government and people had to learn to understand if they were to have any chance of coping successfully with the problems of the postwar world."

Then, on the heels of this secret dispatch by Kennan, Winston Churchill delivered his famous Iron Curtain speech at Westminster College in Fulton, Missouri, on March 5, with President Truman sitting on the platform.

The Churchill speech was a broad and sweeping overview of the state of the postwar world, barely nine months after the Potsdam Conference. Churchill aimed primarily at galvanizing public opinion in the United States to recognize and accept the challenge of history that was bearing down on the nation and rally it to its duty to the free world once again. Kennan was seeking to do much the same within the government, and his Long Telegram achieved almost more than he hoped for – in Dean Acheson's comment: "A long and truly remarkable dispatch that had a deep effect on thinking within the government, although government response, with action, still needed a year's proof of Soviet intentions as seen by Kennan."

Harry Truman had declared himself "tired of babying the Soviets." Now outside and inside the government Churchill and Kennan had defined and crystallized the true nature of the challenge the United States was facing, and at the same time launched the kind of "great debate" by which democracies slowly come to grips with reality and gear up to act.

In October of 1945, as Churchill was preparing a long vacation trip to the United States, he received an unusual invitation from the president of Westminster College, Frank L. McClure, to visit Fulton and address the college, which had a fund to bring famous speakers to its campus. What was unusual about the invitation was a postscript. McClure had gone to Washington to discuss the invitation with an old Westminster graduate, Harry Vaughan, who was in Truman's entourage at the White House. Vaughan took McClure into Truman's office, and when the President read the invitation letter, he immediately wrote in his own hand at the bottom: "This is a wonderful school in my home state. Hope you can do it. I'll introduce you. Best regards. Harry S Truman."

Churchill, with a sense of occasion and history that went well beyond anything that Westminster College anticipated, accepted the invitation on November 8, adding in his reply that to speak "under your aegis . . . might possibly be advantageous from several points of view." He sailed for the United States to settle in private hospitality at Miami Beach in early January, missing the English winter for the first time since 1939. At the end of the month he wrote Truman at the White House:

> I need to talk with you a good while before our Fulton date. I have a
> Message to deliver to your country and to the world and I think it very likely
> that we shall be in full agreement about it. Under your auspices anything I
> say will command some attention and there is an opportunity for doing
> some good to this bewildered, baffled and breathless world. [Churchill
> never missed an opportunity to create a phrase.]

Truman replied at once that he would be coming to Florida in early February for a vacation himself at his favorite getaway spot, Key West. On a stopover in Miami, Truman, Byrnes and Admiral Leahy met with

Churchill to hear the gist of what he had on his mind to say at Fulton. It was then arranged that Churchill would come to Washington in early March, and he and Truman would travel together on the presidential train to Missouri, leaving on March 4, with two Pullman cars of newsmen attached.

On reaching Washington, Churchill sent the text of his speech to Byrnes at the State Department, and Byrnes gave Truman a summary of its contents. Truman, still wary about ganging up against the Soviets, at first decided not to read the speech in advance. Since he was escorting Churchill to Fulton on the presidential train, it is difficult to see what this gesture of innocence could possibly mean to Stalin, but those were early days still. At any rate, since copies had already been distributed to the traveling press, Truman *did* read it as the train sped through the night, telling Churchill that "it would do nothing but good, though it would make a stir." That's exactly what Churchill intended.

In Fulton next day, there was a brief crisis as the greatest orator of this century prepared to turn the stage of a provincial college into a platform of history. Fulton was a dry town, and Winston Churchill seldom spoke without first moistening his throat. While the former prime minister was donning a suitable scarlet English university robe, Truman sent Harry Vaughan out to search the town for a pint of whiskey. He returned just in time, mission accomplished, Churchill commenting gratefully: "I didn't know whether I was in Fulton, Missouri, or Fulton, Sahara."

Churchill titled his Fulton speech "The Sinews of Peace." The "Iron Curtain" passage was not the main focus or thrust of what he had to say, although with half a century of political speechmaking behind him, Churchill certainly knew the headline value of a telling phrase. After opening with a brief and graceful tribute to Westminster as a place he had heard of before, where he had received a large part of his education in politics, dialectic, rhetoric and one or two other things, he laid down the keynote of his address at once:

> The United States stands at this time at the pinnacle of world power. It is a solemn moment for American Democracy. For with primacy in power is also joined an awe-inspiring accountability to the future. If you look around you, you must feel not only the sense of duty done but also you must

feel anxiety lest you fall below the level of achievement. Opportunity is here now, clear and shining for both our countries. To reject it or ignore it or fritter it away will bring upon us all the long reproach of after-time.

Churchill then moved on to talk in general terms about the wisdom of having "an overall strategic concept" to clarify thought, computing available resources while proceeding to the next step. He paid brief respects to the United Nations as a vehicle to keep the peace, but said that "before we cast away the solid assurance of national armaments for self-preservation we much be certain that our temple is built not upon shifting sands but upon rock."

Now, while still pursuing the method of realizing our overall strategic concept, I come to the crux of what I have travelled here to say. Neither the sure prevention of war, nor the continuous rise of world organization will be gained without what I have called the fraternal association of the English-speaking peoples. This means a special relationship between the British Commonwealth and Empire and the United States. This is no time for generalities, and I will venture to be precise.

Fraternal association requires not only the growing friendship and mutual understanding between our two vast but kindred systems of society, but the continuance of the intimate relationship between our military advisers, leading to common study of potential dangers, the similarity of weapons and manuals of instruction, and to the interchange of officers and cadets at technical colleges. It should carry with it the continuance of the present facilities for mutual security by joint use of all Naval and Air Force bases in the possession of either country all over the world. This would perhaps double the mobility of the American Navy and Air Force. It would greatly expand that of the British Empire forces and it might well lead, if and as the world calms down, to important financial savings. Already we use together a large number of islands; more may well be entrusted to our joint care in the near future.

The United States has already a Permanent Defense Agreement with the Dominion of Canada, which is so devotedly attached to the British Commonwealth and Empire. This agreement is more effective than many of those which have often been made under formal alliances. This principle should be extended to all British Commonwealths with full reciprocity. Thus, whatever happens, and thus only, shall we be secure ourselves and able to work together for the high and simple causes that are dear to us and bode no ill to any.

Knowing well the American political susceptibilities about "entangling alliances," Churchill was careful to talk only in terms of special relationship, growing friendship, mutual understanding, kindred systems, common study, interchange and all the rest. Nor did he mention Europe in this context – only Britain and the United States. But he was postulating a major turn in peacetime United States foreign policy.

His mention of joint use of islands and that "more may well be entrusted to our joint care in the near future" was adroit because Churchill knew at that moment – although his audience did not – that the United States had already requested base facilities on a scattering of British islands in the Pacific and elsewhere. He had already advised Bevin to propose "joint use" arrangements to the Americans, and a first exchange on the matter had already taken place between Bevin and Byrnes.

Having called upon America to recognize its "awe-inspiring accountability to the future" and warned against ignoring or frittering away opportunity, Churchill was carefully building on simple and obvious precepts, conditions, facts to point the direction that American policy, American reaction to the realities of the postwar situation should and would have to take. He went out of his way to assure his midwestern listeners that "special associations between members of the United Nations which have no aggressive point against any other country, far from being harmful, are beneficial, and, as I believe, indispensable." Then he struck a note of urgency:

> Beware, I say; time may be short. Do not let us take the course of allowing events to drift along until it is too late. If there is to be a fraternal association of the kind I have described, with all the extra strength and security which both our countries can derive from it, let us make sure that that great fact is known to the world, and that it plays its part in steadying and stabilizing the foundations of peace. There is the path of wisdom. Prevention is better than cure.

Churchill then turned to "a shadow that has fallen upon the scene so lately lighted by Allied victory." He said that "nobody knows what Soviet Russia and its Communist international organization intends to do in the immediate future, or what are the limits, if any, to their expansive and proselytising tendencies."

From Stettin in the Baltic to Trieste in the Adriatic, an iron curtain has descended across the Continent.* Behind that line lie all the capitals of the ancient states of Central and Eastern Europe. Warsaw, Berlin, Prague, Budapest, Belgrade, Vienna, Bucharest and Sofia. All these famous cities and populations around them lie in what I must call the Soviet sphere, and all are subject in one form or another, not only to Soviet influence but to a very high, and in many cases, increasing measure of control from Moscow.... Turkey and Persia are both profoundly alarmed and disturbed at the claims which are being made upon them and at the pressure being exerted by the Moscow government. .... Whatever conclusions may be drawn from these facts – and facts they are – this is certainly not the Liberated Europe we fought to build up. Nor is it one which contains the essentials of permanent peace. ...

On the other hand, I repulse the idea that a new war is inevitable; still more that it is imminent. It is because I am sure that our fortunes are still in our own hands and that we hold the power to save the future that I feel the duty to speak out now that I have the occasion and the opportunity to do so. I do not believe that Soviet Russia desires war. What they desire is the fruits of war and the indefinite expansion of their power and doctrines. But what we have to consider here today while time remains is the permanent prevention of war and the establishment of conditions of freedom and democracy as rapidly as possible in all countries. Our difficulties and dangers will not be removed by closing our eyes to them.

Churchill continued, "The last time I saw it all coming and cried aloud to my own fellow-countrymen and to the world, no one paid any attention." Punching out the words "We surely must not let that happen again," he concluded:

If all British moral and material forces and convictions are joined with your own in fraternal association, the high-roads of the future will be clear, not only for us but for all, not only for our time, but for a century to come.

Churchill, with long direct historic involvement in world affairs of the first half of the century, immense prestige and an unmatched oratorical

* A century earlier, in April 1853, Karl Marx wrote of imperial Russia: "Having come this far on the way to universal empire, is it probable that this gigantic and swollen power will pause in its career? ... The broken and undulating Western Frontier of the Empire, ill-defined in respect of natural boundaries, would call for rectification; and it would appear that the natural frontier of Russia runs from Danzig, or perhaps Stettin to Trieste."

style of originality and intelligence, had said bluntly much that was on the minds of many leaders – Truman and Bevin among them. Out of office, he could say what those in power could not, and he had used the occasion to the full. But those in power were uneasy and not entirely happy. He was ahead of public opinion, while they more or less had to stay in step. If the Fulton speech reads in retrospect, decades later, as an eloquent, prescient statement of the obvious, it was not so at the time. In 1946 Churchill's speech had the impact of a rumbling political earth tremor. For some he had shaken the world with what it needed to hear, in clear and unequivocal terms. For others, it was Churchill the old Tory imperialist trying once again to get the United States to come to the help of Britain. In general, American reaction to the speech was reserved, scarcely an enthusiastic response to a clarion call. Anti-British isolationists would have none of Churchill's ideas about fraternal association, while the liberal left declared itself shocked at his anti-Soviet tone and came out against anything that would supersede the United Nations. *The Wall Street Journal* snapped back: "This country's reaction to Mr. Churchill must be convincing proof that the U.S. wants no alliance, or anything that resembles an alliance with other nations."

Walter Lippmann wrote that "the line of British imperial interest and the line of American vital interest are not to be regarded as identical." Lippmann favored loans to Britain and France, enactment of universal military training in the United States, and the rebuilding of American naval power in Europe and the Mediterranean, but said that "if we do any of these necessary, desirable and inherently constructive things inside an alliance which is avowedly anti-Soviet, they will surely accentuate the antagonism of Moscow far more than they reinforce our own influence for a peaceful settlement."

Truman was asked at a press conference three days after the speech if his presence on the platform at Fulton could be taken as endorsement of what Churchill had to say. He took refuge in a noncommittal and disingenuous response: "I didn't know what would be in Mr. Churchill's speech. This is a country of free speech. Mr. Churchill had a perfect right to say what he pleased."

From Moscow, Stalin struck back in a canned interview with *Pravda*, comparing Churchill to Hitler, voicing racial theories of the Führer:

The English-speaking nations are [supposed to be] the only nations of full value and must rule over the remaining nations of the world. . . . It is a dangerous act calculated to sow seeds of discord among the Allied governments. Mr. Churchill is now in the position of a firebrand of war and Mr. Churchill is not alone here. There is no doubt that the policy of Mr. Churchill is a set-up for war, a call for war against the Soviet Union.

In London, Bevin and Attlee were uneasy and concerned, not about the views Churchill had expressed but fearful of a negative effect on American opinion at a time when the $4.4 billion American loan to Britain was still working its way through a less than enthusiastic Congress. In March of 1946, the pendulum of Anglo-American relations had yet to begin the slow swing back in the direction that Churchill was so forcefully preaching. Just as the Americans were divided over the speech, so the British Labour party was also divided. A party policy resolution, proposed but not adopted, read:

This conference is of the opinion that world peace can only be based on a British policy directed to ensure firm friendship and cooperation with the progressive forces throughout the world, and in particular the USSR. The Conference therefore calls upon the government to maintain and foster an attitude of sympathy and friendship towards the Soviet Union, and to repudiate Mr. Churchill's defeatist proposal to make the British Commonwealth a mere satellite of American monopoly capitalism which will inevitably lead to our being aligned in a partnership of hostility to Russia.

Ernest Bevin had fought too many battles in the Labour party and the trade-union movement with Communists and fellow-travelers to pay much attention to this kind of sniping. He was no man to be blown off course. But like Harry Truman he had to wait, and allow events and the public-opinion debate to shape a judgment before firing off salvos of his own.

Meanwhile, Churchill, back in Washington after the speech and basking in praise from James Forrestal, Averell Harriman and others, sent a personal telegram to Attlee and Bevin through the British Embassy to inform them first of the still-secret American decision to send the U.S.S Missouri to Istanbul, which he had been told about by Forrestal.

This strikes me [Churchill cabled] as a very important act of state and one calculated to make the Russians understand that they must come to reasonable terms of discussion with the Western democracies. It will place a demurrer on what you have called cutting our line through the Mediterranean, through establishment of a Russian naval base at Tripoli. Some show of strength and resistance is necessary to a good settlement with Russia. I predict that this will be the prevailing opinion in the United States in the near future.

The near future, however, was still a good many months away. But Churchill had no worries, and he had another nineteen years of life in which to see his words once again become accepted wisdom. In the meantime, the seed that he had publicly planted at Fulton, watered by onrushing events, was certain to grow. But the making of the alliance that Churchill sought would be a slow and complex evolution.

While Churchill pondered his Fulton speech in the February Florida sunshine, George Kennan, in the arctic gloom of the Moscow winter, received a telegram from the State Department asking, of all things, if the embassy could explain the apparent unwillingness of the Soviet Union to join the World Bank and International Monetary Fund!

Nowhere in Washington [Kennan subsequently wrote] had the hopes entertained for postwar collaboration with Russia been more elaborate, more naïve, or more tenaciously – one might almost say ferociously – pursued than in the Treasury Department. Now at long last their dream seemed to be shattered, and the Department of State passed on to the Embassy, in tones of bland innocence, the anguished cry of bewilderment that had floated over from the Treasury. How did one explain such behavior on the part of the Soviet Government? What lay behind it?*

---

* The official in charge of international policy at the Treasury from 1941 to 1945 was Harry Dexter White, a brilliant monetary and financial expert. In November 1945, the FBI informed Truman that White was suspected of working for the Soviet Union. In 1948, White was then publicly named as a Soviet agent by Whittaker Chambers, in testimony growing out of the Alger Hiss case. White died of a heart attack soon after. No charges were brought and nothing was ever proved.

At the time the telegram arrived, Kennan was in charge of the embassy after Ambassador Harriman's departure. A man of high academic and intellectual bent, he had entered the Foreign Service after graduating from Princeton in 1924. By his own account, Kennan was very much an "outsider" from the Midwest at Princeton – none of the F. Scott Fitzgerald life for him. He had a natural gift for languages, and in the Foreign Service first polished his French in a posting to Geneva and then his German during a tour of duty in Hamburg. In 1928 he became one of a handful of gifted Foreign Service officers who elected to specialize in Soviet affairs and Russian studies – at a time when the United States had no diplomatic relations with the Soviet Union. He learned Russian from German in Berlin, while Charles E. Bohlen was studying Russian from French in Paris. Kennan was next posted to Riga in Latvia and eventually to Russia as the chief career diplomat under Ambassador William Bullitt when Roosevelt reestablished diplomatic relations with Moscow in March 1934.

Kennan loved the Russian language and had a deep compassionate feeling for the Russian people and their unending struggles with tyranny. An uncle, George F. Kennan, after whom he was named, had traveled widely in Russia late in the nineteenth century and had written a classic exposé of the czarist prison and "interior exile" system in Siberia. Face to face with Stalinist tyranny in the 1930s, Kennan formed the strong opinion that "the Soviet Union is not a fit ally or associate, actual or potential, for the United States."

When he returned to Moscow in the summer of 1944, after assignments in Prague, Lisbon and London, everything that was happening reinforced his view that Roosevelt's assiduous efforts to create partnership and understanding with the Soviet Union were politically, historically and morally wrong. His analytical dispatches from Moscow in 1944 and 1945 seeking to expose the fallacies of the policy as he saw it were not what Washington wanted to hear. When the query relayed from the Treasury Department reached the embassy, Kennan was working from his bedroom, fighting off a cold, sinus, fever, tooth trouble and the aftereffects of early sulfa drugs that were supposed to produce relief. The combination of frustration with his sniffles and sputtering indignation over the Washington telegram roused him to fevered action.

For eighteen long months I had done little else but pluck people's sleeves, trying to make them understand. Now my opinion was being asked. The occasion, to be sure, was a trivial one, but the implications of the query were not. It was no good trying to brush the question off with a couple of routine sentences about Soviet views on such things as world banks and monetary funds. It would not do to give them just a fragment of the truth. Here was a case where nothing but the whole truth would do. They had asked for it. Now, by God, they would have it!

The Long Telegram that Kennan dispatched to Washington on February 22, 1946 (actually five separate but related telegrams so it would not look so outrageously long), seized its State Department readers rather as the poet John Keats was seized "On First Looking into Chapman's Homer":

> Then felt I like some watcher of the skies
> When a new planet swims into his ken. . . .

It also lifted Kennan from the outposts of the U.S. Foreign Service into the seminal center of Washington policy-making.

Kennan began his reply by decorously complimenting the State Department on a query that raised questions "so intricate, so delicate, so strange to our form of thought and so important to the analysis of our international environment that I cannot compress the answers into a single brief message without yielding to . . . a dangerous degree of oversimplification." He began his analysis by describing how the Soviets viewed the outside world, as expressed in Soviet propaganda – adding his own caveat that "the premises on which this party line is based are simply not true." Nevertheless, Soviet propaganda was what the Soviet leadership believed, and therefore was the basis of Soviet behavior:

Soviet leaders are driven by necessities of their own past and present positions to put forward a dogma which pictures the outside world as evil, hostile and menacing, but as bearing within itself germs of creeping disease and destined to be wracked with growing internal convulsions until it is given a final *coup de grâce* by the rising power of socialism and yields to a new and better world. This thesis provides justification for that increase of military and police power in the Russian state, for that isolation of the

Russian population from the outside world, and for that fluid and constant pressure to extend the limits of Russian police power, the natural instinctive urges of Russian rulers. Basically this is only the steady advance of uneasy Russian nationalism. . . . But in new guise of international Marxism, with its honeyed promises to a desperate and wartorn world, it is more dangerous and insidious than ever before.

In particular, Kennan warned, this put the United States on a collision course with "a political force committed fanatically to the belief that with the U.S. there can be no permanent modus vivendi, that it is desirable and necessary that the internal harmony of our society be disrupted, our traditional way of life destroyed and the international authority of our state be broken."

How did the Soviets expect to achieve this? Kennan next turned to the two parallel lines of Soviet policy – "official" and "unofficial, or subterranean, the plane for which the Soviet government accepts no responsibility."

As far as "official" Soviet government policy was concerned, out in the open, Kennan told the State Department to "look for the following":

- Priority to increasing in every way the strength and prestige of the Soviet state, with great displays to impress outsiders, along with continued secretiveness about internal matters to conceal weaknesses and keep opponents in the dark.
- Wherever promising, an effort to advance Soviet power territorially against neighboring points that Moscow conceived as of immediate strategic necessity, such as northern Iran and Turkey. (In February 1946, the Red Army was still in northern Iran.)
- Official participation in international organizations where the Soviets saw the opportunity of extending Soviet power, or of acting in a manner to inhibit or dilute the power of others. Moscow, Kennan warned, saw the United Nations not as a mechanism for creating a permanent and stable world society, but as an arena in which it could pursue its own political and strategic aims.
- With regard to colonial areas and backward or dependent peoples, Soviet policy directed toward a weakening of the power and influence of the Western nations, or contacts and advancement of the West.
- Lip service by the Soviet Union to the desirability of deepening

cultural contacts between peoples, but restricted to arid channels of "closely shepherded official visits and functions with a superabundance of vodka and speeches and a dearth of any permanent effects."

Kennan then addressed the "unofficial or subterranean plane for implementation of basic Soviet policies." He first warned that although Stalin had ostensibly abolished the Comintern during the war, "the Communist parties are in reality working closely together in a concealed Comintern tightly coordinated and directed by Moscow." (Stalin would create the Cominform to take the place of the Comintern in the following year, 1947.)

In addition to the Communist parties working under Moscow's direction, Kennan listed for the edification of the State Department all of the various types of potential "front organizations" through which the Soviet Union might be operating to further its political aims with penetration by secret Communist party members: labor unions, youth leagues, women's organizations, cultural groups, religious societies, publishing houses, foreign branches of the Russian Orthodox Church, Pan-Slav societies, racial groups – all available "to undermine general political and strategic potential of the major Western powers, hamstring measures of national defense, increase social and industrial unrest, stimulate all forms of disunity, poor set against rich, black against white, young against old, newcomers against established residents, etc."

Remorselessly Kennan continued:

Where individual governments stand in the path of Soviet purposes, pressure will be brought for their removal from office. In foreign countries, Communists will, as a rule, work toward destruction of all forms of personal independence, economic, political or moral. Everything possible will be done to set major Western powers against each other. Anti-British talk will be plugged among Americans and anti-American talk among British. In general, all Soviet efforts on an unofficial international plane will be negative and destructive in character, designed to tear down sources of strength beyond the reach of Soviet control. This is only in line with the basic Soviet instinct that there can be no compromise with rival power and that constructive work can only start when Communist power is dominant.

Finally he dealt with "practical deductions from the standpoint of U.S. policy." First he pointed out that Soviet power, unlike that of Hitlerite Germany, "does not work by fixed plans, does not take unnecessary risks, is impervious to logic of reason, but is highly sensitive to the logic of force." For this reason, Kennan said, the Soviet Union can easily withdraw "and usually does" when strong resistance is encountered. He therefore judged that "if situations are properly handled, there need be no prestige-engaging showdowns."

> Gauged against the Western world as a whole, the Soviets are still by far the weaker force. Thus, their success will really depend on the degree of cohesion, firmness and vigor which the Western world can muster. And this is a factor which is within our power to influence. All Soviet propaganda beyond the Soviet security sphere is basically negative and destructive. It should therefore be relatively easy to combat it by any intelligent and really constructive program.
>
> Our first step must be to apprehend, and recognize for what it is, the nature of the movement with which we are dealing. . . . We must formulate and put forward for other nations a much more positive and constructive picture of the sort of world we would like to see. It is not enough to urge the people to develop political processes similar to our own. Many foreign peoples, in Europe at least, are tired and frightened by experiences of the past, and are less interested in abstract freedom than in security. They are seeking guidance rather than responsibilities. We should be better able than the Russians to give them this. And unless we do, the Russians certainly will.

Very simply, Kennan in the Long Telegram postulated a complete reversal of the Roosevelt foreign policy of seeking compromise, understanding and cooperation with the Soviet Union. He did not couch his dispatch in those terms, of course, but the message of the Long Telegram was, "Wake up – this is what is *really* happening!" The impact on the State Department, and beyond in the government, was little short of sensational. Kennan's dry, analytical, factual, driving prose was read, moreover, in the context of the Iron Curtain speech two weeks later in which Churchill said publicly in more sweeping, colorful, generalized political terms more or less the same things.

Kennan did not in the Long Telegram formulate the famous "Containment Theory." That came eighteen months later in an article in *Foreign Affairs Quarterly* under the intriguing by-line of "X." But his Moscow dispatch was a first honing of the analysis of the nature and conduct of Soviet foreign policy on which the containment theory would later be based.

Kennan later wrote, not without justification:

> If none of my previous literary efforts had seemed to evoke even the faintest tinkle from the bell at which they were aimed, this one, to my astonishment, struck it squarely and set it vibrating with a resonance that was not to die down for many months. It was one of those moments when official Washington, whose state of receptivity or the opposite are determined by subjective emotional currents as intricately imbedded in the subconscious as those of the most complicated of Sigmund Freud's erstwhile patients, was ready to receive a given message. Six months earlier it probably would have been received in the Department of State with raised eyebrows and lips pursed in disapproval. Six months later, it would probably have sounded redundant, a sort of preaching to the convinced.

Almost at once, the Long Telegram began circulating to a far wider government audience than State Department dispatches usually reach. When it arrived at the department, Averell Harriman was in Washington to clean up affairs after three and a half years in Moscow, before being pressured by Truman to take another assignment as ambassador to London. He read the dispatch, and even sent Kennan a brief laconic telegram of congratulations. Harriman seldom bothered to praise or thank anybody; he simply operated on the principle that working for him was praise enough. But he also sent a copy of the Long Telegram over to James Forrestal at the Navy Department. For Forrestal, Kennan had produced at last, with clear and convincing insight, exactly the explanation of Soviet policy that he had been vainly looking for somewhere in the government. The navy secretary immediately ordered the telegram distributed to the Joint Chiefs of Staff and senior officials and military commanders, and at once it began to spread throughout the government until eventually a thousand or more copies were circulating.

Dean Acheson read and praised the Long Telegram from the somewhat frustrating perspective of an undersecretary trying to conduct foreign policy for Secretary Byrnes. But he also commented rather tartly:

His recommendations – to be of good heart, to look to our own social and economic health, to present a good face to the world, all of which the Government was trying to do – were of no help; his historical analysis might or might not have been sound, but his predictions and warnings could not have been better. We responded to them slowly.

There was, of course, little that a chargé d'affaires sitting in Moscow could do to originate government policy in Washington, but it was not long before Kennan *was* in a position to take a direct hand in shaping events.

Forrestal not only read and circulated the Long Telegram. At his instigation, Kennan was recalled to Washington. A new National War College was about to be established by the federal government at Fort McNair on the southeastern edge of the District of Columbia, and Forrestal proposed to the State Department on the strength of the Long Telegram that Kennan should become its director of foreign-policy studies. It was an assignment perfectly suited to Kennan's fertile academic turn of mind, and he arrived back in Washington in April 1946.

In May of 1947, after he had been at the War College exactly a year, he was summoned to the State Department by General Marshall and given the immediate task of creating a new Policy Planning Staff, with an office adjoining that of the secretary of state. A first urgent assignment was to produce recommendations for American action to deal with the deepening postwar economic crisis in Europe. General Marshall had an intelligent, orderly mind and a soldier's determination about good staff work, even in diplomacy.

After that, it was not long before the exhortations and warnings of Churchill's Iron Curtain speech and Kennan's Long Telegram began to translate into decisive American response and government action.

FOUR

1947: The Truman Doctrine and the Marshall Plan

George Catlett Marshall took office as secretary of state in January of 1947 for the two most decisive years of peacetime in the history of the United States. To Churchill's "bewildered, baffled and breathless" world, Marshall brought clarity, purpose, vision and hope, and above all, firm American leadership. In 1947 and 1948 General Marshall built the base for all that has since followed in America's world role.

General Marshall was one of those rare human beings from whom great authority flowed naturally and effortlessly like breathing out and breathing in. Command decision was his life. He was a tall man of fine bearing, who exuded strength whether he was walking down a corridor or sitting calmly behind his desk. He was a listener rather than a talker, reserved and aloof. No one ever claimed to be close to General Marshall. But his undogmatic open-mindedness, his wide-ranging experience and common sense, the spare clarity with which he expressed himself, his courteous but firm manner with everyone inspired respectful devotion and distant affection in all who served him. Second-raters did not last in his company. Above all, General Marshall was a man of total integrity, without petty vanity or conceit, with no trace of politics or personal ambition in his makeup except to serve his country selflessly and honorably and well. He set the highest standards, and he is the only American soldier ever to be compared with his fellow Virginian, George Washington, in service to the nation. It is fitting that it was under General Marshall that the United States finally turned away from General Washington's famous farewell admonition to the fledgling Republic in 1796 to avoid entangling alliances with Europe.

As Marshall took over in Washington, the worst winter weather of this century locked war-decimated Europe in a prolonged grip of ice and snow and subfreezing temperatures that lasted from December to April. Occasionally there have been brief spells of colder weather in Europe, but never before or since has there been a winter of such unbroken frigid severity. Often weather has affected battles and military history, but seldom has it affected the peacetime fortunes of a nation the way it did in Great Britain in 1946–1947. On the Continent, the weather was a severe interruption to postwar recovery. But in Britain it was a savage blow that brought the nation temporarily to its knees, producing an economic crisis that forced Bevin and the Labour government to an immediate reassessment of British global power commitments that were now the high price of imperial history and victory in the war.

The crisis began in December when the country's largest automobile plant shut down for lack of power. By the end of January, the Thames had frozen solid all the way from Windsor Castle through London to the open sea. Coal barges could not move supplies to power stations. Snow blocked roads and railroads. In February the government was forced to order a three-week shutdown of virtually all industry throughout the country for lack of electricity, and unemployment soared to 2.3 million workers. Electricity for households was cut three hours in the mornings and afternoons. At the time I was starting my third year in the London bureau of the old *New York Herald Tribune*, and in a happy mood, with a growing family, my wife and I had rented a delightful spacious suburban house with a lovely garden near the Wimbledon tennis courts. But it had fourteen fireplaces and no central heating – and in January the coal ration was reduced to one hundred pounds per household per week, barely enough to keep one room warm. Cheese and bacon rations were cut below the wartime level. Bread rationing was introduced for the first time ever. All in all it was a winter to remember.

No government can forecast the weather. Well before the great freeze hit, the Labour government already was agonizing over the precarious state of the economy, the draining overseas commitments, the desperate need for investment to speed industrial reconversion, the paucity of export earnings. Already the government could see the $4.4 billion American loan beginning to drain out like a monetary hemorrhage, barely six months after its approval by Congress. On January 2, 1947, Hugh Dalton, chancellor of the exchequer, wrote almost plaintively to Prime Minister Attlee:

> What shall it profit Britain to have even 1.5 million men in the armed forces and supply services, and be spending nearly one billion pounds a year on them, if we come an economic and financial cropper two years hence.

But the "cropper" was barely a month away. Dalton had just lost a year-end battle in the Cabinet for another 10 percent cut in military spending. Largely on Bevin's insistence, the cut had been held to 5 percent. During 1946, the government had speeded demobilization of a further 800,000 men to bring the armed forces down to 1.1 million, with 650,000 in the work force producing arms and supplies for the military. Yet the British were still maintaining about the same size military establishment as the United States, two years after the war with well under half the population.

Where to cut next? The British Army of several hundred thousand in West Germany, facing the Red Army? British troops in the forward occupation zone in Austria? Troops in Trieste? The largest navy in the Atlantic and the Mediterranean? Nearly 20,000 British bolstering the Greeks in renewed civil fighting with the Communist ELAS forces? Several divisions in seething Palestine? Upwards of 100,000 troops in Egypt and the Suez Canal Zone? British forces in India and the sub-continent? Troops scattered in outposts of the Empire in the Sudan, Kenya, Aden, Ceylon, the Persian Gulf, Malaysia, Singapore, Hong Kong? The sun never set on Britain's burdens.

Already while Bevin was in New York in December 1946, winding up the peace-treaty negotiations with Byrnes, Attlee had written him a long personal letter, which he typed himself on his own typewriter, warning that "we have got to consider our commitments very carefully lest we try to do more than we can – in particular I am worried about Greece." The prime minister continued rather tartly:

I think we have got to be very careful in taking on military obligations in Greece and Turkey when the U.S.A. only gives economic assistance. There is a tendency in America to regard us as an outpost, but an outpost they will not have to defend. I am disturbed by the signs of America trying to make a safety zone around herself while leaving us and Europe in a No Man's Land. While I think we should try to find out what the Americans are preparing to do, we should be careful not to commit ourselves.

For nearly two years, Bevin had been successfully holding the line in the Cabinet against precipitous cuts in military spending that would force a slash in Britain's overseas commitments. Always it was the same argument – if we pull out, who will replace us, what will the consequences be? U.S. occupation forces in West Germany were still being run down, and certainly the United States had yet to show any readiness to entangle itself in any other military commitments beyond what it considered to be its own defense perimeter. But Great Britain without electric power to run its factories was no longer a nation that could go on sustaining and projecting military power indiscriminately across the world. In the freezing February gloom in London, a moment of truth had arrived not only for Britain but for the United States as well.

Attlee, who had sided continuously with Bevin in 1945 and 1946, now decided that commitments had to be cut, and crisply and decisively took charge. Despite the crisis there would be no further immediate military budget cuts, but the process of long-term reductions overseas, both political and military, for future savings would begin at once.

At the top of Attlee's list were India (together with Burma and Ceylon), Palestine and Greece. No problem in British imperial history was ever debated, examined and reexamined, reported, novelized, philosophized, agonized and dramatized with such long and continuous intensity as "what to do about India." In January, Attlee concluded that the only way to bring half a century of discussion and negotiation to an end would be simply to fix a firm and final deadline to end British rule and get out. But as his proposal circulated among the Cabinet ministers, he received a vigorous objection from Bevin that "in the British Empire we knuckle under at the first blow," and warning of "tremendous repercussions" if, as he charged, "we appear to be trying nothing except to scuttle out of it."

Attlee came back with a typically laconic rejoinder to the foreign secretary, of the kind that made him such an unusually strong prime minister:

> We are seeking to fulfil the pledges of this country with dignity and to avoid an ignominious scuttle. But a scuttle it will be if things are allowed to drift. . . . If you disagree with what is proposed, you must offer a practical alternative. I fail to find one in your letter. Yours ever, Clem.

In fact, by pushing through the decision to get out of India, Attlee was also clearing the deck to withdraw from Palestine as well – a burden far more unpopular and onerous, in which British soldiers were getting killed in the intractable and thankless task of trying to maintain peace between Arabs and Jews. And so on February 14, Ernest Bevin announced to the House of Commons that Great Britain would be referring the Palestine problem to the United Nations to work out some kind of agreement to partition the territory, failing which Britain would surrender its mandate and withdraw its forces after forty years of rule. Then on February 20, Attlee announced to the Commons that British rule of India would end, come what may, in June of 1948, whether or not there was constitutional agreement between Hindus and Muslims. In the end, the subcontinent was partitioned between India and Pakistan.

These announcements in the February gloom with British industry shut down and the Thames frozen solid outside the Houses of Parliament marked the beginning of the end of the greatest empire in all history – a process of withdrawal and dismantling that took all in all another twenty years to effectively conclude, carried out on the whole with statesmanship, good grace and political courage and skill. Nothing in the history of the empire became the British like the leaving of it.

On the day Bevin made the Palestine announcement in the House of Commons, he invited a small group of American correspondents to the Foreign Office to discuss the action the government was taking after so much bitter controversy not only between Arabs and Jews but also between Britain and the United States. I was there for the *Herald Tribune*. In later years, Dean Acheson would write that "life with Ernie was gay and turbulent, for his temper could build up as suddenly as a summer storm, and could flash and thunder as noisily, and then disappear as the sun broke through." As we walked into the foreign secretary's great office, I was walking unwittingly into one of those summer storms.

In those days, an enormous portrait of King George III hung behind the foreign secretary's desk.* But on this occasion the great chandelier in the center of the room was turned off to save electricity, and the scene was gloomily lit by low-watt floor and desk lamps as we settled into leather easy chairs. Bevin was a short, squat man of large girth and hulking, powerful shoulders and arms from his days as a farm laborer and horse-cart driver. He had the appearance of a knotty, gnarled trunk of old English oak. In his colorful worker's speech, he launched into an explanation of why Britain had concluded that it was now up to the United Nations to take over the Palestine problem, and questions began.

As the discussion progressed, I asked the foreign secretary, perhaps injudiciously, if he was not concerned that the Soviet Union might attempt to grab the Palestine Mandate in the United Nations if Britain were to give it up, and "cut across the throat of the Empire" – using the phrase that Bevin had used when the Russians had attempted to obtain a mandate over the Italian colony of Tripolitania. I ignited a very short fuse. As I formed my question, Bevin began pounding his chin with his fist in irritation, and then the fist came crashing down on his desk.

"It's BOTH our throats – BOTH our throats I tell you," he almost seemed to bellow. "That's what I've been tryin' to tell you people for two years! It's BOTH our throats in this!" And then he launched into an impassioned defense of his efforts to obtain a peaceful solution to the Palestine problem, the strategic importance of the whole Middle East to the West, and the dangers of Soviet penetration of the area, which an Arab-Jewish conflict would only increase. I slumped lower and lower in the deep leather armchair, but there was no place to fade away as the foreign secretary thundered on. When he finished there were a couple of further desultory questions, and we all got up to troop out. I felt particularly chastened, but Bevin came out from behind his desk and clamped a great arm around my shoulder, grinned at me and said: "Well,

---

* Acheson also relates how Bevin once poured him a drink in his office and then turned to the portrait and said: "Let's drink to 'im. If 'e 'adn't been so bloody stoopid, you wouldn't 'ave been able to come to our rescue with the Marshall Plan!"

now, that was just the price of admission, I guess, wasn't it?" I could understand why the Foreign Office was so devoted to him.

None of us knew on that February 14 in Bevin's office that he was agonizing over the most important and far-reaching foreign-policy decision to be taken in London since the end of the war – the cutoff of British economic and military support for the embattled government of Greece. It was a move that would have immediate political and strategic impact on the United States and the world situation, far greater than the longer-term decisions for eventual British withdrawal from India and Palestine.

Bevin had long felt that the Labour party and even Attlee did not fully grasp how much was at stake in Greece, the effect that a Communist takeover would have on the balance of power in the Middle East, and how much a British withdrawal would affect Anglo-American relations if it was clumsily handled. When the war ended in 1945, Britain had 80,000 troops in Greece to bolster changing Greek governments that managed generally to combine incompetence, complacency and defeatism. By February of 1947, troops had been cut back to around 16,000, but as far as Attlee, Dalton and the British Treasury were concerned, it was increasingly a waste of men and money. Once the decisions were taken in the February crisis to withdraw from Palestine and India, Bevin knew that he could no longer carry the case for holding on in Greece. All he could do was play as best he could to get the Americans to take over. On February 18, he accepted in the Cabinet that the Greek commitment would have to be wound up, but it was agreed to say nothing to the Greek government and keep the decision secret until the Americans had first been informed and given time to react.

In fact, Bevin had begun preparing the groundwork for such an eventuality several months before. In earlier discussions while Byrnes was still in office, the Americans had accepted in principle British urging that they should do more to help the Greeks, and a special U.S. economic mission was already in Athens and had made a preliminary study of the situation. In the State Department, Loy Henderson, the astute Near Eastern director and a specialist on Soviet affairs, had already prepared a paper on "Crisis and Imminent Possibility of Collapse" in Greece.

Nevertheless, when the British ambassador asked to see the secretary of state on the morning of Friday, February 21 – the day after the announcement of British withdrawal from India – to deliver an urgent message from London, it was, in Dean Acheson's words, "a shocker." The message was "brief and all too clear – British aid to Greece and Turkey would end in six weeks."

Under Acheson, the State Department went into feverish weekend activity to prepare recommendations for General Marshall, who was away from Washington to deliver a speech at Princeton University. When Marshall arrived at the department on Monday morning, he needed no briefing on the strategic importance of Greece and the gravity of the situation were it to slip under Communist control. The question was what the United States would do. Marshall first sent a polite protest to Bevin at the short notice with which he had thrust the problem on the United States, and inquired whether this meant some basic change in British policy. Bevin cabled immediately that Britain's view was unchanged – the freedom of Greece and Turkey as well as Iran and Italy from Soviet domination was absolutely essential to Western European security and Middle East stability, but Britain could no longer carry the burden alone. Marshall then assured Bevin that the United States would accept its full share of responsibilities, but he said it would take five or six weeks, at least, to get congressional approval for a special aid program, and could the British not find additional funds and keep their remaining troops in Greece to hold the fort in the meantime? This Bevin agreed to do, with relief. He could now be sure that the torch would be successfully passed. In fact, the last British troops did not leave Greece until 1950 when the civil war was over.

By Monday evening, basic policy recommendations for emergency aid for Greece and Turkey had been approved by Marshall for submission to President Truman on Tuesday. Truman wasted no time agonizing over a decision, and convened a White House meeting with congressional leaders on Thursday, February 27. All that was involved was a simple aid bill. But a full year had now passed since the warnings of the Long Telegram and the Iron Curtain speech. There was no doubt in the minds of Truman, Marshall, Acheson and the Washington policymakers that the time had come to act, and this would be a major turning point in U.S. foreign policy. After two years of reaction, aid to Greece and Turkey would clearly commit the United States to action on the front line in Europe.

When the congressional leaders gathered in the Oval Office, Marshall of course led off the discussion. But his style was always restrained and somewhat flat, avoiding histrionics and relying on clearly presented facts to speak for themselves. Unfortunately, this was not quite enough to stir congressmen who, in Acheson's phrase, "had no conception of what challenged them." So Acheson asked to speak, and launched into an impassioned dissertation that would have had Tom Paine cheering, as he rolled on about the threat to freedom that a Soviet breakthrough into Greece would pose to the Middle East, Europe and Africa, and how "we alone are in a position to break up the power play." According to Acheson's account, a long silence followed, and then Senator Arthur H. Vandenberg spoke up in his mellifluous senatorial manner: "Mr. President, if you will say that to the Congress and the country, I will support you and I believe that most of its members will do the same."

Despite Vandenberg's weighty assurance, it was far from clear sailing. The following week the newly elected Republican-controlled Congress voted a cut of $4.5 billion in the Truman budget for the coming fiscal year. When the President held a second enlarged White House meeting on March 10 to go into more detail on the request he would be making for $400 million for Greece and Turkey, he got a very cool and skeptical hearing.

By now General Marshall had left Washington for Paris and Moscow and another Council of Foreign Ministers meeting with Molotov, Bevin and Bidault. A final draft of what became the Truman Doctrine speech was sent to Marshall in Paris. Acheson had prepared the first draft, which George Kennan criticized for being too strong, and Clark Clifford, Truman's close political adviser in the White House, thought was too weak. Clifford went to work to get it more into Truman's speaking style, and more important, to invest the aid request with the rhetoric of a crusade.

In Paris, Marshall went over the speech with Bohlen, who was accompanying him to Moscow to interpret and advise, and both felt that even though the Soviet Union was not specifically mentioned, the tone was too flamboyantly anti-Communist for what they thought should be handled as a Greek problem and not a crusade. Marshall cabled Washington to this effect, but Truman had now taken over the draft himself, remarking later, "I wanted no hedging, it had to be clear and free of hesitation or double-talk."

And so President Truman's address to Congress on March 12, 1947, continues to reverberate in history today:

> At the present moment in history, nearly every nation must choose between alternative ways of life. The choice is too often not a free one. One way of life is based on the will of the majority. The second is based upon the will of a minority forcibly imposed upon the majority. It relies upon terror and oppression, a controlled press and radio, fixed elections and the suppression of personal freedom.
>
> I believe that it *must* [italics added] be the policy of the United States to support free peoples who are resisting attempted subjugation by armed minorities or by outside pressures.
>
> I believe that we *must* [italics added] assist free peoples to work out their own destinies in their own way.
>
> I believe that our help should be primarily through economic and financial aid which is essential to economic stability and orderly political processes. . . .
>
> Should we fail to aid Greece and Turkey in this fateful hour, the effect will be far-reaching to the West as well as to the East. We must take immediate and resolute action.

By now Marshall was in Moscow and the first meeting of the Big Four foreign ministers had taken place on March 10. The conference went on for seven weeks. Yet in all that time, in all the formal and informal discussions with Molotov and others, including Stalin himself, not once was the Truman speech mentioned to General Marshall by any Soviet leader. They left it to *Izvestia* to make a routine denunciation of "a fresh intrusion of the U.S.A. into the affairs of other states."

As Ernest Bevin wearily and warily prepared to go to Moscow, he had been told firmly that for medical reasons, in those days before pressurized aircraft, he would have to travel by train – a four-day journey across the frozen snow-covered continent. His doctor, Sir Alexander McCall, once said that the only sound organ in Bevin's body was his feet. At the age of sixty-seven, he had angina pectoris, cardiac failure, arteriosclerosis, sinusitis, enlarged liver, damaged kidneys, high blood pressure and he smoked and drank more than was good for him, took no exercise and was a poor sleeper. Fortunately he and McCall were close friends, because Ernie was a cantankerous and difficult patient. "I know, I know," he once joshed McCall as he poured a drink, "if I do's your don'ts I'll be in trouble."

But at least when Bevin departed from London's Victoria Station on March 4, with British industry only just beginning to start up again after the February power crisis, he had the relief of knowing that the New World had once again begun to come to the rescue of the Old World. And Bevin had an important and constructive diplomatic act of his own to perform when he crossed the English Channel: a stop first at the French port of Dunkirk, famous in the history of World War II, where he would sign a new Anglo-French Treaty of Alliance with Foreign Minister Georges Bidault.

This had come about at last through one of those brief moments of opportunity that often make history. In the last week of 1946, the veteran French Socialist leader, Léon Blum, who had spent most of the war in Vichy and Nazi prisons, briefly formed an interim minority government in Paris. He immediately wrote his fellow Socialist, Attlee, pleading for extra supplies of coal for France from the Ruhr mines in the British occupation zone of Germany, and proposing a quick visit to London to discuss relations between the two countries. Attlee invited him to come as soon as he could.

Alfred Duff Cooper, the experienced and astute British ambassador in Paris, at once suggested to both Bevin and Blum that this might be the moment to revive the question of a treaty between the two nations for the first time in their long and not always fraternal history. Bevin had always felt that any long-term security arrangement for Europe would have to begin with an Anglo-French alliance. But General de Gaulle had refused to consider such a move until the future of Germany was settled. This had remained French policy, even though de Gaulle had now been out of office for a full year. But when Blum reached London, with the terrible winter adding to European malaise and uncertainty, he quickly seized on

the treaty proposal to give some kind of political uplift and success to his
visit. All that actually happened in London was a communiqué simply
stating that the two governments had agreed to enter into negotiations to
conclude a treaty of alliance. When Blum then got back to Paris, his
caretaker government lasted only three more days! But at least when
Georges Bidault returned to the Quai d'Orsay as foreign minister in the
next government, he sent assurances – to Bevin's relief – that he would
adhere to Blum's decision and negotiations could begin.

In Dunkirk, when Bevin and Bidault arrived for the signing, the
sous-préfecture where the ceremony was to take place was one of the very
few undamaged buildings standing in the snow and biting, windy cold.
Bevin recalled a War Cabinet meeting at the end of May 1940, when
Churchill grimly reported that they would be fortunate if 10 percent of the
British Army could be got off the Dunkirk beaches, where they had
retreated at the time of the fall of France. But in the end, 338,000 British,
French and Belgian soldiers were evacuated to England. Now on those
same snow-covered beaches, Bevin and Bidault exchanged deeply emo-
tional pledges that the two nations would remain allies "for all time." And
Bevin reboarded his train for the long Moscow journey.

The Moscow conference from March 10 to April 24 was the last Big
Four meeting at which it might have been possible to avoid an irrevocable
division of Germany and Europe had the Soviet Union been interested.
But almost certainly there never had been any chance anyway of prevent-
ing the cleavage of Europe into Communist and non-Communist spheres
once the Red Army reached the Elbe River in April 1945. Nevertheless, it
had been laid down at the Potsdam Conference that Germany would be
treated on a unified basis as one country by the four occupying powers,
and up to the Moscow meeting the Western powers were still trying and
even occasionally hoping to make the policy work. After Moscow they
turned to the more realistic course of making their own part of Germany
an economic and political success instead of holding back in pursuit of a
German unity that never was going to happen. Events of two years, Soviet
intransigence and the outcome of the Moscow meetings all slowly pushed
the Western Allies into this basic change of course, but it was General
Marshall who galvanized the change into action.

Marshall, as Army Chief of Staff, of course had been present at the major wartime conferences at Teheran, Yalta and Potsdam, but this was his first direct experience of diplomatic negotiations with the Russians. From the outset he was incensed at the useless exchanges of accusations and time-wasting propaganda debates that Molotov forced on the Allies. Endlessly they had to repeat charges and countercharges about what became known as the four German D's – disarmament, demilitarization, denazification and democratization. Unlike Byrnes, who was a natural political debater, Marshall left it largely to Bevin to do the table pounding and counterpunching against Molotov, while seeking to make his effectiveness felt with cold and sparing responses and rebuttals. If the Russians could not read him, or read him incorrectly, that was their problem. For Marshall, a decisive point was reached in Moscow on the afternoon of April 14.

One year earlier, in the spring of 1946, Byrnes had proposed – and the British and French had somewhat reluctantly gone along – that the four wartime allies conclude a twenty-five-year treaty to keep Germany disarmed. This, the Americans assumed, would constructively address a major security concern of the Soviet Union. But Molotov had simply brushed it aside without, however, having totally rejected it. Now it was again on the agenda in Moscow, and Bevin and Bidault had both hardened their support. On April 14, Marshall asked Molotov for a clear decision – did he want such a treaty or not? Molotov responded by saying that the American proposal did not go far enough because it did not put the Ruhr industry under four-power control and did not guarantee establishment of a "democratic" German state. Marshall replied coldly that those were matters for a peace treaty, not a disarmament treaty. He had "asked plainly" if Mr. Molotov was prepared to negotiate, and in reply he had gotten further qualifications "but no answer." He would now draw his own conclusions, and the ministers should pass on to their next business. The Byrnes proposal – and a last chance for some act of four-power unity on Germany – was dead.

Next evening Marshall went to the Kremlin for his one and only diplomatic face-to-face with Stalin. The meeting lasted barely an hour and a half. Marshall, speaking with habitual calm restraint, began with pleasantries about their earlier wartime meetings and regrets at the cooling of American feeling toward the Soviet Union. He had concluded, he told Stalin, that the Soviet Union did not want a treaty with its wartime allies on the demilitarization of Germany, and he would report accordingly to the President. He made no attempt to reopen the question with Stalin. Then, without mentioning the Truman Doctrine speech, Marshall firmly told Stalin that it was the determination of the United States to give all the assistance it could to countries that were threatened with economic collapse, and with it the hope of preserving their democracies. It was the U.S. intention to help, not to dominate, he said, and he hoped that his speaking frankly might improve understanding.

Stalin had listened impassively, puffing on a cigarette and, Bohlen noted, doodling wolf's heads with a red pencil. He also spoke calmly and quietly. Defending the Soviet positions, he told Marshall that it would be wrong to give too tragic an interpretation to their present disagreements because as a rule "when people exhaust themselves" in disputes they come to recognize the need for compromise. These were "only first skirmishes" and it was necessary to have patience. There was no urgency about settling the German question and "if we don't agree the next time, then maybe the time after that."

General Marshall silently drew his own conclusions and did not waste time in further discussions before a courteous good-bye.

A few days later as the conference came to an end, totally without results, Bevin wrote a personal letter to Attlee: "There is courtesy, there are no high words being used, no tempers, but all of it is cool, calculated, and between the two big boys it looks to me to be pretty determined." Bevin was certainly right.

"All the way back to Washington," Bohlen wrote, "Marshall talked of the importance of finding some initiative to prevent the complete breakdown of Western Europe. He came to the conclusion that Stalin saw that the best way to advance Soviet interests was to let matters drift. This was the kind of crisis that Communism thrived on."

On his return, after talking with the President, Marshall went on the air with a stark report to the nation, and a reply to Stalin:

We cannot ignore the factor of time. The recovery of Europe has been far slower than had been expected. Disintegrating forces are becoming evident. The patient is sinking while the doctors deliberate. So I believe that action cannot await compromise through exhaustion. New issues arise daily. Whatever action is possible to meet these pressing problems must be taken without delay.

Next day, Marshall summoned George Kennan and instructed him to assemble a new Policy Planning Staff "immediately" and produce a report on what ought to be done for Europe "without delay."

In the eight weeks that Marshall had been away from Washington, reports had been pouring in from United States embassies all over Europe about the devastating effect of the terrible winter, along with alarmist warnings of the political effect that the slowdown of recovery and the parlous economic malaise were beginning to have on the strength and stability of governments – many of which in 1947 included at least token membership of Cabinet ministers drawn from the upper ranks of the Communist parties. Marshall's instructions to Kennan did not go much beyond what he had already said in his radio address to the nation – the patient was sinking while the doctors were deliberating, and he wanted a clear staff recommendation of what to do, and he wanted it quickly. He told Kennan that others would take the initiative if he did not, and he wanted to avoid this and not be put on the defensive. General Marshall was as much a strategist of democracy as he was of war. His terse and typical final instruction to Kennan was: "Avoid trivia."

Like the State Department query that had produced the Long Telegram fifteen months earlier, this was a moment and an opportunity that George Kennan had instinctively been preparing for, waiting for. He quickly pulled in a dozen old friends and associates from the ranks of the State Department and academia and got down to work. Chip Bohlen joined him temporarily, and John Paton Davies, an old China hand recently returned from a Moscow assignment, and Burton Berry, just back from Eastern Europe. There was Joseph Johnson, a history professor on temporary State Department duty, James Angell, an economics professor from Columbia, and George McGhee, a thirty-five-year-old Rhodes scholar with a distinguished war record, then working as a special assistant to Will Clayton, undersecretary for economic affairs in the department. It was a very strong team intellectually and in terms of expertise and experience, and this made Kennan's role as the intellectual catalyst all the more remarkable.

"We met very very rapidly and very very frequently and very informally," one of the staff later recalled. "Original drafts were nearly always made by Kennan. He was always open-minded for other views and we'd gather round the table and George would start talking. Just by watching us he'd seem to know what we were thinking, like bouncing ideas off us and noticing the angle at which they bounced."

Kennan says that "my associates, able, honorable and intellectually hard-headed people, spared me no complications and forced me into an intellectual agony more intensive than anything I had previously experienced." The result was a staff report titled "Certain Aspects of the European Recovery Problem from the United States Standpoint" that went to General Marshall on May 25. Like the Long Telegram, it is probably one of the most important basic policy-shaping documents in the American archives. It set a course not only for a historic and fundamental new American involvement in Europe but, of equal importance, a new course of European unity as well. It went far beyond a mere economic-assistance program. It accelerated the transformation of United States foreign policy and a political transformation of Western Europe at the same time.

With its political and economic expertise, the Policy Planning Staff was not greatly agitated by the mere economic problem. If it were only a matter of economic aid, this could be dealt with piecemeal with loans, grants-in-aid, the Export-Import Bank or other devices. What was needed, Kennan wrote, was a much wider recovery program, the value of which "will lie not so much in its direct economic effects, which are difficult to calculate with any degree of accuracy, as in its psychological and political by-products." Such a program should aim "not to combat Communism, but the economic maladjustment which makes European society vulnerable to exploitation by any and all totalitarian movements, which Russian Communism is now exploiting."

Therefore, the policy planners concluded, it required a clear distinction between a program for economic revitalization of Europe on the one hand, and a program of American support. It was the business of the Europeans to devise their own program with "friendly aid" from the

United States, the report said, but in the end: "The program which this country is asked to support must be a joint request from a group of friendly nations, not a series of isolated and individual appeals." Kennan later elaborated on the reasoning behind this, which really lay at the heart of what became the Marshall Plan:

> Had this not been insisted upon, the United States would have been confronted with a whole series of competing national demands, all padded and exaggerated for competitive purposes, all reflecting attempts to solve economic problems within national frameworks rather than on an all-European basis. This would have forced us to make choices bound to be politically unpopular in many quarters, with respect to European governments in a position to shift onto our shoulders the blame for any features of the programs that were particularly disagreeable to sections of their electorate. But beyond this, we had serious doubts about the success of any movement toward European recovery that rested merely on a series of uncoordinated national programs; we considered that one of the long-term deficiencies of the European economy as a whole was its excessive fragmentation, the lack of competitive flexibility in commercial exchanges, the lack in particular of a large consumer's market. By insisting on a joint approach, we hoped to force the Europeans to think like Europeans, and not like nationalists in their approach to the economic problems of the continent.

Of course this knitting together of Europe inevitably involved the German question, at a time when the Americans were still preoccupied with war criminals, denazification, breaking up the I. G. Farben cartel, et cetera, and the French were determined to hold down German steel production and prevent some illusory revival of German militarism. Addressing this aspect of European recovery, Kennan's memorandum to Marshall said bluntly:

> To talk of the recovery of Europe and to oppose the recovery of Germany is nonsense. People can have both or they can have neither. This is the real choice for people like the French, and they may as well be brought to recognize it now.

As to the uncomfortable prospect of Russia and its satellites joining such a Pan-European program simply to wreck it, the planning-staff report simply proposed that the whole project should be advanced "in such a form that the Russian satellite countries would either exclude themselves by unwillingness to accept the proposed conditions, or agree to abandon the exclusive orientation of their economies" – in other words, turn from Russia to the West. Both Kennan and Bohlen felt, without any doubt, that the Russians would certainly refuse to join the kind of program they envisaged, generously open to all but in concept totally at odds with Communism and Soviet aims in Europe.

The genius of the Kennan report lay in its combination of altruism, expediency and common sense. It encompassed a whole range of problems and challenges facing the United States and synthesized it all into a dynamic policy objective, a proposal easy to grasp, politically unassailable and of self-evident compelling need. The recovery of Europe served American self-interest, anti-Communism, unity of Europe, the German problem, humanitarian considerations, the jingo idealism of the American Century – all of it recognizable by any politician or commentator or diplomat or economist or statesman who wanted to see in it his own particular crusade.

General Marshall lost little time translating the Kennan report into policy and action. The planning study was reinforced by a report of agitated alarm that Will Clayton brought back from a trip around Europe and submitted to Marshall about the same time the Kennan report was completed. Then on May 28, Marshall's secretary asked him if he wished to confirm a tentative commitment he had made to address the graduating class of Harvard University on June 5, only one week away. Marshall said yes.

Marshall turned to Chip Bohlen, a Harvard graduate, to prepare the draft of the speech, telling him simply to base it on the ideas in the Policy Planning Staff paper and the economic findings on the situation in Europe that Will Clayton had brought back. Bohlen was then forty-three years old, and after prewar years in Moscow and Tokyo, he had been at the center of power in Washington for seven years. He had known and worked directly with all of the senior Americans concerned with foreign policy in that period from Franklin Roosevelt and Harry Hopkins on down. He had an easy conviviality, charm and sophistication, quick humor and a love of the poker table. He did not pretend to be as intellectually intense as his good friend George Kennan, but he and Kennan were usually in close agreement on the reading of the Soviet situation, and Bohlen was solid and steady in his advice and influence and did not make mistakes. In particular at this juncture he was handling the State Department's congressional relations, and he was shrewd and experienced in the *political* dimension of American foreign policy, unlike Kennan, who found Congress and the democratic process to be largely a pain in the neck for diplomats and diplomacy. The political hazards of another major foreign-policy initiative by the secretary of state were very real. It had taken nearly three months to get the aid package for Greece and Turkey through Congress, under fire from both the left and right. The isolationist wing of the Republican party under Senator Robert A. Taft remained hostile to anything that seemed to be dragging the United States ever more deeply into foreign commitments and European involvements. The Henry Wallace liberals inside and outside the Democratic party were hostile to the anti-Soviet crusade aspect of the Truman Doctrine and the supposed bypassing of the United Nations. All of this was certainly on the minds of Marshall and Bohlen, though the extent to which they actually talked over the approach the speech should take is not clear.

Probably there was not much need for a discussion, because Bohlen had a clear understanding of how Marshall's mind was running. Indeed, much earlier, when General Marshall had retired as Army Chief of Staff on November 26, 1945 (to be recalled almost immediately by Truman to take on the abortive China mission), he had drafted his own "farewell" speech to his country that virtually forecast the Harvard speech:

> Today this nation with good faith and sincerity, I am certain, desires to take the lead in the measures to avoid another world catastrophe, such as you have just endured. And the world of suffering people looks to us for such leadership. Their thoughts, however, are not concentrated alone on this problem. They have the more immediate and terribly pressing concerns – where the mouthful of food will come from, where they will find shelter tonight and where they will find warmth from the cold of winter. Along with the great problem of maintaining peace we must solve this problem. . . . Neither can be solved alone. They are directly related, one to another.

Now, barely eighteen months later, the moment had come when Marshall's long grasp of the central problem was to be translated into a call for action. It was one of those moments when men make history. Much later, after forty years in the diplomatic service, Bohlen wrote:

> I have never gone in for hero worship, but of all the men I have been associated with, including presidents, George Catlett Marshall is the top of the list of those I admire. He had a power of command I have never seen equaled. Once a decision was made, there was no turning back. It did not take long for his character to permeate the Department. We knew we were working for a great man. There was greater clarity in the operation of the Department than I had ever seen before or have ever seen since.

There is no record to show whether Marshall discussed the speech with President Truman at all. Nevertheless, he was a most punctilious man in his relations with the President of the United States, and it seems almost certain he would have advised Truman what he had in mind to say at Harvard, if only in a brief phone conversation.

The master stroke of the speech that outflanked and disarmed potential domestic political opposition lay very simply in the fact that General Marshall did not *really* propose any great new American initiative or program at Harvard at all. Instead he simply posed the problem and suggested that Europe take the initiative and come up with a program for its own recovery, which the United States would then be glad to consider sympathetically to see how it could help. Marshall could not be accused of launching any Santa Claus giveaway program because he gave nothing away at all at Harvard except a promise of sympathy and a message of hope.

At the same time, the speech disarmed the critics of the left by deliberately avoiding the anti-Communist rhetoric of the Truman Doctrine that had been the work of Dean Acheson and Clark Clifford. At the time of the Truman speech, both Marshall and Bohlen had voiced reservations on this point to the White House. In shaping the Marshall speech, Bohlen drafted what in effect was a refocus of United States foreign policy objectives:

> Our policy is directed not against any country or doctrine, but against hunger, poverty, desperation and chaos. Its purpose should be the revival of a working economy in the world so as to permit the emergence of political and social conditions in which free institutions can exist.

Acheson in his memoirs subsequently wrote somewhat sourly, "If General Marshall believed, which I am sure he did not, that the American people would be moved to so great an effort as he contemplated by such a Platonic purpose, he was mistaken." In the last analysis, Acheson said, "citizens and representatives in Congress alike always wanted to learn how Marshall aid operated to block the extension of Soviet power."

But this misses the real point and the real problem in June of 1947. The Marshall speech was addressed to Europe, not Congress. Its political altruism was far more in tune with international idealism and the hopes that were still prevailing for a cooperative world instead of Acheson's confrontational world.

Europe would never have rallied to another Truman Doctrine speech as it was able to rally to Marshall's Harvard speech. By the time Acheson succeeded Marshall eighteen months later, the political division of Europe was complete, Czechoslovakian democracy had been snuffed out by Stalin and the Berlin blockade was at its height. Of course, when Acheson was lobbying for appropriation votes for the Marshall Plan in Congress, the anti-Soviet, anti-Stalin, anti-Communist crusade was the overwhelming selling point. But if Marshall had started out that way there would never have been a Marshall Plan.

Bohlen spent two days on the initial draft of the speech, which remained basically unchanged although lightly edited by Marshall himself. The key rallying cry to Europe was lifted almost intact from Kennan's policy report:

> It is already evident that before the United States Government can proceed much further in its efforts to alleviate the situation and help start the European world on its way to recovery, there must be some agreement among the countries of Europe as to the requirements of the situation and the part those countries themselves will take in order to give effect to whatever action might be undertaken by this Government.
>
> It would be neither fitting nor efficacious for this Government to undertake to draw up unilaterally a program designed to place Europe on its feet economically. That is the business of the Europeans. The initiative, I think, must come from Europe. The role of this country should consist of friendly aid in the drafting of a European program and of later support of such a program so far as it may be practical for us to do so. The program should be a joint one, agreed to by a number, if not all, European nations.

Marshall insisted to Bohlen that the speech be kept short, and it took less than ten minutes to deliver. If the speech lacked memorable eloquence, the message was clear, and Marshall himself worked over the final passage:

> With foresight, and a willingness on the part of our people to face up to the vast responsibilities which history has clearly placed upon our country, the difficulties I have outlined can and will be overcome.

Marshall had given strict instructions at the State Department that there was to be no advance publicity or briefings on his Harvard appearance. He was not after all looking for domestic impact, sensing that it might be largely negative anyway, against another lecture about the need to help Europe. The reaction Marshall sought was from Europe.

However, Dean Acheson, in his final days as undersecretary before returning to his private law practice, did discreetly breach Marshall's instructions. Acheson had advised Marshall against using the Harvard graduation as a platform "on the grounds that commencement speeches were a ritual to be endured without hearing." Acheson himself had already delivered a major speech on the economic plight of Europe and its inevitable effect on the United States and the world a month before, in early May, and he was greatly concerned that what Marshall now had to say would indeed go unnoticed. He therefore arranged to accept a standing invitation for a quiet lunch with three top British journalists in Washington – Leonard Miall of the British Broadcasting Corporation, Malcolm Muggeridge, then Washington correspondent of the *Daily Telegraph* and René MacColl of the *Daily Express*. They met two days before Marshall was due to go to Harvard.

Without even referring to the forthcoming speech at all, Acheson talked about his earlier speech and how difficult it was becoming to get Congress even to think about aid for Europe when, as in the case of the British loan, the money seemed to run out without doing any good. With the Republican Congress so economy-minded, Acheson said, "there must be some kind of a cooperative and dramatic move from the Europeans in order to capture the imagination of Congress."

The three British journalists were greatly impressed with the urgency of what Acheson had to say – far more so when they saw the text of the Marshall speech two days later and realized that this was what Acheson had been talking about. Muggeridge cabled the full text to the *Daily Telegraph* with a note to his editors to deliver a copy to the Foreign Office, since he had been told that it had not been cabled by the British Embassy, which was under instructions to hold down on communications costs! Leonard Miall held an excited conversation with the BBC news editors to explain that Marshall was making a major proposal to Europe, and they agreed at once to give him the lead time in an expanded evening news bulletin and commentary.

One of Miall's listeners that evening in London was Ernest Bevin.

FIVE

Bevin Takes the Initiative

"I remember with a little wireless set alongside the bed, just turning on the news, and there came this report of the Harvard speech. I assure you, gentlemen, that it was like a lifeline to a sinking man. It seemed to bring hope where there was none. The generosity of it was beyond my belief. It expressed a mutual thing. It said, 'Try and help yourselves and we will try to see what we can do. Try and do the thing collectively, and we will see what we can put into the pool.' I think you can understand why, therefore, we responded with such alacrity, and why we grabbed the lifeline with both hands, as it were. To us it meant the beginning of Europe's salvation, and Europe will go on until it has restored itself and reestablished its culture, its influence and in turn that gift will become an investment, because in the years to come we will return to the United States, for all of the gifts you have made, the blessings that Europe can still give."

So Ernest Bevin recounted some months later to an audience at Washington's National Press Club his feelings when he heard the news of Marshall's speech. He had tuned in on Leonard Miall broadcasting from Washington a ten-minute special commentary, quoting or paraphrasing large segments of the speech, and in particular punching home to Britain Marshall's essential message that Europe must take the initiative and further help from the United States could not be made to work on a piecemeal basis. Bevin heard Miall say, quoting Marshall:

"Any assistance that this government may render in the future should provide a cure rather than a mere palliative. . . . Before the United States can proceed much further, there must be some agreement among the countries of Europe as to the requirements of the situation. . . . The initiative, I think, must come from Europe. . . . The program would need to be a joint one, agreed to by a number, if not all, European nations. . . ."

Then, to drive Marshall's point home, Miall continued: "The plan would be for Europe to determine its own needs, design its own program for recovery, and then come to the United States with a single request. Of course, Marshall said, the United States would be willing as the Europeans considered just what their needs might be to offer, as he put it, 'friendly aid in drafting a European program.'"

Bevin was an early riser all his life from his days as a farm boy in Somerset in the west of England where he was born in 1881. His father, unnamed on the birth certificate, died before he was born and his mother died when he was seven. His formal education ended when he was eleven and went to work on a farm for a shilling a week and board. In his teens he headed for the port city of Bristol and worked as a kitchen boy in a restaurant, a hotel porter, an errand boy in a grocery store, a streetcar conductor. When he was eighteen he got a job as a horse-cart driver, delivering mineral water to the pubs and restaurants and hotels of Bristol, and he continued driving for the same firm until he was twenty-nine. Then in 1910 he became an organizer for a local branch of what later merged into Britain's largest union, the Transport and General Workers. Bevin's real life now began. Hardworking, persuasive and efficient, he moved rapidly from the local union branch to regional offices and finally to union headquarters in London. By the 1920s he was a major figure in the trade-union movement, of growing national reputation. When he became head of the Transport and General Workers he also became a major power broker in the Labour party. In 1940 when Winston Churchill formed the wartime coalition government at the time of the fall of France, Bevin entered the Cabinet as minister of labor and took a seat in the House of Commons. While Churchill ran the war, Bevin mobilized the home front. He was a big man in the fullest sense of the word. If his learning was untutored, his grasp of issues was acute, his intelligence intuitive and far-ranging, his negotiating experience vast, his vision wide. He was a rocklike figure of certitude and common sense, and no man to be blown off course.

When Bevin lumbered into the Foreign Office the morning after hearing of the Marshall speech, one official said later that "it was astonishing the way in which he, with his elephantine frame, seemed to spring into action." From the news on the BBC, Bevin had already formed a much clearer sense of historic opportunity than his officials. One of the first to see him was Sir William Strang, an august figure who was undersecretary and an expert on Germany. Strang suggested that in view of the fact that Marshall's speech had not been officially communicated by the American government, the British should first inquire in Washington what the secretary of state had in mind, what he meant. Bevin brushed this aside like a dock-workers' leader.

"Look 'ere, Bill," he said (and nobody in the Foreign Office but Ernie would have dreamed of calling Sir William "Bill"), "we know what 'e *said*, don't we? If you ask questions you get answers you don't want. Our problem is what we *do* – not what 'e *meant*!"

Instead, a telegram was drafted instructing the embassy in Washington to inform the State Department that Mr. Bevin had noted with great interest the speech of the secretary of state, and was approaching the French government to discuss an appropriate response to Marshall's suggestion for a European initiative. He hoped this would be coordinated in the shortest possible time, and he trusted this course of action would be welcomed in Washington. No questions were asked, and within twenty-four hours the initiative that Marshall sought *had* come from Europe and the launching of the Marshall Plan had begun.

When Bevin then proposed to Georges Bidault that they meet in Paris the following week, the American ambassador to France, Jefferson Caffery, reported to Washington that Bidault was put out by what he regarded as a British "attempt to steal the show – the truth is Bidault wanted to steal the show and Bevin beat him by a day or two." But Bevin's move to go to Paris probably made agreement easier with the French. At least that is the way it happened.

By the time Bevin flew to Paris on June 17 (at low altitude in an old wartime workhorse DC-3), officials in both the Foreign Office and the Quai d'Orsay had worked out preliminary ideas and proposals on how to respond to Marshall's offer. The first problem clearly was the Soviet Union. Marshall had already made it clear at a news conference following his speech that it was indeed open to the Soviet Union to join if it was prepared to accept the European approach he had outlined. This was a relief to Bidault and Bevin, and without this the Marshall Plan would never have gotten off the ground – for it would have been politically impossible for Britain and France to have taken the initiative of excluding the Soviet Union from any European recovery program. Both Bevin and Bidault then took care to advise Molotov in Moscow of their plan to meet and promised to communicate further as soon as they had discussed what to do.

For the French, with a large Communist party hostile and active in the country and the National Assembly, it was vital to make the effort to include the Soviet Union if it was ready to be included. Bevin's point of view was slightly different. After two years of postwar diplomatic stalemate, he was well aware of the immense difficulties the Soviets would cause if they did join, but he was nevertheless anxious to make a maximum effort without jeopardizing the whole affair. It was clear to the Foreign Office that if the Russians stayed out, it would probably be impossible for the countries of Eastern Europe to join, and this would harden the division of Europe. But if Russia stayed out, it also might well make it very difficult to carry the program forward in Western Europe, France and Italy in particular, in the face of Soviet hostility and the certainty of major Communist party disruptive tactics.

When Bevin and Bidault got down to cases in Paris, they in fact had little trouble agreeing quickly on immediate tactics and basic strategy.

A cordial and unconditional invitation would be sent to Molotov to come to Paris to discuss with Britain and France the terms of reference for convening a conference of European states to draw up a European response to the Marshall offer. It would be left to Molotov to fix the date for a meeting, so he could scarcely accuse the British and French of holding a pistol to his head. At the same time Bevin and Bidault agreed that if the Russians arrived in Paris merely to delay or obstruct, this would not be tolerated, and they would get on with the job of preparing a plan with European governments ready to cooperate. The French were relieved at Bevin's readiness to invite the Russians and the British were relieved at French readiness to stand firm when the Russians got there.

Molotov's reply was prompt. On June 22 he proposed a Paris meeting on June 27, and Bidault and Bevin immediately accepted. The Soviet foreign minister then arrived with an excessively large party of nearly a hundred advisers, security men and Communist hangers-on. The British theorized that this was designed as a kind of diplomatic show of force against the French, but the French simply theorized that it was only a maximum shopping expedition to Paris. At any rate, when the talks opened at the Quai d'Orsay, the East-West split was immediate from the outset.

Bidault opened by proposing a plan worked out jointly with the British to convene a conference under a directing committee of France, Britain and the USSR, with six subcommittees involving other European states, which would then draw up a program of European self-help for submission to the United States. Molotov in his opening remarks said that since none of them apparently knew any more than they had heard in the Marshall speech, they should jointly ask the U.S. government exactly how much money it was prepared to spend on aid to Europe and whether it could be sure that Congress would vote such a credit!

Bevin and Bidault at once told Molotov that no American government – or indeed any other parliamentary government – could ever make such a commitment in advance, and in any case, in Bevin's words, it was not for borrowers to lay down conditions when asking for credit. This lesson in democracy and economics did not impress Molotov, and the first meeting adjourned. Next day Molotov switched his attack on the British-French proposal to the supposed "sovereignty issue" – his contention that it was an interference with the national sovereignty of states to expect them to get together and discuss their collective requirements for aid. Next, he said, ex-enemy states should be excluded from the program – meaning in particular, of course, Germany and Italy. Molotov proposed simply that each country then draw up its own "shopping list" and send it off to Washington.

By the third day of discussions, chasing these arguments round and round, Bidault was calling the talks "fruitless," but it was essential as far as the French and British were concerned that Molotov be maneuvered into making the final break. Bevin wanted the break on the fourth day, but the French offered a new proposal that at first gave rise to rumors they were weakening. Maurice Couve de Murville, senior adviser on the

French delegation, quickly explained to the American ambassador that the French were simply making one last effort, which they were sure Molotov would refuse but which would disarm the French Communists and make it easier for the French government to go ahead without the Russians. Bevin later was full of praise for Bidault, telling Caffery that he had "shown great courage and given the fullest and even surprisingly solid and whole-hearted support, having in mind the present critical state of French internal politics."

Molotov duly consulted Moscow overnight on the French proposal, and the decisive fifth day of the meeting took place on July 2.

When the final meeting got under way, an intervention by Stalin from Moscow relieved Bidault and Bevin of any anxieties over how the break would come. At the outset, Molotov launched into what at first seemed to be another propaganda delaying attack, again accusing Britain and France of trying to set up an organization to force other countries to sacrifice their national independence for American aid. As this was being rebutted back and forth by Bidault and Bevin, a Soviet aide entered the room with a communication for Molotov. Bevin later recounted to Dean Acheson what happened next:

"It seems that Molotov has a bump on his forehead which swells when he is under emotional strain. We were debating away at various points when this telegram was handed to him. He turned pale and the bump on his forehead swelled. After that his attitude changed, and he became more harsh. I suspect that Molotov must have thought that the instruction sent him at the table was stupid."

At any rate, instead of keeping things bogged down in more debate, Molotov launched into a wholly irrelevant attack on the Western powers for trying to organize a European recovery program while ignoring Soviet claims for German reparations. He announced Soviet rejection of the final French proposal, and wound up with a menacing warning that if Britain and France persisted with the proposals he had been listening to, then it would lead not to a united effort in the reconstruction of Europe but to "grave consequences and very different results." Bidault replied first to repudiate Molotov's charges, and then Bevin followed:

"Nobody has striven more than I have for the unity of Europe, including the political and economic unity of Germany. I regret that Mr.

Molotov has ended with a threat. Great Britain on other occasions has been threatened with grave consequences. Such threats have not and will not cause us to hesitate to pursue what we consider our duty."

As Molotov flew back to Moscow the next day, Bidault and Bevin turned to cleaning up the business at hand – invitations to twenty-two states of Europe, East and West, to convene quickly in Paris in nine days' time, on July 12, to map jointly a European recovery program. Meanwhile, a telegram arrived at the American Embassy from General Marshall, marked "personal and private," for Ambassador Caffery to deliver to Bidault and Bevin:

> I have followed with complete understanding the course of your patient efforts to find agreement with the Soviet Government. We realize the gravity of the problem with which you have been confronted and the difficulty of the decisions which you have been forced to take. We are prepared to do all in our power to support any genuine and constructive efforts toward the restoration of economic health and prosperity in the countries of Europe.

As Molotov left Paris and the invitations went out, Stalin lost no time rounding on the hapless states of Eastern Europe. Of the twenty-two states invited to the Paris conference, eight refused – all of them in direct compliance with Moscow's dictates. The Finns, however, managed skillfully to decline and at the same time keep the door open with a response stating that since the Marshall proposal was "a matter of serious disagreement between the great powers," Finland wished to remain outside the conflict "but will make its needs known and wants to contribute to cooperation in Europe." Hungary declined, and a Hungarian official in Budapest told the British that they had been told by Stalin that if they accepted, then Russia would suspend the return of Hungarian prisoners of war it was still holding, and demand immediate maximum delivery of reparations. Poland hesitated until July 9 while consulting Moscow, and then sent its regrets.

But on July 7, an acceptance was received in London and Paris from Czechoslovak Foreign Minister Jan Masaryk, well known in almost every Western capital from prewar days and the wartime Czech government-in-exile in London. But Masaryk and Klement Gottwald, the Communist Czech prime minister, then journeyed to Moscow where they faced a sinister and brutal Stalin in the Kremlin. He accused the Czechs of "participating in an action designed to isolate the Soviet Union," and when Gottwald attempted to plead that the country was dependent on the West for 60 to 80 percent of its raw materials and needed foreign exchange to pay for this, Stalin burst out laughing, and turned to Molotov in harsh mockery: "They thought they could lay their hands on some dollars, and they didn't want to miss the chance!" On July 10, Czech acceptance was withdrawn.

But Stalin did not confine his counteroffensive simply to forcing Eastern Europe to refuse to take part in the Paris talks. On July 10, the Bulgarians – most loyal and servile of Stalin's client states – signed a trade agreement with the Soviet Union. The Czechs, having been forced to back down on going to Paris, were then required to sign a similar agreement on July 11 before Masaryk and Gottwald returned to Prague. Hungary signed on July 14, Yugoslavia (later to break away from Stalin's grip) signed on July 25, Poland on August 4, and finally Romania on August 26. These agreements, around which the Comecon bloc was subsequently proclaimed, forced a complete reorientation of Eastern European economies away from trade exchanges with the West, and locked them totally into the control of the Soviet Union in all economic planning.

In the wake of Molotov's exit from Paris, Stalin also began speeding up the final liquidation of the last remnants of independent political parties and democracy in Eastern Europe. Bela Kovacs, secretary-general of the Hungarian Smallholders Party, had already been arrested on February 26, 1947, and was never seen again. More now quickly followed.

In Bulgaria, Nikolai Petkov, leader of the Agrarian Union, was arrested in June 1947 and tried and executed in September. Iuliu Maniu, leader of the Romanian National Peasant Party, was arrested in July 1947 and condemned at the age of seventy-four to solitary confinement for life. In Poland, Stanislaw Mikolajczyk, leader of the Peasant Party and a former minister in Poland's wartime government-in-exile in London, was warned in October 1947 that his arrest had been ordered and managed to escape once again to London. All over Eastern Europe, the old Social

Democratic parties were being systematically broken from within by secret Communists or their supporters, who would force splits over policy issues, rally against the old democratic leaders, and finally force party purges and take over in the name of democracy. The regimes of Eastern Europe were rapidly being molded into one-party Communist states.

Stalin's response to the launching of the Marshall Plan culminated in the formation of a new Communist Information Bureau, the Cominform, in effect a revival of the old Comintern that Lenin had established as an instrument of international revolution in 1919, and Stalin had ostensibly dissolved out of deference to his wartime Allies in 1943. On Stalin's orders, the first secretary of the Polish Communist party, Wladyslaw Gomulka, reluctantly invited nine European Communist parties to send delegates to a country estate at Wilza Gora in Polish Silesia on September 22, 1947. In charge of the proceedings for Stalin were Andrei Zhdanov and Georgi Malenkov. The meeting lasted seven days, and a number of the speeches were subsequently published by the newly formed Cominform, while other details eventually leaked out from participants such as Milovan Djilas of Yugoslavia, who broke with Communism in the 1950s. In setting up the Cominform, Stalin's main aims were to mobilize the Communist parties behind a tough Soviet policy against the United States around the world, and in particular to reestablish tighter Soviet control over international Communism and the parties.

The lengthy speeches of Zhdanov and Malenkov denouncing "the ruling clique of American imperialists on a path of outright expansion, of enthralling the weakened capitalist states of Europe and the colonial and dependent countries, an embodiment of the American design to enslave Europe" soon became the stereotyped routine standard line of Communist propaganda wherever the Cominform could reach. But the real, fundamental purpose of the meeting was to discipline the Communist parties in a new organization and make them toe the line. In Europe, the Communists had emerged from the war in most countries with new indigenous strength and national pride, and by 1947 Stalin could see the growth of incipient diversities, away from what he was determined would be an international monolithic movement under Kremlin control. This trend was accentuated by the launching of the Marshall Plan, which the

Polish Communists, the Czech Communists and the Hungarian Communists all would have happily joined if they had been allowed. In September of 1947 there was still a semblance of multiparty coalition government in Eastern Europe under Communist leadership, but not for much longer.

At the Cominform meeting, an attack was launched first of all on the French and Italian Communist parties, represented by Jacques Duclos and Luigi Longo. The two party leaders – Maurice Thorez and Palmiro Togliatti – had stayed home, perhaps sensing what might be coming. The vilification was led off by Edvard Kardelj of Yugoslavia, egged on by Zhdanov and Malenkov. The French and Italians were flayed for having allowed themselves to be kicked out of democratic governments after two years, failing to use their full strength, and losing positions of power from which they might have served Soviet interests by stopping the Marshall Plan. Zhdanov could rant at the French and Italians with scorn and invective, but there was not much he could do to change French and Italian democracy. This, however, was only a warmup for attacks on the Eastern European Communist parties, where the Soviets were in control, and could dictate.

In particular, Zhandov rounded on Gomulka, who had not wanted to have Poland host the meeting in the first place, and had even been committing heresy by talking about "a Polish road to socialism." Zhdanov laid it on the line for everybody that there would be no more such deviationism, that there had to be an end to any ideas of "national Communism." To drive home the new Stalinist discipline, he then forced the Cominform to endorse the collectivization of agriculture, one of Stalin's favorite devices of suppression and terrorism, as "the only appropriate way to socialism" throughout Eastern Europe. It was a policy dictated by Stalin that was to cost the peoples and regimes dearly for the next ten years.

Other important decisions subsequently emerged from that first meeting. An instruction was given to the Czechoslovak Communist party to prepare to seize power. In 1947, Czechoslovakia had a coalition government of Socialists and others under a Communist premier, a pluralistic political system of free speech, a cautious but free press, freedom to travel and open access to the West. The Communists were advancing in an atmosphere of political gradualism. But Stalin knew perfectly well that there was no Communist majority in the country (or anywhere else in Eastern Europe). After his experience with the Czechs over the Marshall Plan invitation, and the democratic ousting of the French and Italian parties from government office, gradualism and democracy for the Czechs was over and preparations began for the Czech coup five months later.

The Cominform meeting also decided to step up the civil war in Greece, now that the Americans were involved there, and the Greek Communists were ordered to proclaim a "Provisional Democratic Government of Free Greece." This was duly done at Christmas 1947.

A Cominform journal was launched – called *For a Lasting Peace, for a People's Democracy* – to be the new bible of Stalinist discipline and the propaganda battle against the United States. Zhdanov declared in its first issue:

> A special task devolves on the fraternal Communist parties of France, Italy, Great Britain and other countries. If, in their struggle against the attempts to economically and politically enthrall their countries, they are able to take the lead of all the forces prepared to uphold national honor and independence, no plans for the enslavement of Europe could possibly succeed.

In accordance with Zhdanov's dictate, when the French and Italian Communist leaders returned home after being raked over the coals at the Cominform meeting, they launched a major outbreak of political demonstrations and labor strikes in both countries in October and November 1947. In France, the response of the government, on the initiative of a Socialist interior minister, Jules Moch, who fully understood the ideological dimension of what was at stake, was the rapid formation of a special anti-Communist riot force called the Republican Security Companies, the CRS. To avoid ever having to call out the French Army against civilian demonstrators, Moch wanted the Interior Ministry to have under its direct orders its own shock troops, and the CRS has continued in that role in France, for better or worse, ever since.

Stalin decided to locate the new Cominform headquarters in Belgrade. Marshal Tito at once ordered a crash building program to put up a low-rise office block on the edge of his dusty capital to accommodate the new organization. But Tito was a strong *national* Communist, the kind of independent-minded leader Stalin was determined to bring into line. Perhaps this was Stalin's reason for putting the Cominform in Tito's capital. At any rate, before the building was completed, Yugoslavia rejected Stalin's dictates and broke out of Soviet enthrallment in the first major postwar schism in the Communist bloc. In April of 1948, Yugoslavia was thrown out of the Cominform only seven months after it had been formed. The unoccupied headquarters building was eventually turned into a hotel to attract Western tourists.

In the summer of 1947, as the division, or consolidation, of Europe into contending power blocs, East and West, reached its final stage, a new word entered the American political-diplomatic lexicon: containment.

It leaped into headlines and the permanent jargon of Soviet-American relations from an article that appeared in the prestigious *Foreign Affairs Quarterly*. Titled "The Sources of Soviet Conduct," it was signed or by-lined simply under the intriguing letter "X." But it quickly became known that this lucid and persuasive prose had flowed from the fluid pen and fertile mind of George F. Kennan. When read as the views of the director of the State Department's Policy Planning Staff, and not some anonymous savant, the article immediately took on added intellectual and political weight, and soon was elevated in popular and even official perception as the expression of a logical and convincing new doctrine of U.S. foreign policy. This was something that Kennan regretted, never intended and came almost to abhor for the rest of his days, asserting tersely at one point later on in the never-ending discussions that the article stimulated: "When I think about foreign policy, I do not think in terms of doctrines – I think in terms of principles."

Nevertheless, like Kennan's secret Long Telegram from Moscow, which had had the effect of crystallizing and clarifying much thinking *within* the American government about the Soviet Union, his "X-Article" eighteen months later had a very similar effect on American public opinion and political thinking at large at this very decisive and volatile period in the postwar development of U.S. foreign policy. As Kennan regretfully acknowledged: "In the years that have passed since that time,

the myth of the 'doctrine of containment' has never fully lost its spell."
His permanent lamentation was that because of "serious deficiencies
that I might have corrected by more careful editing and greater fore-
thought," he had failed to be precise as to exactly what he meant by
"containment" and how it should be applied and what it could – and
could not – achieve.

In particular, Kennan found himself soon after his article appeared
under heavy counterattack from Walter Lippmann, the most cerebral
American journalist of this century, over the diplomatic wisdom and
efficacy of a policy of containment, and the unending and unworkable
commitments and burdens it was likely to impose on the United States if
logically pursued to the extent that Kennan appeared to be advocating.
This, Kennan subsequently wrote, was "a misunderstanding almost
tragic in its dimensions," since he found himself in basic agreement with
much of Lippmann's riposte "to which I had led squarely with my chin in
the careless and indiscriminate language of the X-article."

Lippmann's response to Kennan came in a series of twelve lengthy
columns that appeared in the *New York Herald Tribune* in September of
1947 and were then quickly reprinted in book form under the title *The
Cold War: A Study in U.S. Foreign Policy*. Thus, the term "Cold War" also
became part of political vocabulary at the same time as "containment."
This public intellectual jousting between two of the foremost political
writers and thinkers of the period had and still has a quality of penetrating
and lucid analysis that continues to apply today in any interested examination of the politics and diplomacy of the Soviet-American confrontation.
It epitomizes the high quality of the public debate that went with that great
period of American leadership.

The Kennan article was actually written more than six months before it
appeared. While still assigned to the National War College, he wrote it at
the request of Navy Secretary Forrestal, in effect as a sequel to the Long
Telegram, to carry his analysis of Soviet conduct further into the realm of
how American policy should respond. He wrote, therefore, before either
the Truman Doctrine or the Marshall Plan had been launched. Then, in
the spring of 1947, at the request of Hamilton Fish Armstrong for an
article for *Foreign Affairs Quarterly*, Kennan obtained Forrestal's permission and State Department clearance to declassify and publish. The

article went off, Kennan says, with "X" as the anonymous by-line "and I thought no more about it."

Until the appearance of the X-article, Kennan was little known outside government and academic circles. He had spent almost his entire diplomatic career abroad, and his only public exposure had been limited forays on the lecture circuit after his return from Moscow in the spring of 1946. Inside somewhat cocooned official circles, his influence had been considerable, particularly after the Long Telegram, but he was not prepared for the impact of his free-flowing and unedited thoughts in public print for the first time. It was not that anything Kennan had to say in the X-article was particularly spectacular or unusual or exaggerated – it was simply that once his analysis was out in the open it became exaggerated in ways that Kennan had never anticipated. In particular, for Americans who are forever looking for simplistic answers or formulas to resolve complicated foreign-policy problems, Kennan unwittingly provided a simple catchword. Suddenly, it seemed, America's leading Soviet specialist had come up with the answer to all of America's troubles with the Soviet Union. *Life* magazine quickly reproduced the Kennan article in full for its wide readership, and *Reader's Digest* enthusiastically jumped in with a condensed version that of course made Kennan's ideas even more simplistic and underdefined. Because of his official position in the State Department, Kennan had already found General Marshall considerably less than pleased with the unexpected appearance of an article by the head of his Policy Planning Staff. Kennan was in no position to "go public" once again to clarify or elaborate or respond to the public debate. From the left, he was being assailed for providing an intellectual cloak for aggressive military designs against the Soviet Union. Right-wing critics assailed him for offering a doctrine of passivity, lack of aggressiveness and failure to promise anything like victory. Meanwhile politicians came to realize that "containment" was a catchword that could justify anything aimed at the Soviet Union from minor aid appropriations to preventive war.

The article began with a lengthy examination of Communist thought in the exercise of Soviet power, and the extent to which all Soviet actions internal and external were imbedded in the antagonism, or struggle, between capitalism and Marxist socialism. He reviewed how Stalin, through terrorism and wartime leadership, had imposed his own principle of infallibility on the Soviet Union, and how this in turn rested on iron discipline and unquestioning acceptance of Stalin's word. This meant, Kennan wrote, that "facts speak louder than words to the ears of the Kremlin, and words have the greatest weight when they are backed up by facts of unchallengeable validity." But Soviet power, he declared, "bears within itself the seeds of its own decay, and the sprouting of these seeds is well advanced." He then came to his central theme:

> In these circumstances it is clear that the main element of any United States policy toward the Soviet Union must be that of a long-term, patient but firm and vigilant containment of Russian expansive tendencies. It is important to note that such a policy has nothing to do with outward histrionics, with threats or blustering or superfluous gestures of outward "toughness." Like almost any other government, the Kremlin can be placed by tactless and threatening gestures in a position where it cannot afford to yield even though this might be dictated by its sense of realism. . . .
>
> It will be clearly seen that the Soviet pressure against the free institutions of the Western world is something that can be contained by the adroit and vigilant application of counter-force at a series of constantly shifting geographical and political points, corresponding to the shifts and maneuvers of Soviet policy, but which cannot be charmed or talked out of existence. The Russians look forward to a duel of infinite duration, and they see that they have already scored great successes. . . .
>
> It would be an exaggeration to say that American behavior unassisted and alone could exercise a power of life and death over the Communist movement and bring about the early fall of Soviet power in Russia. But the United States has it in its power to increase enormously the strains under which Soviet policy must operate, to force upon the Kremlin a far greater degree of moderation than it has had to observe in recent years. . . .
>
> Russia, as opposed to the Western world in general, is still by far the weaker party, Soviet policy is highly flexible, and Soviet society may well contain deficiencies which will eventually weaken its own total potential. This would of itself warrant a policy of firm containment, designed to confront the Russians with unalterable counter-force at every point where they show signs of encroaching upon the interests of a peaceful and stable world.

Kennan in his own subsequent analysis of the "deficiencies" of his article conceded that he had "failed to make clear that I was talking about not the containment by military means of a military threat, but the political containment of a political threat," although he says that he believed that this was implicit in what he wrote. And, he says, he did not distinguish between various geographical areas and make clear that he was not talking about containment everywhere, or even a need to attempt containment everywhere in order to be successful. It was a failure also, he acknowledged, not to have mentioned the strains on Soviet power, on Stalinist discipline and Soviet infallibility that would go with its imperialist takeover of Eastern Europe and could be aggravated by effective containment measures.

Walter Lippmann came back with a withering counterattack against these "deficiencies" and Kennan had to wait a long time before being able to acknowledge them. American military power, Lippmann wrote, is marked by "mobility, speed, range and its effective striking force" and therefore "is not an efficient instrument for a diplomatic policy of containment." He continued:

The United States cannot by its own military power contain the expansive pressure of the Russians "at every point where they show signs of encroaching." The United States cannot have ready "unalterable counterforce" consisting of American troops. Therefore the counterforces which Mr. X requires have to be composed of Chinese, Afghans, Iranians, Turks, Kurds, Arabs, Greeks, Italians, Austrians, of anti-Soviet Poles, Czechoslovaks, Bulgars, Yugoslavs, Albanians, Hungarians, Finns and Germans.

A containment policy, Lippmann wrote, "can be implemented only by recruiting, subsidizing and supporting a heterogeneous array of satellites, clients, dependents and puppets." Weak allies are not an asset but a vulnerable liability, Lippmann warned.

A diplomatic war conducted as this policy demands, that is to say indirectly, means that we must stake our own security and the peace of the world upon satellites, puppets, clients, agents about whom we can know very little. Frequently they will act for their own reasons and on their own judgments, presenting us with accomplished facts that we did not intend, and with crises for which we are unready. The "unassailable barriers" will present us with an unending series of insoluble dilemmas. We shall have to either disown our puppets, which would be tantamount to appeasement and defeat and loss of face, or must support them at an incalculable cost on an unintended, unforeseen and perhaps undesirable issue.

Instead of "reaching out for new allies on the perimeter of the Soviet Union," Lippmann said, American policy should concentrate on "natural allies – the nations of the Atlantic Community, that is to say the nations of Western Europe and the Americas." It was not leadership "to adapt ourselves to the shifts and maneuvers of Soviet policy at constantly shifting geographical and political points, and allow Moscow and not Washington to define the issues, make the challenges, select the ground where conflict would be waged and choose the weapons."

Lippmann saw in the Truman Doctrine a reaching out for a weak client state as an instrument of containment, while he praised the Marshall Plan, which "treats European governments as independent powers we must help but cannot presume to govern." Lippmann did not know, and Kennan was in no position to enlighten him then, that Kennan had opposed the features of the Truman Doctrine speech to which he was objecting, and virtually drafted the features of the Marshall speech he was praising.

Lippmann's basic conclusion was that instead of a policy of containing Soviet power, the United States and its Allies should bend every effort to reach a German settlement that would produce a withdrawal of the Red Army and other occupation forces, and permit Europe to find a new unity instead of living under the threat of Soviet-American confrontation and conflict. If, as he acknowledged, "the ransom is set in terms which mean that Russia does not intend to evacuate Europe," then, he contended, the situation would be no more dangerous "but our energies will be concentrated, not dispersed all over the globe, and the real issues will be much clearer."

This in fact was exactly what the Western Allies had been attempting to do for two years, and when Lippmann wrote these words the best efforts to achieve a German settlement were already dead and in a matter of months would be buried forever. In line with Lippmann's urgings to concentrate on natural allies instead of reaching out for weak and tiresome client states on the Soviet perimeter, the United States would soon also embark on negotiations for the North Atlantic Treaty.

In reply to Lippmann, Kennan was eventually able to write:

> No one was more conscious than I was of the dangers of a permanent division of the European continent. The purpose of "containment" as then conceived was not to perpetuate the status quo to which the military operations and political arrangements of World War II had led; it was to tide us over a difficult time and bring us to a point where we could discuss effectively with the Russians the drawbacks and dangers this status quo involved and to arrange with them for its peaceful replacement by a sounder one.

So the Kennan-Lippmann debate ended in 1947 with both men, in fact, in intellectual accord. But it was not until several years later, when Kennan was giving up government service, that he encountered Lippmann in a Pullman car leaving New York for Washington, and they talked it all out for four or five hours.

This did not prevent succeeding American administrations and secretaries of state from pursuing containment to excess in endless application of bloody battles and diplomatic dead ends that Lippmann had warned about and Kennan had never intended. There was the fateful advance of American forces north of the 38th Parallel in the Korean War, the ill-starred Baghdad Pact and the now-defunct Southeast Asia Treaty Organization (SEATO) of the John Foster Dulles days, the Vietnam War of the 1960s, the American buildup in the Indian Ocean and the Persian Gulf of the 1980s following the Iranian Revolution and the Soviet invasion of Afghanistan, the Reagan administration's aid to the Contra rebels to "contain" the Marxist regime in Nicaragua, and endless other major and minor ventures around the globe over forty years, launched by the United States and justified under the label of containment.

It was Kennan's final summing up in his *Memoirs*:

> If I was the author in 1947 of a "doctrine" of containment, it was a doctrine that lost much of its rationale with the death of Stalin and the development of the Soviet-Chinese conflict. I emphatically deny the paternity of any efforts to invoke that doctrine today in situations to which it has, and can have, no proper relevance.

At the end of September 1947, as Stalin hammered the nations of Eastern Europe into the Cominform, sixteen states of Western Europe completed their Marshall Plan report in Paris. It had not been easy going. In the words of the conference chairman, Britain's Sir Oliver Franks, the report to Washington "involved four years of crystal gazing; it had to be completed in eight weeks; it had to be agreed to by sixteen governments." And he might well have added that it had to be thrashed out in the face of "friendly aid" from American emissaries that often seemed neither friendly nor realistic to the Europeans, and pretty hard to take. But everyone *was* aware that historic new ground was being broken in both European unity and transatlantic relations, and this had to prevail.

Although the Marshall Plan was still far from an established fact and far from assured, its launching had nevertheless clearly marked a watershed turn in United States foreign policy. It was a watershed for the Soviet Union as well. Until Marshall's Harvard speech, the tide of events in Europe since the end of the war had been almost entirely in Moscow's favor, with good promise of continuing that way in the future. The one thing that could effectively alter the prospect was American intervention to arrest the economic decline and restore European confidence – and now this had happened, subject still to approval and appropriations in Washingon. Stalin had counterattacked with the formation of the Cominform, and all of the resources of Soviet and Communist pressures and propaganda were being orchestrated to obstruct and defeat this prospect of European recovery through United States aid and intervention.

Much had changed in outlook, therefore, since the Moscow Council of Foreign Ministers in March and April 1947, and now another Big Four meeting with Molotov loomed ahead in London in November. Bevin and Bidault were both worried at the thought of some Soviet diplomatic move to disrupt this new momentum in the West and sow confusion, perhaps with a proposal for a four-power settlement of the German problem. A year earlier, in December 1946, the Western ministers had seen the Russians reverse field suddenly on an Italian peace treaty and agree to a settlement after eighteen months of deadlock. It could not be ruled out that Stalin would now find it to his advantage to come up with surprise "concessions" on the German question that could halt progress toward a fusion of the Western zones of occupation, hamper the inclusion of

Germany in the Marshall Plan, and by making a new major ploy for East-West understanding, manage to sabotage the objectives of Western European unity and recovery that the Americans were trying to achieve.

It would have been quite possible, for example, for the Russians suddenly to reduce their demands for reparations, offer food shipments to Germany, open up the question of withdrawal of occupation forces and offer negotiable arrangements to set up an all-German government. They would no doubt demand at the same time that they be given a role in some new international arrangements for control of heavy industry in the Ruhr Valley, but a Soviet "package offer" of this kind at this juncture would certainly have put the cat back among the pigeons. It would have given the Communist party of France something to campaign for and would have been embarrassing and difficult for the Western powers to reject. And if the German question had been reopened again it would have brought the Marshall Plan to a halt.

In the event, not for the first time and not for the last time, Soviet intransigence once again made the forging of Western unity an easier and simpler problem. The London foreign ministers conference opened on November 25, and continued for seventeen sessions until December 15. Molotov did indeed open up with a bid for German support by calling for the immediate creation of an all-German government – but he offered absolutely nothing in the way of concessions to achieve this, and simply used it as the takeoff point for a denunciation of supposed Western plans for "using one piece of German territory or another as a base for the development of a war industry" in the guise of a recovery program to enslave Europe and serve the ends of Anglo-American imperialism. It went on like this for almost the entire conference, with Bevin remarking after one such speech that "Mr. Molotov might at least have thanked us for listening to the end." Not only were there no potentially embarrassing or disruptive diplomatic moves from Molotov – each time that he spoke he was making it easier for the Western foreign ministers to cut the nonsense and bring things to an end. This they decided to do on December 15, with Bevin in the chair.

Marshall did not feel that the onus for the actual break should rest on the United States, and Bevin readily agreed that he would take the initiative to adjourn the meeting. But an unfortunate mixup then occurred. Bevin opened by reviewing the discussions of their sixteen meetings so far, and expressing doubts as to whether the Council of Foreign Ministers was a body that could ever reach a settlement of the German problem. Molotov delivered his standard broadside, and Marshall then replied in his concise, no-nonsense soldierly style and turned to Bevin to await the decision to adjourn. Bevin missed his cue. As Dean Acheson later recounted the incident:

> Bevin was no split-second operator. He moved slowly; he was often distracted. He could easily miss a cue and in the resulting confusion not know how to pick it up again. To a soldier, trained to precision in maneuver, what was really clumsiness appeared deliberate. The General felt that he had been let down, and that Bevin was not reliable, a black mark in the General's scale of judgments. This was a misjudgment. Ernest Bevin was as honorable and loyal a colleague as one could wish.

Instead of moving the adjournment, Bevin resumed the discussion, and finally, with concealed exasperation, Marshall moved that they adjourn on the grounds that Soviet obstruction had made progress impossible. Molotov at once retorted that Marshall was trying to gain a free hand for the United States to do whatever it wanted in Germany. But he did not oppose the adjournment. Had Bevin not missed, he could have adjourned the meeting as chairman without any motion or discussion from the other participants. It was a small incident, but it did rankle with Marshall. Chip Bohlen, who was translating, later related to the author that when he got into the official car with Marshall after the meeting to return to the embassy, Marshall said to him in irritation: "Well, Bohlen, I suppose that kills my dinner with Molotov tonight." Bohlen hastened to say that the Soviets seldom allowed things that went on in formal meetings to interfere with social contacts, and that Molotov almost certainly would turn up as arranged – which he did.

Whatever problems Marshall may have felt with Bevin, he did not allow such things to interfere with a working relationship, as was quickly shown after the foreign ministers had adjourned without fixing a date to meet again. Bevin asked Marshall to stay on in London for a few days of further talks, and Marshall readily agreed. The foreign secretary then arranged bilateral meetings on December 17, first with Bidault, then with the respected and influential Canadian high commissioner in London, Norman Robertson, and finally with Marshall at the end of the day. Bevin's preoccupation was not European recovery but European security.

The *Manchester Guardian* commented at the time that "like the Greek historian Thucydides, the more interesting Mr. Bevin is, the more obscure and difficult he becomes." On that day at the Foreign Office, Bevin decided that the moment at last had come for the most crucial move of his long-term foreign policy – the initiation of discussion to draw the United States into some new multilateral security arrangement for the West. But it was to be kept vague, diffuse and obscure. Bevin told his staff that he felt the essential thing was simply to start the idea and let the outcome emerge, much as Marshall had done with the recovery program. So he played like an experienced fly-fisherman trying to hook a big salmon at the end of a long line cast over rapid waters, taking care to entice and attract without scaring the fish away.

When he began with Bidault in the morning, he talked about the need for some sort of federation in Western Europe "to save civilization." But, he said, it should be a flexible and unwritten association, although it was essential to bring in the Americans. It was not good enough, Bevin said, for the Americans to expect the French and British to bear the brunt again while they waited to come in. As Bevin was only throwing out ideas at this point, Bidault only had to say that he was interested and would think about it.

In his conversation with Robertson during the afternoon, Bevin said that "unfortunately" the Americans had no plan about what to do following the breakdown of the Council of Foreign Ministers and "this meant that the U.K. must produce a plan for them." Again he talked about "informal federation" that would include first of all Western Europe. But it had to include the Americans and he was thinking of the Dominions also, since it perhaps should cover the Pacific as well as the Atlantic to secure U.S. interests. Bevin was really bringing the Canadians in from the outset to establish the transatlantic linkage with North America.

Marshall arrived at 6:00 P.M. and Bevin, well warmed up on his subject, plunged in at once. The British record of the meeting reports Bevin saying to Marshall:

His own idea was that we must devise some western democratic system comprising the Americans, ourselves, France, Italy, etc., and of course the Dominions. This would not be a formal alliance, but an understanding backed by power, money and resolute action. It would be a sort of spiritual federation of the west. . . . He preferred, especially for this purpose, the British conception of unwritten and informal understandings. If such a powerful consolidation of the west could be achieved, it would then be clear to the Soviet Union that having gone so far they could not advance any further. . . . The essential task was to create confidence in Western Europe that further Communist inroads would be stopped.

Bevin had a "containment" policy too. But this was pretty vague and cryptic for Marshall's practical turn of mind. He was cautious but certainly not negative. He told Bevin at once that "they must take events at flood stream and produce a coordinated effect," but this needed an understanding first between the two of them as to what their immediate objective was. Bevin said he had yet to put his own ideas before the Cabinet, and suggested that when he had some more definite suggestions, then perhaps their officials might start discussions either bilaterally or with the French. Marshall agreed, saying he had no criticism of Bevin's general ideas, but no definite approval either.

That evening, Marshall discussed his talk with Bevin at dinner with several State Department officials who had accompanied him to London, including John D. Hickerson, chief of the Division of European Affairs, who would play a key role in the events of the next fifteen months. Marshall said he was impressed by Bevin's ideas, but he felt that any "union" would have to be solely European, and United States participation would have to be confined to material assistance to members of a Western European security pact. In particular, Marshall said he did not want to complicate congressional approval of the European Recovery Program by bringing in the security question. He then told Hickerson to visit the Foreign Office and see if he could get some elucidation of Bevin's thoughts.

Next day Hickerson met Sir Gladwyn Jebb, then an influential under-secretary dealing with peace treaty and security questions. Jebb told Hickerson that Bevin had in mind a two-circle arrangement, "one a small tight circle including treaty engagements between the U.K., the Benelux countries and France." Surrounding this would be a larger circle involving lesser commitments, but with some treaty form that would bring in the U.S. and Canada.

Despite Marshall's hesitations, Hickerson from the outset became a strong proponent of a direct military alliance between the United States and Europe. As General Marshall flew back to Washington, most of the U.S. delegation returned by ship – including Hickerson and John Foster Dulles, the influential Republican party foreign-policy guru. They had long confidential talks on the voyage home about Bevin's vague ideas, Marshall's cautious but positive interest and readiness "to take events at flood stream" and the policy America could or should adopt. By the time the *Queen Elizabeth* reached New York, Hickerson had laid a basis with Dulles for a bipartisan approach to the great fundamental historic decision to take America into an entangling alliance. Bevin's initiative was taking hold.

SIX

1948: Talks Begin

Until January of 1948, no one in the State Department or anywhere else in the American government had ever given any serious thought or consideration to the far-fetched proposition that the United States should enter a military alliance with Europe. The very idea ran completely counter to a century and a half of United States history and deeply embedded tenets of its foreign policy. Simply to pose the suggestion to almost anybody anywhere in the country would have produced an automatic response that "entangling alliances" were out of the question for America – unnecessary, unthinkable, impossible.

And in any case, was America not doing enough already to ensure the security of Europe with the maintenance of an occupation army in West Germany, and the revival and recovery of Europe with the Marshall Plan? What could paper assurances or treaty guarantees really add to these realities? The situation was much as a French marshal saw it in 1914 before World War I when he was asked how many British troops he would like to see on the Continent as a guarantee to France: "One soldier, and I will make sure that he is killed in action on the first day."

Of course, "alliance" was not a new idea or a forbidden subject. There had been endless wartime and postwar policy discussions and political speechmaking about the need for closer American involvement with Europe and stronger commitments to preservation of peace. Ever since the Atlantic Charter was drawn up by Roosevelt and Churchill in 1941, the Western world had been awash in a variety of idealistic movements of One World, Union Now, Europe Unite, World Federalists, etc. etc., led by Clarence Streit, Count Kudenhov Calergy and others, all dedicated in one way or another and one form or another to increasing and enhancing and strengthening transatlantic linkage between the United States and Europe. In that sense, there are almost as many "fathers" of the Atlantic Alliance as there were fathers of the tribes of Israel.

Nevertheless, just as Winston Churchill had been very careful in his Iron Curtain speech to go no further than the word "association" in sketching out his ideas for greater American involvement and commitment to security and peace, so almost everyone else who had addressed the question publicly, politically, officially or unofficially had instinctively and automatically avoided using the brutal word "alliance" until Ernest Bevin took the initiative to bring the whole question into focus and make it a matter of Anglo-American discussion.

It is true that there had already been a breakthrough to some extent for the United States in "entangling alliances" when it signed the Treaty of Rio de Janeiro in 1947, in which it joined twenty-one American republics in a mutual pledge "to take positive action to assist in meeting an armed attack against any American state," whether such attack came from outside the Western Hemisphere or within. However, from a political and historic perspective, the United States had always been pledged to oppose any outside intrusion into the Western Hemisphere under the Monroe Doctrine. The Rio pact, therefore, was viewed by Americans not so much as an "entangling alliance" but as simply a logical restatement of the Monroe Doctrine in multilateral-treaty form. Nevertheless, the existence of the Rio Treaty and the wording of its mutual-defense obligations was to be of decisive political importance in the drafting and eventual ratification of the North Atlantic Treaty.

When General Marshall returned to Washington from his talks with Bevin, he found that his undersecretary of state and long-time close associate Robert A. Lovett was also of the firm opinion that any idea of a military alliance between the United States and Britain and other Western European states was, at the very least, premature. In London, Bevin already realized from Marshall's cautious reaction that he should move carefully, not rush things with the Americans or try to jump fences too fast. This was shown by his next move.

On January 13, after discussions and approval by the Cabinet, Bevin sent instructions to British ambassadors in Washington, Paris and Ottawa to inform the respective governments of proposals he would soon be announcing to the House of Commons, along the following lines:

> The Soviet Government had formed a solid political and economic bloc. There was no prospect in the immediate future of re-establishing and maintaining normal relations between countries either side of the Soviet line. It would only be possible to stem the further encroachment of the Soviet tide by organizing and consolidating the ethical and spiritual forces of Western civilization. This could only be done by creating some form of union in Western Europe, whether of a formal or informal character, backed by the Americans and the Dominions.
>
> In Europe this union should comprise, in addition to the U.K.: France, the Benelux countries, Italy, Greece, the Scandinavian countries and possibly Portugal. As soon as circumstances permitted, the British Government would also wish to include Spain and Germany, without which no Western system could be complete. . . .
>
> The Soviet Government would react against the proposed union as savagely as they had done against the Marshall Plan. But in the face of Russian policy, half measures were useless. Peace and safety could only be preserved by the mobilization of such moral and material force as would create confidence and energy on one side and inspire respect and caution on the other. The alternative was to acquiesce to continued Russian infiltration and witness the piecemeal collapse of one Western bastion after another.
>
> This policy would require a lead from Britain. . . .

This was the diplomatic communication that launched the making of the Atlantic Alliance. Bevin certainly knew where he wanted to go – even to the inclusion of Spain, which came about only thirty-five years later. In that first message Bevin spoke only of "creating some form of union in Western Europe," and with due regard for American caution, he said only that this could be "backed by the Americans and the Dominions." Neither "association" nor "alliance" was mentioned. He went one step further with Bidault, however, and proposed specifically that France and the U.K. should formally offer a treaty to the Benelux countries along the lines of the Anglo-French Treaty of Dunkirk, as a starting point for a Western Union.

At the State Department there was no doubt about the direction in which Bevin was heading, whatever the caution of his communications. The question was how to respond, and what the *American* objective should be. This produced an immediate and serious split in the department between Marshall's senior policy advisers – on the one hand the two Soviet experts, Kennan and Bohlen, and on the other hand the two senior men in the Office of European Affairs, John D. Hickerson and Theodore C. Achilles.

Kennan at once sent a memorandum to Marshall urging that Bevin's proposal for a Western Union "is one we should welcome just as warmly as Mr. Bevin welcomed your Harvard speech – only such a union holds out any hope of restoring the balance of power in Europe without permitting Germany to become again the dominant power." But having said this, Kennan went on to add:

> Military union should not be the starting point. It should flow from the political, economic and spiritual union – not vice versa. . . . People in Europe should not bother themselves too much in the initial stage about our relationship to this concept. If they develop it and make it work, there will be no real question as to our long-term relationship to it, even with respect to the military guarantee. This will flow logically from the consequences.

Kennan, in short, was all for the United States encouraging the Europeans to get on with the job – but he wanted America to keep its distance. Basically, as he was to write later, he "saw no real necessity" for the United States to go beyond "a unilateral guarantee, in partnership with the Canadians if the Canadians were willing, of the security of those Western European nations that chose to associate themselves with the Brussels Union, if this was the only way the Europeans could be given the reassurances necessary for them to proceed confidently with the task of economic and domestic-political recovery."

Kennan's position that a "unilateral guarantee" to the Europeans would be sufficient was based on his own firmly held judgment that "the Russians had no idea of using regular military strength against us." Kennan's judgment almost certainly was correct, but this was too risky to be widely shared as a basis for policy. As Bohlen later put it, "Whether or not European fears of an armed Soviet attack were exaggerated, they were genuinely felt." The Europeans were faced with the reality of the Red Army and not a theory as to whether it would be used or not.

Hickerson, a sharp-minded and incisive Texan who had been dealing with Western Europe in the State Department for more than a decade, took a very different view from Kennan's. At once he sent a memorandum to Marshall that if the Europeans drew up a defense pact, then "to be really effective, the United States would have to adhere – I believe this country could and should adhere to such a treaty if it were clearly linked up with the UN."

Hickerson on his own then set out to urge the Europeans to shape a treaty that would take the American position into account. To the British ambassador, soon after Bevin's speech, he suggested that the model for the proposed Western Union treaty should not be the Anglo-French Treaty of Dunkirk, which was specifically directed against German aggression, but rather should follow the Rio Treaty of the American States that provided for mutual assistance against *any* aggression from any quarter.

In the face of this fundamental division in the State Department, Marshall's reply to Bevin on January 20 was scarcely the enthusiasm the British were hoping for. The best Marshall could muster was:

> Your initiative will be warmly applauded in the United States. I want you to know that the proposal has deeply interested and moved me and I wish to see the United States do everything which it properly can in bringing a project along this line to fruition. I hope you will feel free to consult with me from time to time when you think I can be of assistance.

Marshall was a little warmer in a personal talk with the British ambassador. He was, he said, "already turning over in my mind the question of participation of the United States in the defense of Europe." But he asked that the British not press the question.

Meanwhile, Bidault had responded immediately and favorably to Bevin's initiative. By January 22, when Bevin rose in the House of Commons to deliver what was probably the most important speech of his five-year tenure as foreign secretary, joint invitations from Britain and France had already been sent to Holland, Belgium and Luxembourg to join in talks on a mutual-defense treaty "along the lines of the Anglo-French Treaty of Dunkirk."

Bevin was far from a natural House of Commons speaker, at his worst when in effect he had to read Foreign Office briefs to members of Parliament. But on the occasion of the launching of the Western Union, forerunner of the NATO Treaty, his speech bore the stamp of his own personality and the imprint of history. I was listening in the press gallery, covering for the *New York Herald Tribune*, and I wrote at the time that "he was in vigorous and forceful form, speaking with authority and confidence that had been missing from his earlier pessimistic reviews of the world outlook." Winston Churchill rose at once from the opposition front bench to praise Bevin's initiative as "the best chance of avoiding war," although it did not help Bevin very much with his own left wing when Churchill went on to say: "I cannot help feeling content to see that not only the British but the American government has adopted to a very large extent the views which I expressed at Fulton nearly two years ago."

Bevin deliberately avoided any reference at all as to how he would like to see the United States associate with the Western Union grouping he was setting out to create. He confined himself to praise and appreciation of the Marshall Plan, saying only that the "resources" of America would be needed to ensure European recovery and security.

The speech was widely praised in Washington. Senator Vandenberg called it "terrific." But having ruffled no feathers across the Atlantic, Bevin was perhaps overgratified, for he now cast caution aside with a sudden new approach to the State Department. On January 26, he instructed Lord Inverchapel (Sir Archibald Clark-Kerr had been given a peerage) to see Undersecretary Lovett with a proposal that the United States "consider with Great Britain entering into a general commitment to go to war with an aggressor and reinforce the Western European defense project." He wanted secret talks and a secret understanding with Washington.

Lovett poured very cold water on this at once. "You are now suggesting a military alliance," he told the British ambassador, and this would entail very long and complicated consideration. In a formal written response to the British on February 7, Lovett said, "When there is evidence of unity with a firm determination to effect an arrangement under which the various European countries are prepared to act in concert to defend themselves, the U.S. will carefully consider the part it might appropriately play in support of such a Western Union." But until then, he went on, "if it became known in Congress that in addition to the economic commitments involved in the European Recovery Program the United States is being asked to assume new and extensive military and political commitments, it might well adversely affect the prospects for approval by Congress of the ERP." More colloquially, Lovett remarked, "They are asking us to pour concrete before we see the blueprints."

Bevin had overreached, perhaps out of excessive confidence at the way his European Union speech had been received – but also certainly because of the mounting political tensions in Europe at the bludgeoning pressures and intimidations coming from the Soviet Union. Barely two weeks later, in mid-February, whatever momentum Bevin might have lost was swiftly regained when the Soviets launched the brutal Communist coup that snuffed out the last vestiges of democracy in harmless, helpless Czechoslovakia.

> We are now in a crucial period of six to eight weeks which will decide the future of Europe. I have no fear of the future provided we get through it. But I am really anxious lest the period immediately before us should turn out to be the last chance for saving the West.

With these weighty words the British foreign secretary began an emergency discussion with American Ambassador Lewis W. Douglas at the Foreign Office on the evening of February 25, 1948, as the Czech crisis reached its tragic climax. Bevin was far from an emotional man in his judgments, but he spoke with all the heavy portent of the famous remark of his predecessor, Sir Edward Grey, in that same room one evening at the fateful end of August 1914: "The lamps are going out all over Europe; we shall not see them lit again in our lifetime."

In Czechoslovakia, no two democratic statesmen in all of Europe had tried more anxiously, more desperately or with greater sincerity (whatever the naïveté) to gain the friendship and trust of Joseph Stalin than President Eduard Beneš and Foreign Minister Jan Masaryk. Thrown out of their country by the Nazis in 1938, they had constituted the wartime government-in-exile in London, and had assiduously cooperated every step of the way with the Soviet Union on their return to Prague in 1945. Czechoslovakia was to be the model bridge between West and East – a little country with a democratic constitution and a multiparty political system with a Communist prime minister under a democratic president. Now Beneš and Masaryk were forced to drink the poison truth that it was servitude and not friendship that Stalin demanded of them and their nation. Bevin's ambassador to Prague, Sir Pierson Dixon, telegraphed London on February 27: "The whole character of the State has been changed in less than a hundred hours." Although the Czech coup had been foreseen for several months in London, Washington and Paris, the end had come with a swiftness and ruthlessness that stunned governments and political leaders – and, as Stalin intended, sent a wave of fear and despair across Europe.

The coup had been in preparation ever since the Cominform meeting in Poland in September, and a tested Stalinist hatchet man, Vice Foreign Minister Valerin Zorin, arrived in Prague two weeks before the end to take charge. The country was due to hold democratic elections in May of 1948, but Stalin was not going to let this happen. At a cabinet meeting on February 21, Social Democratic party ministers complained that the Communist minister of the interior was failing to carry out an earlier Cabinet decision to halt the packing of the police force with Communist party members. They got no satisfaction on this from Communist Prime Minister Klement Gottwald, and they then made the fatal error of resigning. At once Gottwald declared that he had uncovered a plot against the State, and proclaimed emergency powers.

Communist-led mobs took to the streets and sacked the headquarters of the Social Democrats while the police looked on. Beneš, a tragic figure, frail and old anyway, declined to call out the army as he could have done with presidential powers, because he felt it would bring on civil war. Gottwald then handed Beneš a new slate of Cabinet ministers composed of Communist loyalists except for Jan Masaryk, who would stay on as foreign minister. Beneš held out briefly before accepting the new government, and for the second time in a decade saw democracy snuffed out in his country.

Three weeks later, on March 10, 1948, Jan Masaryk's pajama-clad body was found dead in the courtyard of Czerin Palace, the Czech Foreign Ministry, below an open fourth-floor window of the minister's private apartment. It was announced as suicide and looked like suicide, but it was difficult for many of Masaryk's myriad of friends in the West to believe that it was suicide. I had known him casually in London, a large and vigorous man physically, of great charm, sharp intelligence and irrepressible wit and humor, so much life and vitality and sophistication about him that it was impossible to see suicide in his being.

There is little doubt, long after, that it was a GPU murder. Masaryk had an American mistress, who was living in Prague at the time of the coup, Marcia Davenport, a journalist and author. He got her out of the country almost immediately, telling her, in her apartment, that he was also making secret preparations to flee, and would join her in about ten days at Claridge's Hotel in London. Instead, she got a phone call that he was dead. If Masaryk had been allowed to escape, he would have been able to reveal all that had taken place. At the same time, he was the last impediment to a complete Communist slate of government ministers. If he had been kicked out of the government but kept in Czechoslovakia he would have been a rallying point for democratic opposition. To have put on trial the son of Thomas Masaryk, founder of modern Czechoslovakia, would have been monstrously ludicrous even by Stalin's crazed standards. His elimination by political murder resolved all these problems, and also drove home to the Czechs and Europe at large the message of fear – that nothing could stop the Communists and the Communists would stop at nothing in imposing total power.

Edward Taborsky, who was private secretary to President Beneš to the end, while all these events were taking place, and who later got out to the West, was certain that if everything were ever revealed "it would show that Masaryk was disposed of by the Soviet Secret Police" (then called the GPU, today the KGB). In 1983, Taborsky told an interviewer:

> There is evidence for it. There was disorder in Masaryk's room. The argument is that had he wanted to commit suicide he would have taken pills and certainly would not have jumped from a window in his bathroom which was so hard to have access to. I talked to Dr. Klinger who was his personal physician, and he produced some evidence about this. He noted for instance that Masaryk's clothing was soiled, which was an indication that he

was in fear of his life and might have had some struggle. There were plenty of cigarets in the room which seemed to have been smoked not only by Masaryk but by other people. And the doorman in the building saw some other people come in.

So I think that when they began to examine all that in the archives in 1968 (during the brief "Prague Spring" before Soviet troops moved in to crush the Dubček regime) they were obviously coming to the conclusion that he did not commit suicide but was simply disposed of. But before they could do anything or say anything it was stopped and the Soviet invasion came. After that they then produced something which is also indicative of guilt. They said it was neither suicide nor anything else: It was just sheer accident. He just fell from the window by accident – which is the least likely explanation of all.

The death of Masaryk had a devastating effect in the West, not only among political leaders but with the public at large, for he had long been a public embodiment of Czech liberty and resistance to Hitler and of "bridge-building" between East and West, and now he was gone. Whether it was murder or suicide, no one was in any doubt that the cause of death was the Communist takeover of his nation.

Tension and fear were increasing everywhere in Europe. One week before Masaryk's death, General Lucius D. Clay cabled Defense Secretary Forrestal from Berlin:

For many months, based on logical analysis, I have felt and held that war was unlikely for at least ten years. Within the last few weeks, I have felt a subtle change in Soviet attitude which I cannot define but which now gives me a feeling that it may come with dramatic suddenness. I cannot support this change in my own thinking with any data . . . other than to describe it as a feeling of a new tenseness in every Soviet individual with whom we have official relations. I am unable to submit any official report in the absence of supporting data but my feeling is real. You may advise the Chief of Staff of this for whatever it may be worth if you feel it advisable.

It was not long until this "Clay warning" was being judiciously leaked, particularly on Capitol Hill as Congress edged toward the decisive vote to approve the European Recovery Program.

Bevin had certainly not overdramatized when he told Ambassador

Douglas that the next six to eight weeks would "decide the future of Europe."

Under the impact of events in Prague, Bevin's proposal for the creation of a Western Union must have set a diplomatic record for the speedy negotiation of a multilateral treaty of alliance. A proposed draft of the treaty, based on the Anglo-French Dunkirk Treaty that had been signed a year earlier, was circulated to the governments of Belgium, Holland and Luxembourg on February 19. But in Washington, Hickerson had already "called the attention" of those three governments to the Rio Treaty. Just as he had advised the British, they were also told that it would be preferable to formulate a treaty against *any* outside aggression, rather than a European treaty directed solely at Germany or German aggression.

The French, however, had objected to this approach for the rather curious reason that they were committed by some past prewar understanding with both Poland and Czechoslovakia not to negotiate alliances in Europe except on the basis of defense against German aggression. On the other hand, when talks opened in Brussels, the Belgians, under Paul-Henri Spaak, and the Dutch had decided firmly on the Rio model rather than the Dunkirk model. As the Brussels deliberations began, the Prague coup got under way. Whatever its other effects, this suddenly removed any French sense of diplomatic obligation to the Czech government. Experts turned rapidly to drafting a treaty along the lines preferred by the Americans, and completed their work in barely two weeks. The treaty was initialed on March 13, ready for a signing ceremony in Brussels on March 17. Much stronger than the Rio Treaty, it provided for an "automatic" military response to an act of aggression against any signatory. It did not mention Germany, but in deference to the French it was worded to apply (with a view to possible future admission of Germany) if one signatory were to attack another.

From the 1947 Dunkirk Treaty to the 1948 Brussels Treaty of Western Union, Bevin now had one large step to go to the 1949 North Atlantic Treaty. And again Stalin played quickly into his hands.

While Gottwald, Zorin and company were hacking up democracy in Czechoslovakia, Stalin turned on Finland. The same week the Czech coup was taking place, he sent a formal letter to Finnish President Juho

Paasikivi in Helsinki requesting him to come to Moscow to "negotiate" a pact of "friendship" similar to those that the Soviet Union had imposed on Hungary and Romania. Paasikivi was seventy-eight years old and in poor health, and Stalin did offer him the alternative of receiving a Russian delegation in Helsinki for immediate talks. Devastated by the war, the Finns had no choice but to comply. But they were and are a tough and united people, and there was no chance of any internal Communist coup such as had taken place in Prague and Stalin knew this. Nevertheless, to preserve their precarious independence and freedom, the Finns had to sign a friendship treaty which made the Soviet Union their major trading partner, and they had to cede naval-base rights to the Soviets on Finnish territory at a strategic point on the shipping lanes in the Baltic Sea.

While the Finns succumbed to Stalin's demands, Norwegian Foreign Minister Halvard Lange summoned the British and American ambassadors to the Foreign Ministry in Oslo for separate interviews of a crucial and very different tenor on March 11. Lange told the two ambassadors that Norway had received information from three different sources that it was to be next – that it was likely to be asked very soon, perhaps even before the Soviet-Finnish pact was concluded, to negotiate a similar "treaty of friendship" with Stalin. Lange then informed the ambassadors that the situation had already been considered by an inner circle of the Labor government, and the Cabinet had taken a firm decision to refuse any such Soviet treaty demand.

To the American ambassador, Lange confined the discussion to stating the Cabinet's decision. But he went much further with the British ambassador. It was possible, Lange said, that the Soviets would make demands on Norwegian territory, or seek base rights in the far north in the Finnmark region, which the Red Army had "liberated" and occupied all the way to the North Cape in the final stages of the war. Norway would refuse any concessions to the Soviet Union, Lange said firmly, and if this were to lead to a Soviet armed attack on Norwegian territory, then Norway would resist. He therefore wished to inquire of the British government "what help Norway might expect to receive if attacked."

This was a request of major significance at a time of grave tension throughout Europe. Lange did not raise the question of help from the United States in his talk with the American ambassador, probably because he already knew from earlier general discussions with the American Embassy that the United States at that point was not prepared to consider military assistance. Great Britain was close at hand and still had strong naval forces at the ready. Norway had been a heroic ally in the war, and Lange knew that the seriousness of his demarche to the British ambassador would start alarm bells ringing in London. But he could not have guessed at the decisive impact on the future of Atlantic security his move would have.

There is no indication of what attention, if any, the report by the American ambassador on his conversation with Lange roused when it reached Washington. But when the British ambassador's report reached London, in the crisis atmosphere of the Czech coup and increasing indications arriving of Soviet action building up against Berlin, Bevin went into action at once. World War II had engendered strong affinity between Britain and Norway, and the strategic interests of the two nations were totally intertwined. When the Germans seized Norway in 1940, their control of the long Norwegian coastline extending far above the Arctic Circle had given them an enormous strategic advantage in the submarine warfare against Britain in the Atlantic Ocean. This could not be allowed to happen again. Norwegian resistance during the war had been a heroic saga, and now a wartime ally was again posing the stark question to Britain: If attacked, we will resist – what will you do to help?

Although Bevin himself, as well as his military and intelligence advisers, doubted that the Soviets would actually attack Norway, the question that Lange posed could not simply be ducked. Bevin's greater concern was that if some reassurances were not offered to Norway, then this would make it very difficult for Lange and the Norwegian government to hold out against any Soviet demands. Any "turning of the Norwegian flank" by the Soviet Union would affect the strategic interests of the United States as well, and any assurances or guarantees to Norway would have to involve United States power to have any reality.

Despite the rebuff from Lovett only a month earlier, when Bevin had somewhat hastily proposed a secret bilateral pact to fight aggression, he now returned to the whole alliance question with the dispatch of a lengthy *aide-mémoire* that the British ambassador was instructed to deliver to General Marshall on March 11.

It was of decisive importance in producing the North Atlantic Treaty. After reviewing what the British knew of the Soviet pressures then being applied to Finland, and the Norwegian foreign minister's deep concerns that Norway would be next, Bevin sent this assessment to Marshall:

A defection by Norway would involve the appearance of Russia on the Atlantic and the collapse of the whole Scandinavian system. This would in turn prejudice the chance of calling any halt to the relentless advance of Russia into Western Europe. Two serious threats may thus arise shortly: The strategic threat involved in the extension of the Russian sphere of influence to the Atlantic, and the political threat to destroy all efforts to build up a Western Union.

Bevin told Marshall that he had "thought carefully" about bringing the Scandinavian countries into the five-power system of the Western Union (the treaty negotiations in Brussels having been concluded the same day his message was being sent to Washington), but he had decided against it partly because the five European states would not themselves be able effectively to defend Scandinavia. Instead, the *aide-mémoire* continued:

Mr. Bevin considers that the most effective steps would be to take very early steps, *before Norway goes under* [italics added], to conclude under Article 51 of the Charter of the United Nations a regional Atlantic Approaches Pact of Mutual Assistance, in which all of the countries directly threatened by a Russian move to the Atlantic could participate, for example, U.S., U.K., Canada, Eire, Iceland, Norway, Denmark, Portugal, France (and Spain when it has a democratic regime).

We could at once inspire the necessary confidence to consolidate the West against Soviet infiltration and at the same time inspire the Soviet Government with enough respect for the West to remove temptation from them and to ensure a long period of peace. The alternative is to repeat our experience with Hitler and to witness helplessly the slow deterioration of our position, until we are forced in much less favorable circumstances to resort to war in order to defend our lives and liberty. In Mr. Bevin's view, we can turn the whole world away from war if the rest of the nations outside the Soviet system become really organized, and in turn save Russia herself.

The Prague coup, the death of Masaryk, the Clay warning from Berlin, the demands on Finland, the pressures on Norway – this time there was no hesitation or internal debate in Washington. Marshall needed no map explanation in geopolitical strategy. The very next day, March 12, a message from the secretary with the approval of the President was handed to the British ambassador for the foreign secretary:

> Please inform Mr. Bevin that in accordance with your *aide-mémoire* of 11 March, we are prepared to proceed at once in the joint discussions on establishment of an Atlantic security system. I suggest prompt arrival of British representatives early next week.

Whatever difficulties and delays still lay ahead, there would be no turning back now. Bevin replied two days later that a British delegation would arrive in Washington on March 22. He proposed that the Canadians be included, and this was quickly agreed with Ottawa.

Events raced on. The focus swung to Italy, where the Communists were mounting an all-out wave of strikes and political agitation with a crucial general election due to take place on April 18. After the events in Czechoslovakia, there was almost hysterical anxiety – particularly among Italian-Americans – that Italy might be next. The prospect was indeed dire, for an election result that would bring the Italian Communists into the government in Rome would have a toppling effect which all could see on the entire European Recovery Program.

At this point, George Kennan was in the Far East on an extended tour of appraisal for the Policy Planning Staff. But from Manila, he sent a frantic analysis back to Marshall on March 15, declaring, "It would clearly be better that elections not take place at all than that the Communists win in these circumstances." Then, for a supposedly cool intellectual head, Kennan made the extraordinary proposal that "the Italian government outlaw the Communist party and take strong action against it before the elections."

> Communists would presumably reply with civil war [Kennan continued] which would give us grounds for reoccupation of Foggia airfields or any other facilities we might wish. This would admittedly result in much violence and probably a military division of Italy; but we are getting close to

the deadline and I think it might well be preferable to a bloodless election victory, unopposed by ourselves, which would give the Communists the entire peninsula at one coup and send waves of panic to all surrounding areas.

To this alarmist message, Hickerson attached a handwritten notation before it went to Marshall: "Action would be certain to cause civil war. Non-Communist parties have a good chance of winning without such drastic steps. Therefore action recommended by GFK seems unwise." The memorandum was more hysteria than wisdom, and General Marshall saw no wisdom in the United States stirring up a civil war in order to intervene to save democracy in Italy, particularly with the limited American military resources available at the time.

The incident is a curious one in the Kennan record. Earlier from the Philippines he had sent a telegram to the department remonstrating strongly against General Clay's "Berlin war warning," and he had been highly critical from a distance of what he considered "overreacting in a most deplorable way" to the Czech coup – which he had correctly forecast to Marshall much earlier as a probable Soviet reaction to the Marshall Plan. Yet in the case of Italy, he had suddenly produced a reaction and recommendation far more extreme than anything anybody else at the top in the U.S. government contemplated. Of course Berlin and Prague were already behind the Iron Curtain, while Kennan had taken alarm at the prospect that Rome might fall from the Western camp to Communism. Hickerson, directly responsible for Italian affairs, took a cooler view – not the first or last time he and Kennan were in disagreement.

On March 17, the foreign ministers of Britain, France, Holland, Belgium and Luxembourg gathered in Brussels to sign the Western Union treaty. After a discussion of "Where do we go from here?" they adjourned to tune in through shortwave static to listen to the President of the United States make an important address to Congress.

They first heard Truman ask Congress for immediate legislation to establish peacetime selective service to bring the United States armed forces up to necessary strength to meet the deepening security crisis. Then, referring to the signing of the Brussels Treaty only a few hours earlier, Truman said:

This development deserves our full support. I am confident that the United States will, by appropriate means, extend to the free nations the support which the situation requires. I am sure that the determination of the free countries of Europe to protect themselves will be matched by an equal determination on our part to help them do so. The recent developments in Europe present this nation with fundamental issues of vital importance. I believe that we have reached a point at which the position of the United States should be made unmistakably clear.

After listening to Truman, the five foreign ministers of the new Brussels Union quickly drafted and dispatched a message to Secretary Marshall before leaving for their home capitals:

We are ready together to discuss with you what further steps may be desirable and we should welcome your views on the form these steps should take and on the time and place of such discussions. They might perhaps best be opened with your official representatives in Washington and we should of course be very ready to meet you personally as soon as this seemed advisable.

Bevin had *not* informed his new Brussels Treaty partners that he had already received Marshall's agreement to trilateral talks with Canada on a regional "Atlantic Approaches Pact of Mutual Assistance" to begin secretly only five days later. (He did, however, secretly and personally inform Robert Schuman, who had become French premier and was in Brussels for the treaty signing.) The telegram to Marshall was therefore something of a diplomatic charade. It was, however, consistent with Bevin's intention that the forthcoming trilateral talks should lead as quickly as possible to broader multilateral negotiations that would include all the Western Union powers.

From Washington, Marshall diplomatically joined in this little game with a reply to each of the Brussels Union powers on March 24, which of course made no mention of the secret talks with the British and Canadians that had by then already begun. He simply said that the United States was "urgently studying" the Brussels Treaty and "I hope we shall be in a position to undertake discussions very shortly."

Meanwhile, on March 22, the most elaborate precautions had been taken to maintain total secrecy when the British and Canadian negotiators began the talks in Washington. The meetings were held not at the State Department but somewhere in the bowels of the Pentagon, where the diplomats could arrive in the secrecy of the underground parking lot and be whisked by special elevators to a secure area where "unauthorized personnel" never penetrated.

Ambassador Douglas came from London to act as chairman of the Pentagon talks. With him were Jack Hickerson from the State Department, General Alfred M. Gruenther (later a Supreme Allied Commander in Europe) representing the secretary of defense, and George Butler from the Policy Planning Staff, in the absence of George Kennan, who was off in the Far East and would certainly have expressed reservations if he had been present. From Ottawa, the Canadians were represented by Lester Pearson, then undersecretary in the External Affairs Ministry, together with the minister at the Canadian Embassy in Washington, Thomas A. Stone, and the chairman of the Canadian Chiefs of Staff, General Foulkes.

On the British side, the ambassador, Lord Inverchapel, was present at the opening, but he handed over largely to Sir Gladwyn Jebb, who had been sent from London by Bevin, and General Sir Leslie Hollis from the Ministry of Defense. Last but not least on the British side was a quiet but highly regarded second secretary from the embassy in Washington – Donald Maclean, who was a Soviet spy.

Donald Maclean sat in on the Pentagon talks and the subsequent negotiations until August of 1948 when he was promoted by the Foreign Office and transferred to the British Embassy in Cairo. He was then recalled to London early in 1951 after a series of drunken brawls and other carryings-on that were put down to psychiatric problems. By that time he had also come under secret security investigation by MI5, the counterintelligence agency. From within MI5 he was tipped off by yet another secret Soviet agent, Kim Philby – and in May of 1951 Maclean and a close cohort also spying for the Russians, Guy Burgess, bolted together for the Soviet Union. They slipped away by boat across the English Channel on a weekend, and had a three-day clear run before their disappearance became known. Years of investigation gradually unfolded the devastating story that Maclean, Burgess, Philby and another "mole" named Anthony Blunt all had been recruited as Soviet agents in the 1930s through a secret society in Cambridge University called The Apostles. Originally the society had been a kind of super-intellectual snob circle, but in the interwar Depression years its atmosphere was dominated by homosexuality and anti-Fascist political radicalism that made it a happy hunting ground for Communist activists as the war clouds gathered. Philby also escaped from a closing MI5 net in 1963 to live out his life with Burgess and Maclean in Moscow. Philby died in June 1988. Blunt bargained with MI5 for his freedom from prosecution in return for cooperation, and died in disgrace in London in 1985.

It is therefore to be taken as certain that, as Sir Gladwyn Jebb later wrote, "however secret the negotiations were, the Soviet Government had a pretty full record of what happened from the very moment when they took place." Assuming this is so, it is difficult to find that this spectacular intelligence coup had the slightest effect at all on any of Stalin's actions or on Soviet foreign policy. It may have interested or even amused the Kremlin to learn that America's two senior Soviet experts, Kennan and Bohlen – both well known in Moscow – were against the United States entering treaty arrangements with Europe or going any further than supplying arms and declaring unilateral support in Europe's defense.

It is possible that when the Soviets learned that the Pentagon talks had been triggered by a warning from the Norwegian foreign minister, they decided to refrain from mounting a diplomatic offensive against Norway that would spur on Britain and the United States. In the event, no such demands on Norway to conclude a "treaty of friendship" ever materialized from Moscow, though dire threats were later thrown at Norway for signing the North Atlantic Treaty. But at the same time, on the very day the Pentagon talks ended – April 1, 1948 – the Soviets first halted U.S., British and French military trains en route to Berlin to signal the start of the buildup to the full blockade.

Meanwhile, at the opening of the talks, Sir Gladwyn Jebb, acting on Bevin's instructions, proposed that the French should be brought in. But the Americans refused because they considered the French a security risk, with Communists running around all over the place. Maclean must have enjoyed transmitting that to Moscow.

*

The Pentagon talks lasted only eleven days. Almost certainly the discussions moved rapidly to broad general agreement because both Lew Douglas and Jack Hickerson were strong proponents of an Atlantic Alliance, and neither Kennan nor Bohlen took part. But that did not mean an end to the division in the State Department that had already surfaced in the matter of an American response to the Western Union treaty. The British later came to feel that it had been a mistake not to have included Bohlen, in particular, on the American delegation from the outset since his exclusion "merely nourished his hostility, which he reserved to exercise with great effect at a later stage," in the words of an official Foreign Office summary. However, the task of the Pentagon talks was not to negotiate but simply to make recommendations as to what to negotiate about and how to proceed. The final memorandum was largely the work of Jebb and Hickerson.

There were five principal recommendations:

First, the President of the United States would invite thirteen other countries (U.K., France, Canada, Belgium, Luxembourg, Holland, Norway, Sweden, Denmark, Iceland, Eire, Portugal and Italy) to join in a negotiation for a collective defense agreement for the North Atlantic.

Second, pending conclusion of such an agreement, the President would issue a unilateral declaration that the United States would consider an armed attack against a signatory of the Brussels Treaty as an armed attack against itself and would act accordingly.

Third, the United States would declare its readiness to extend similar support to any other European state joining the Brussels Treaty.

Fourth, the United States and Great Britain would jointly declare that they would not countenance any attack on the political independence or territorial integrity of Greece, Turkey or Iran.

Fifth, when circumstances permitted, Germany (or its three Western zones) and Spain should be invited to adhere to the Brussels Treaty and to the North Atlantic defense agreement.

In addition to these specific proposals, it was agreed in the Pentagon talks that the model for a North Atlantic agreement should be the Rio Treaty, under which each party would regard an armed attack on any party to the treaty as an attack on itself. It was also agreed at the experts level that such a pact should run for ten years with automatic renewal for further periods of five years unless denounced.

This result was a considerable leap forward for Bevin and the British. The Canadians were so excited about the speedy success of that first meeting that they went back to Ottawa enthusiastically predicting that a treaty could be concluded by the end of May. Instead it was to take a full year.

In fact, Hickerson and Douglas, anxious to advance toward an alliance with Europe, had pushed their cause by agreeing to these recommendations without having consulted fully with Lovett or Marshall, who was away at a conference in Bogotá at the time. They were well aware of the Kennan-Bohlen opposition in the State Department, and they knew that selling the alliance all the way to the White House would not be easy. But by agreeing with the British and Canadians at the "experts level" on the *objective* of an alliance at this very first stage, Hickerson and Douglas were in effect attempting a diplomatic preemptive first strike against their own government.

They knew that they were taking a chance, for Hickerson specifically told Jebb that the outcome of the Pentagon talks "represents only a concept of what is desired at a working level, and British expectations should be based on nothing more than this." The official Foreign Office summary of the negotiations also records:

> At the final meeting the Americans entered a warning that it was by no means certain that the idea of a pact would in fact be approved by the higher authorities concerned. Hickerson said that some presidential declaration might in practice be all that the Americans would be able to offer. Much would depend upon whether some fresh Soviet action maintained the present tense atmosphere. If complete calm prevailed, it would be much more difficult to sell the idea of a pact to the senatorial leaders. He would, however, do his utmost to push the idea.

If Maclean, the spy, transmitted this to Moscow, Stalin certainly paid no attention. Indeed, he obliged by halting Allied trains into Berlin for the first time that same day.

When the Pentagon proposals reached London, Bevin quickly dispatched a lengthy comment of fervent endorsement to the British

Embassy and the State Department – after which all he could do was sit back and wait. The British hoped that the early and logical outcome of the Pentagon meeting would be a summons at least to the five Brussels Treaty powers to open discussions on an Atlantic pact – thus merging the initial three-power preliminaries in a wider forum. This, they hoped, could begin as early as mid-April.

Instead, to the disappointment and frustration of the British, the Canadians and others, a deliberate pause on the American side now replaced the momentum of the previous three months. When Lovett in Marshall's absence took the Pentagon report to President Truman, the President at once saw that his first problem was political – not diplomatic. Truman had carefully nurtured bipartisanship in foreign policy, and this had paid off with appropriations for Greece and Turkey, and now the Senate and House of Representatives were in the final stages of consideration of the European Recovery Act to implement the Marshall Plan. Moreover, the 1948 presidential election was barely six months away. Here was yet another major foreign-policy initiative in the making. Truman's first reaction and first priority was to maintain bipartisanship – and in any case, neither he nor Marshall nor Lovett yet felt certain as to exactly what form an "Atlantic security arrangement" should take. Truman therefore decided that he should stay well in the background, while Lovett undertook first to open discussions with Senator Vandenberg, and in effect negotiate a political agreement with the Republicans before negotiating a diplomatic agreement with the European Allies. Lovett's first meeting of delicate soundings with Vandenberg took place on April 11.

Meanwhile, by mid-April both the Senate and the House completed action on the European Recovery Act, and although appropriation battles still lay ahead, there could no longer be any doubt about the American commitment to aid Europe. Then on April 18 in the Italian general election the Communist party was effectively beaten back and fear gave way to jubilant relief. These developments, at least in the view of Lovett and others, made the question of a new security commitment to Europe less urgent. That, however, was not the view in Europe.

At the end of February, as the Prague crisis was unfolding, Bevin had told Ambassador Douglas, "We are now in a crucial period of six to eight weeks which will decide the future of Europe." By mid-April, with the recovery aid beginning to flow from America and the Communists checked by the voters of Italy, this "crucial period" had been passed. But the major test had already begun in Berlin and Germany. When Stalin launched the next crisis, he also ensured the forging of the Atlantic Alliance.

SEVEN

Decision in Germany

In the center of Europe lies Germany, and at the heart of Germany lies Berlin. For two and a half centuries, the diplomacy of Europe, its wars and history, revolved around German political geography. Never was this more true than in 1948–1949.

When Joseph Stalin arrived for the Potsdam Conference in July 1945, Averell Harriman greeted him with the remark that it must give him satisfaction to be in Berlin after four bloody years of war. Stalin's laconic and somewhat ominous reply was: "Czar Alexander got to Paris."* Stalin was never in any doubt as to what he intended to do with the Soviet occupation zone in Germany. In fact, Yugoslav Communist Milovan Djilas, who later broke with the party, quoted Stalin as once saying in his presence: "*All* of Germany must be ours, that is, Soviet and Communist." From the time he reached Potsdam, Stalin was utterly determined that East Germany would be hammered, shackled and welded into a total Communist puppet state. On the Western side, a kind of postwar immobility surrounded Allied policy in Germany. Initially, of course, everything stood still because the policy was to treat Germany as a whole.

---

* Harriman also related to the author that Stalin later told him that he wanted to acquire the Hotel Talleyrand on the Place de la Concorde in Paris for a new postwar Soviet Embassy because the czar had stayed there at the end of the Napoleonic Wars in 1815. "I did not want to see the Red Flag flying in the heart of Paris," Harriman said to me, so he at once cabled Washington and U.S. officials in Paris urging that the United States get possession of the historic mansion first. Somehow it was done, and to Harriman's satisfaction he was then able to set up his headquarters for European adminstration of the Marshall Plan in Talleyrand's old residence, which remains an American Embassy annex today.

Accordingly, during 1945, 1946 and 1947 the endless futile discussions in
the Allied Control Council in Berlin served as a useful cover for the
Soviets to proceed with the political and economic subjugation of East
Germany, while the Western Allies diddled, debated and did very little to
revive or restore their own occupation zones with viability and hope.

In May of 1946, General Lucius D. Clay summarized in a cable from
Berlin:

> After one year of occupation, zones represent air-tight territories with
> almost no free exchange of commodities, persons and ideas. Germany now
> consists of four small economic units which can deal with each other only
> through treaties, in spite of the fact that no one unit can be regarded as
> self-supporting, although the British and Russian zones could become so.

And earlier that March, George Kennan, in the wake of his famous
Long Telegram to Washington, had warned from Moscow against
"undue optimism about central agencies serving to break down exclusive
Soviet control in the Soviet zone" in Germany.

> We have only two alternatives – to leave the remainder of Germany
> nominally united but extensively vulnerable to Soviet political penetration
> and influence, or to carry to its logical conclusion the process of partition
> which was begun with our acceptance of the Oder-Neisse line in the east
> [giving German territory to Poland], and to endeavor to rescue the Western
> zones of Germany by walling them off against eastern penetration, and
> integrating them into an international pattern of Western Europe rather
> than into a united Germany.

But the policy then was to seek a peace treaty for a united Germany.
Part of the problem for the United States during this period lay in the fact
that Germany was basically the responsibility of the War Department and
the American military governor. The State Department was largely
confined to giving "political advice" in Germany, not to the initiation of
any major policy change such as Kennan and others were already urging.
It was not until General Marshall became secretary of state that the State
Department really began to assert its primacy over German affairs.

For the Allies, there was also the incessant problem of the attitude of the French, adamantly against any moves that seemed to hint at "German revival" and tirelessly trying to detach, annex or otherwise take over the contentious German Saarland and make it part of France, while refusing to consider including their occupation zone in any Western merger.

French governments of course were constantly looking over their shoulders against a political stab in the back from the Communist party. Then in 1947 General Charles de Gaulle suddenly marched back into the political arena when he launched a new movement grandly called "Rally of the French People," which swept to a remarkable initial success, capturing 40 percent of the total vote in municipal elections in October. If it had been a general election, and General de Gaulle had returned to power at this point, then French history and European history would be very different. Instead, his political movement soon began to fragment and fade, but de Gaulle remained a force to be reckoned with – and not a constructive force where Germany and the making of the Atlantic Alliance were concerned.

First steps to break out of the German stalemate had been initiated by Secretary Byrnes in the summer of 1946, but the results had been meager. The merger of the British and American occupation zones had not produced much change, and the economy remained mired in inflation, with a huge black market in which coffee and American cigarettes seemingly were the country's real "hard currency." Byrnes had also asserted in his important Stuttgart speech in September of 1946 that the time had come to restore local government to the Germans without control by the occupiers, and that this start to political life should be followed by "early establishment of a provisional government" to draft a new constitution. However, refusal of the French to join in the merger of the Western occupation zones meant that progress even in starting up democratic local government had been uneven and slow, and the basic situation remained stagnant both economically and politically.

The launching of the Marhall Plan brought things to a head. Hesitancy, confusion and uncertainty over Allied policy toward West Germany had to change. As Kennan minuted to Marshall: "The French and others must be brought to acknowledgment of their responsibility for integrating Western Germany into Western Europe, and to a detailed agreement as to how this shall be done."

General Marshall fully concurred in this attitude, but political realities required that it be carefully applied. When the fourteen original Marshall Plan states sent representatives to Paris in July of 1947 to draw up their joint economic needs to present to Washington, it was automatically agreed that European recovery would have to include West Germany, which would be represented at this stage by officials of the three occupying powers. The Soviet Union, of course, had conveniently excluded itself and East Germany from the Marshall Plan. From this point on, therefore, the creation of a West German state became as inevitable as it was logical and necessary. But it was many months before the French were ready to accept this logic as policy.

Marshall first moved, therefore, to assert the new American muscle and leadership in Europe in that part of the German arena where he could act – to prod the stagnant economic situation in the merged Anglo-American Bizonia. For two years, German coal production had been languishing, in part because the Labour government in London had been pushing to nationalize the privately owned coal mines of the Ruhr Valley, in line with the socialist policies it was pursuing in Britain. At the end of June 1947, Will Clayton, the American undersecretary of state for economic affairs, arrived in London on a first visit of "friendly advice" in shaping the Marshall Plan. He brought unusually blunt instructions from Marshall "to make it quite clear to Mr. Bevin that we regard British management of the Ruhr coal problem as pathetic – we cannot sit by while they try out ideas of socialization, time does not permit experimentation." Clayton reported back that "the points you asked me to make were accepted soberly and without rancor by the British and with only weak rebuttal." Bevin was far from happy at this American demarche, but nationalization was dropped in Germany, and the German owners of the mines could start getting on with the job. As part of the Marshall Plan, the United States intended West Germany to be made safe for free-enterprise capitalist democracy.

Next the American and British commanders in Germany were told to draw up a revised Bizonal level-of-industry program, in line with the European recovery studies under way in Paris. This, of course, meant increases in the level of coal and steel production that were then permitted in the British zone in particular – and when Bidault learned of this, he went through the roof. To Harriman he raged: "We have 180 Communists in the National Assembly who are saying that the Marshall Plan means Germany first, and I tell you that if you take this action and it permits them to say this again, whether with ostensible or real reason, then this government will not survive."

A major row now broke out. General Clay threatened to resign if the new production levels were not approved. (By State Department count, Clay threatened to resign eleven times in all during his tenure in Germany.) The French began staying away from Marshall Plan meetings in Paris until they got "satisfaction" on the German question. Will Clayton reported after a meeting with Bidault: "If France should withdraw or if her present government should fall as a consequence of deep dissatisfaction over decisions relating to Germany, the whole Marshall program would probably be gravely jeopardized."

General Marshall was not a man to be impressed or intimidated by threats from other general officers to quit their posts. He did not even deign to communicate with Clay, but he decided to make a tactical retreat in the wider interests of European recovery. He firmly told the army secretary, Kenneth Royall, after a Cabinet meeting in Washington, that the State Department was fixing German policy, not the army. It was then announced that the Bizonal industry program would be held in abeyance "until the French government has had a reasonable opportunity to discuss these questions." Clay floundered and forgot about his resignation. Another French crisis was past, but the problem would not go away.

The breakup of the London Council of Foreign Ministers meeting in December 1947 removed any lingering diplomatic impediment or political excuse for the Western Allies about setting their own house in order in West Germany. Marshall tackled Bidault on the subject immediately after the four-power meeting ended, on December 17. He told Bidault firmly that important questions for the Allies in West Germany could not be avoided, in particular the relationship between the French occupation zone and the Anglo-American Bizonia. He suggested that the French examine the Bizonal agreement, and offer any criticism of it they might wish to make, but in the meantime, as a step to merger, could they not adopt procedures "to bring the zones into greater harmony by evolutionary process"? He cited the question of currency reform for all of West Germany, which was already under discussion and would soon have to be tackled as a matter of economic necessity. Bidault responded that Marshall's suggestion "was reasonable but it would take time," and at once he added that such an "evolution" would have to take into account French claims for annexation of the Saar, and the establishment of some kind of an international authority to exercise control over German heavy industry in the Ruhr to meet French security concerns.

Marshall then proposed, and Bidault quickly agreed, that the Western Allies convene a special high-level conference of their own early in the new year to examine collectively for the first time the whole range of their economic and political policies in shaping the future of West Germany, now that any four-power agreement was dead. In nudging the French, Marshall's hand was strengthened by the fact that the American Congress had just completed the passage of an emergency aid appropriation for France, urgently requested by President Truman, to tide things over until the full Marshall Plan program could be enacted.

Five days after this discussion in London, Bidault sent a formal communication to Marshall in Washington on steps that the French were preparing to take toward an eventual fusion of their occupation zone. This was motion, but it still turned out to be complex and frustratingly slow before motion became action.

Meanwhile, the Bizonal military commanders – General Clay and General Sir Brian Robertson – arrived in London from Berlin to review in detail with Marshall and Bevin the situation in Bizonia. Meeting on December 18, they went over plans for an administrative reform for the two zones to create a centralized Bizonal economic ministry, which would have a German advisory council to give the new administration a certain cachet of political democracy under military control. After a full discussion of this and other problems, including procedures and possible timing for currency reform, Marshall and Bevin gave their ready approval to the new Bizonal plans and Clay and Robertson flew back to Germany to launch the changes during the first week of January 1948.

The Bizonal administration and its Economic Council would be headquartered in Frankfurt, the council to be appointed by the military governors from the ranks of economists, academics, trade unionists, and would-be political leaders of the new Germany, with political parties then still carefully licensed and controlled by the occupation authorities. The council's dominant figure soon became Ludwig Erhard, a free-enterprise Christian Democrat and future chancellor of the Bonn Republic. But a West German government was still a long way away, and even this modest elemental first step ran into flak. On the one hand, there were German expressions of apprehension that this evolution in Bizonia would prejudice all-German unity – a theme that was certainly encouraged by the Communists and the Soviet Union to frustrate political progress in West Germany. On the other hand, the French immediately fired off a protest to London and Washington that "a German government is in fact being created, contrary to the understanding reached in London."

Bevin responded to the French complaints with the formal invitation to meet in London in mid-February to coordinate German policy. In the meantime, the Bizonal military commanders had their orders and moved straight ahead. The French would not be allowed to hold things up. However, with the aim of encouraging the French to come out of their corner, Britain and the United States both informed Paris in advance of the London talks that they were "now ready to recognize de facto separation of the Saar from Germany and incorporation of its economy with that of France, subject to agreement on related issues and to confirmation of this arrangement in a final peace settlement." Without further ado the French promptly moved their border control and customs posts from the western frontier of the Saarland across the valley to its eastern border and proclaimed a "customs union" of the territory with France. But when the London meeting opened, France still would not budge on fusion of the Western occupation zones. However, with the Tricolor now flying grandly, if only temporarily, over the Saarland, and its coal and steel production now ostensibly added to that of France, the French did quietly acquiese in the decision to increase the level of German heavy-industry production in the Ruhr, in the interests of European recovery.

The French then held on to the Saarland until 1954, when it was quietly returned to German sovereignty as part of the negotiations to bring the Federal Republic into the North Atlantic Treaty.

Top officials of the three Western powers began their London meeting on February 19, and at the end of the first phase on March 6 they issued a communiqué announcing "substantial agreement on full association of the Western zones in Germany in the European Recovery Program." This, however, was a diplomatic cover for the more important discussions that had taken place about how to proceed with the creation of a West German government.

At the end of February, while the London talks were under way, Stalin launched the Communist coup in Prague to take over the government of Czechoslovakia. At this same time, in Brussels, the five-power negotiations began on Bevin's proposal for a Treaty of Western Union. After the Brussels Treaty was signed, the Western Allies decided to enlarge the second phase of their talks on Germany to include the Benelux countries and thus give a wider European base to the vital long-term decisions they expected to take when they reconvened on April 20. Both the Belgians and the Dutch had an added claim to take part because they were also providing small military contingents to the occupation forces in the British zone of Germany (which remain there to this day as part of NATO defenses). So, by the end of March, uncertainty and hesitation in Western Europe were at last being replaced by policies of clarity, firmness and unity – and none too soon.

By mid-March in this torrent of events and diplomatic activity, the Russians certainly knew through their spy in the British Embassy in Washington, Donald Maclean, that Marshall had agreed on Bevin's initiative to open super-secret talks on an Atlantic security agreement, together with the Canadians, in the Pentagon on March 22. The Soviets proceeded nevertheless with a new offensive against the West that was bound to push the Allies closer to a full-fledged military alliance.

On March 20, 1948 – ten days after the death of Jan Masaryk in Prague; three days after the signing of the Brussels Treaty; two days before the start of the secret Pentagon talks – the Soviet military commander in East Germany, Marshal Vasili Danilovich Sokolovsky, broke up a meeting of the four-power Allied Control Council in Berlin, and it never met again.

Sokolovsky opened that last meeting of the four military governors with a demand that General Clay, General Robertson and General Pierre

Koenig inform him of the purpose of the London three-power talks, and the decisions taken by the Western Allies. He launched into an accusation that they were "treating quadripartite authority in Germany as a suitable screen behind which to hide unilateral actions in the Western zones directed against the peace-loving people of Germany" – an accusation that precisely mirrored how the Soviets had been running their zone of Germany for nearly three years. When the Western commanders objected to "using the meeting for propaganda purposes," Sokolovsky produced a prepared statement of denunciation of the West, which he proceeded to read at such a rapid pace that the interpreter could not keep up with him. Racing to the end of what he had been instructed to deliver, he swept up his papers, rose to his feet and strode out of the room declaring: "I see no sense in continuing today's meeting and announce that it is adjourned."

To the military commanders on the spot, to government leaders and foreign ministries in Washington, London, Paris and every capital in Western Europe, the intent and implications of the breakup of the Allied Control Council were clear. To the east of the Elbe River, the only territory that remained free of total Stalinist control following the coup in Prague was West Berlin, and Berlin was now targeted for a complete Communist takeover. Everywhere Western governments braced for a test of wills, with the clear danger that it could escalate into a test of arms.

Ten days later the Soviet noose around Berlin began to tighten. On April 1, 1948, the regular American Army overnight train from Frankfurt to Berlin was halted after it crossed into the Soviet zone. Soviet troops surrounded the train and the commander was told that the documents of every single passenger would be checked before it would be allowed to proceed to Berlin.

The American train commander had his orders too. No inspection of Americans would be permitted, he told the Soviet commander, and if Soviet troops attempted to board the train, this action would be resisted and American MPs would open fire if fired upon. The Russians then shunted the train to a siding where British and French trains were also stranded without engines. Fourteen hours later, after a flurry of messages between the Pentagon and Berlin and Frankfurt, the trains were hauled back to West Germany. After this first test-case shot-across-the-bows, trains to Berlin resumed but delays and harassments continued on a rising scale until the full blockade was imposed by the Russians in late June.

The eleven weeks that ensued until the full blockade began were not exactly a breathing space for the Western Allies, but it did give time for assessment of what was coming, and to determine in Washington, London and Paris the stance each government would take, individually and collectively, as the Berlin crisis moved to a climax. Despite differences of diplomatic style and method, nuance and timing, there was clear and automatic basic unanimity. There was unanimity that the three Western powers would stay in Berlin. There was unanimity that the Soviet Union did not intend to go to war to seize Berlin, but neither should the West act in any way that might force the situation to a choice of war. And there was unanimity on pressing ahead with new policies to shape the future of West Germany.

On the other hand, to the particular frustration of Ernest Bevin, progress apparently had ground completely to a halt in Washington on an Atlantic security agreement, just as Europe was plunging into the major security crisis of the postwar period. Accordingly, Bevin and Bidault sent a joint appeal to Marshall on April 17, 1948, for the United States to begin security talks, as promised, with the Brussels Treaty powers. After informing Marshall that they were "taking all possible steps to prepare measures for defense as contemplated in the Treaty," including "military talks in the near future," they struck a note of urgency:

> It is clear that simultaneously we shall require the assistance of the United States in order to organize the effective defense of Western Europe which at present cannot stand alone. It seems imperative that the United States should now take an initiative and at least begin conversations, if the situation in Europe, of which the recent events in Berlin are symptomatic, is not still further to deteriorate.

But Marshall and Lovett were not yet ready to move. Lovett had only just begun his delicate secret tentative political talks with Senator Vandenberg to shape a bipartisan base on the whole question of how far America could or should go in an Atlantic security arrangement. Within the State Department, in the wake of the Pentagon talks, Kennan and

Bohlen had stiffened their heavyweight advice against the idea of any actual *treaty* with Europe, while Hickerson and Achilles were both strongly urging that anything less than a treaty would be meaningless and ineffective for both Europe and the United States. So the response to both London and Paris was temporizing.

To Bidault, Marshall replied that he "fully agreed on the desirability and urgency of coordinated planning to meet possible emergencies," but he then pointedly added that "the present talks in London on Germany will provide an opportunity to discuss the current situation and its implications." In effect, the secretary's message to the foreign minister was that if France wanted progress on an American security commitment to Europe, the Americans were waiting for progress from the French on the more immediate German question. And, Marshall added, "it is vital to the success of the aim we all have in mind that any assurances from this country on this matter have maximum countrywide support and the backing of the Congress – this is a complicated matter, but Mr. Lovett advises me he is making good progress."

There the matter rested in Washington until the start of the Berlin blockade.

Winston Churchill in his Iron Curtain speech two years before the Berlin crisis had said: "I do not believe that Soviet Russia desires war. What they desire is the fruits of war and the indefinite expansion of their power and doctrines." This, in fact, was also the conclusion of almost every military-intelligence estimate and political analysis of Soviet intentions and the probable course of Soviet action against Berlin. The closest to a direct "war warning" had come from General Clay in his widely circulated dispatch to Washington in early March at the time of the Czech coup, in which he said that although he had believed that the danger of a war was at least ten years away, "within the last few weeks I have felt a subtle change in Soviet attitude which I cannot define but which now gives me a feeling that [war] may come with dramatic suddenness." At the time this was received, Kennan remonstrated strongly against what he regarded as an overreaction from Clay. Moreover, when Clay wrote his memoirs four years later, he blandly acknowledged that his dispatch was primarily intended to drum up congressional support for passage of the

Marshall Plan and for President Truman's call for peacetime selective service to beef up the armed forces! By way of justification, Clay wrote that the change in Soviet attitude that he had noted turned out to be preparation for the blockade, not preparation for war.

Apart from this "warning" by Clay, it appears that no responsible Allied intelligence service, Soviet experts, top-level diplomats or political leaders believed that the world was heading for war when the Berlin crisis unfolded. Of course under the circumstances no one could be totally categorical in ruling it out. It was Georges Bidault's summation:

> I am *almost* convinced that the Soviet Union will not attack us. But that's not the same thing as saying, "I believe it's going to be a fine day and I'm not taking my umbrella." . . . Our information does not permit us to conclude in the absolute impossibility. . . .

Kennan said at the time that "it would be frivolous to say that there is no danger of war with Russia" and that "the chances of war would have been greatly increased" if the United States had failed to launch its aid program for Europe and the Communists had won the Italian election in April. But in a State Department paper, he gave this assessment, on which it was noted "no disagreement anywhere":

> A military danger, arising from possible incidents or from the prestige engagement of the Russians and the Western powers in the Berlin situation does exist, and it is probably increasing rather than otherwise. But basic Russian intent still runs to the conquest of Western Europe by political means. In this program, military force plays a major role only as a means of greater intimidation. The danger of political conquest is still greater than the military danger. If war comes in the foreseeable future, it will probably be one which Moscow did not desire but did not know how to avoid.

In London, Field Marshal Montgomery, then Chief of the Imperial General Staff, always didactic and never in doubt about his wisdom, simply pointed to the fact that the Soviets had ripped up so much railway track in Poland and Eastern Europe to cart off to Russia, and had suffered so much wartime destruction of industrial centers still being rebuilt that "they do not have the capacity to make war now – the critical time might well be in four or five years during the 1952 American presidential elections, if they wish to fight that would appear to be the danger period."

Bevin, in a message to Marshall at the end of April, said "there could be no question" of being forced out of Berlin, but the Allies would have to show firmness with "a determination not to be provoked into any ill-considered action which might result in an impossible position from which it would be difficult to retreat." He continued:

> They intend to do all they can to wreck the ERP and to cause us the greatest political embarrassment everywhere, *but without pushing things to the extreme of war.* [Italics added] The danger of course is that they may miscalculate and involve themselves in a situation from which they feel they cannot retreat. That is why we are called upon to show particular prudence at the danger points.

On the other hand, General Omar Bradley, then Army Chief of Staff in the Pentagon, transmitted a telecom message to Clay in Berlin of a rather different thrust on April 10:

> Will not Russian restrictions be added one by one which eventually would make our position untenable unless we ourselves were prepared to threaten or actually start a war to remove these restrictions? Here we doubt whether our people are prepared to start a war in order to maintain our position in Berlin and Vienna. If you agree, should we not now be planning to avoid this development and under what conditions – for example, setting up Trizonia with capital at Frankfurt, we might ourselves announce withdrawal and minimize loss of prestige rather than being forced out by threat.

In a purely military sense, of course, the position in Berlin *was* untenable and it was General Bradley's clear duty to consider *all* the options and *all* the military risks. In April of 1948 no one had given any serious thought yet to the preposterous idea of supplying a city of two million people by air. Nor was it General Bradley's responsibility to assess the political considerations of a retreat from Berlin. Perhaps his message to Clay was simply designed to provoke the answer he wanted and expected. At any rate, Clay's reply was immediate and unequivocal:

> After Berlin will come Western Germany, and our strength there relatively is no greater and our position no more tenable than Berlin. If we mean that we are to hold Europe against Communism, we must not budge. ... I cannot believe that the Soviets will apply force in Berlin unless they have determined war to be inevitable within a comparatively short period of time.

After the first train stoppage, Clay gave secret orders to prepare plans for a small U.S. Army task force of armor and engineers to be ready to move to the main autobahn to Berlin, and force its way through the Soviet checkpoint at the Helmstedt zonal boundary if the Soviets ordered total closure of the border. As the showdown approached in Berlin, the British and French became almost more apprehensive about the Americans triggering a war than they were about the Russian blockade.

The high-level diplomatic experts' discussions on future moves in West Germany resumed in London on April 20, with the three Allied military governors present along with senior diplomats from Belgium, Holland and Luxembourg. Under the impact of the walkout of the Soviets from the Allied Control Council, events in Prague and the necessities of the Marshall Plan and European recovery, the reluctant French were at last accepting that they could hold out no longer against creation of a West German government. But they fought a dogged diplomatic rearguard action to extract their final price.

The main basic agreement reached in London, after a month of very searching and intense discussions, was the procedure and a timetable for the Germans to draft their own democratic constitution and establish a federal government. Under the plan, the military governors would invite the minister presidents of the German Länder (states) to nominate members of a special Constitutional Assembly, to begin work by September 1, 1948, on a "basic law" or constitution for a new Federal Republic. This would follow general guidelines laid down by the occupying powers. After final approval by the Allied governments and promulgation, elections would be held, and once a government was in place, the Allies would relinquish to German authority a whole range of powers they had been exercising under unconditional surrender. However, external relations and defense and security would continue exclusively in the hands of the Allies while the new government in effect "worked its passage" back to eventual full sovereignty.

The French, as their price for agreement, won two further provisions to meet their political and supposed security needs – both of which were quietly abandoned or overtaken by much larger developments in the next three years.

First they extracted an agreement to establish a special International Authority for the Ruhr, to impose special control machinery on West German heavy industry. Under the powers of unconditional surrender, this authority, with the Germans ostensibly participating but the Allies in control, would fix production levels and export quotas over the coal, coke and steel industries of the Ruhr. The British and Americans went along reluctantly, but the Benelux states supported the French. The Ruhr Authority imposed by the Allies on behalf of the French was hated by the Germans, and eventually became meaningless and lost all *raison d'être* and was liquidated when France itself had the wisdom to launch the Schuman Plan and the creation of the European Coal and Steel Community in 1952.

Next, to satisfy the French, the Allies jointly pledged that they would maintain their occupation forces in Germany until the peace of Europe was secured, and would make no withdrawals from their forces without prior consultation. They also agreed to establish a tripartite Military Security Board as a watchdog to make sure that West Germany would remain demilitarized and disarmed. Within a year, these "security concessions" to France lost any practical meaning with the signing of the North Atlantic Treaty.

The sighs of relief in Washington and London when the French signed the London agreements did not last very long. Britain and the United States could approve the documents simply by executive action, but the French government had to submit them to a vote in the National Assembly. An unholy alliance against the very idea of creating a West German government now quickly formed between the Communists and the resurgent Gaullists. From his country home at Colombey-les-Deux-Églises, General de Gaulle fulminated against a "weak government" bowing to "Anglo-Saxon pressures" to allow a revival of German power without extracting either territory or security for France in return. It was well that de Gaulle was in his exile period at the time.

Georges Bidault was an intelligent and brave man, who had been head of the Council of National Resistance in France during the war. But he was also excitable and generally more flexible under pressure than he was solid and stable. The London agreements had scarcely been brought across the Channel to Paris before Bidault began pleading for more concessions, or for an approach to Stalin over the Berlin situation before he had to ask the National Assembly for their approval. The United States and Britain responded immediately – not with concessions, but by announcing their formal approval of the package. They made it absolutely clear to the French that they would adhere to the timetable to proceed with a West German government whether France went along or not. Ernest Bevin then sent a posse of senior political figures from the Labour party over to Paris to lobby the French Socialists, including President Vincent Auriol, on the National Assembly vote. At last, on June 18, 1948, the Assembly passed a motion loaded with reservations but approving the agreements by 300 votes to 286.

In Germany the day before the Assembly vote, the three Western military governors issued final secret orders for a sweeping currency reform, long in preparation, which would transform the entire German economic outlook. Without yet agreeing to fusion of their occupation zone, the French had gone along because obviously there could be only one currency in West Germany. So, on the evening of Friday, June 18, after the banks had closed in West Germany and the National Assembly was nearing its crucial vote in Paris, the German radio stations broadcast the surprise announcement by the Allied authorities that beginning at 7:00 A.M. Monday a new currency, the deutsche mark, would be issued to replace the reichsmark at a whopping deflationary rate of one new for ten old.

On Sunday, Clay received a letter from Sokolovsky protesting the currency reform and declaring ominously: "With regard to Greater Berlin, I consider it to be economically integrated with the Soviet Zone."

The Allies had deliberately omitted West Berlin from the initial stage of their currency reform, and Clay replied to Sokolovsky with a proposal that the economic advisers of the defunct Allied Control Council meet to discuss the situation. The Russians accepted, but it was apparent that they had been taken by surprise by the Western move and were stalling for time while they prepared to counter. On Monday, Sokolovsky issued a unilateral decree to the Berlin authorities that only East German currency would be valid throughout the city. On Tuesday the Control Council economic advisers met to discuss currency reform for the city, but predictably got nowhere. On Wednesday, June 23, the Berlin City Council convened at the Rathaus in East Berlin and the Russians tried to ram through a law to block the new West German currency. A Communist rabble was turned loose to intimidate the 130 city councillors, but at the end of a wild and stormy meeting a counterresolution was approved, 106 to 24, specifying that the currency question was a matter for decision by the occupation authorities and not the Berlin city government. Only the Communists voted against.

That evening at 11:00 P.M. the news agency in the Soviet zone clattered out a Teletype message: "The transport division of the Soviet Military Administration is compelled to halt all passenger and freight traffic to and from Berlin tomorrow at 0600 hours because of technical difficulties."

The Berlin blockade had begun.

Next morning, General Clay made a quick trip to Heidelberg to discuss at U.S. Army Headquarters the preparations he had ordered for a military convoy to push through to Berlin. He returned to Berlin later in the day, and General Sir Brian Robertson came to confer with him. When Clay told Robertson what he had in mind, the British commander was appalled.

"If you do that, it will be war – it's as simple as that," Robertson told Clay. He then added with British soldierly exactitude: "In such an event I am afraid my government could offer you no support, and I am sure that Koenig and the French will feel the same way."

In fact the feeling was the same in Washington. Lovett, who had been a pilot in World War I and at the War Department throughout the Second World War, simply dismissed Clay's idea as "silly." It did not take much military foresight to conclude that the bridge across the Elbe River in the Soviet zone could quickly be blown by the Russians if a convoy ever did get past the Helmstedt checkpoint without shooting. Going to the rescue of an ambushed American Army force in the Soviet zone of Germany would indeed mean going to war. At one State Department conference Lovett remarked: "The Soviets would just sit up on a hillside and laugh."

Nevertheless, on June 25 General Clay cabled the Pentagon: "I am still convinced that a determined movement of convoys with troop protection would reach Berlin, and that such a showing might prevent rather than build up Soviet pressures which could lead to war."

Still he could find no takers in Washington. As Dean Acheson later wrote: "General Clay's confidence was based not on the belief that the Russians could not stop a convoy, but that they would not." That was certainly not good enough to run a risk of war.

When General Robertson bluntly informed Clay that Britain would not support any effort to run the blockade on the ground, he then proposed immediately the idea of supplying the city by air. He told Clay that the Royal Air Force had already studied the problem at his instigation, and the officer who had produced the study, Air Commodore Waite, was summoned to brief Clay. Waite had worked out rough tonnage figures for an airlift to cover civilian needs as well as the British military garrison. While there was no question of Britain's having such a capacity, he had concluded that an airlift to sustain the city could be organized and would work.

The RAF had already been ordered by Robertson to prepare contingency plans to increase its airlift capacity into the small airfield at Gatow in the British sector of Berlin. Air Commodore Waite went over his estimates with Clay, and together he and Robertson convinced the American commander that he had to give it a try. In fact it was the only immediate response possible to the blockade once it was clear that the convoy idea would not get off the ground. So Clay got on the scrambler telephone to General Curtis LeMay at Air Force headquarters in Wiesbaden and said: "Curt, have you got any planes that can carry coal?" Robertson gave his orders too, and the RAF was in fact the first into Berlin with an airlift supply delivery to Gatow on June 26.

That same June 26 in London, Bevin saw Ambassador Douglas to urge that Washington give priority consideration to ordering that Berlin be supplied by air. He also proposed that the United States dispatch to Europe some of its B-29 strategic bombers, capable of delivering the atomic bomb over great distances at what in those days was the extreme operational altitude of 29,000 feet. General Clay had cabled a similar proposal to the Pentagon to send the bombers to West Germany. From either Britain or Germany, the B-29s would be within striking distance of Moscow – a fact the Soviets clearly understood. Marshall replied immediately to Bevin on June 27, assuring him that the feasibility of an airlift was being urgently examined, and asking whether, if the B-29s were flown to Europe, could some of them be stationed in Britain. The British replied affirmatively, and a first force of sixty bombers reached England on July 17. By then, the workhorse C-54 cargo planes of the U.S. Air Force were arriving in Germnay for airlift duty from as far away as Hawaii and Japan.*

President Truman also met with his senior Cabinet advisers on June 26 for a full-scale review of all the risks and options. After listening to everyone, Truman's first comment, according to Forrestal's diary, was: "We are going to stay. Period." When Army Secretary Kenneth Royall remarked that he didn't feel the problem had been thought through, Truman cut him off: "We will have to deal with the situation as it develops. The Russians have no right to get us out."

In imposing the blockade on Berlin, the Soviet Union did *not* make any direct or open demand on the Western Allies that they withdraw from the city. Of course the intention of the blockade was indeed to force the Allies out – or perhaps at a minimum negotiate some reduced presence under which they could stay in the city if they withdrew their currency from West Berlin, integrated the whole of the city into the economic control of the Soviet zone of Germany and gave up plans to create a West German government. Such a surrender was unthinkable.

The full blockade had begun on Thursday, June 24, at 6:00 A.M. On Saturday, while Truman was telling his Cabinet, "We are going to stay. Period," Bevin issued a formal Foreign Office communiqué: "The statement that we intend to stay in Berlin holds good." Four days later he went before the House of Commons to outline the steps being taken to institute an airlift to supply the Western sectors of the city and to tell the House in very serious and heavy tones:

---

* In fact, none of the B-29s sent to Europe was configured to carry the atomic bomb. In 1947, the United States had only thirteen atomic bombs, and this had about doubled by the time the Berlin blockade began.

We recognize that as a result of these decisions a grave situation might arise. Should such a situation arise, we shall have to ask the House to face it. His Majesty's Government and our Western Allies can see no alternative between that and surrender – and none of us can accept surrender.

The Allies would stay. But how would they stay? That was still to be proven. Whatever the general appraisal of political-diplomatic-intelligence estimates that the Soviet Union did not want a war, the risk of war was growing higher. If they could block roads and railroads and waterways into Berlin, they could also block the three air corridors into the city from the West. This would mean shooting down Allied aircraft and that clearly would be an act of war, but there also could be an accidental war. It was a risk that the Allies had to take, and were confidently prepared to take.

In the face of these risks and tensions in Berlin, the Western Allies moved promptly to underscore their commitment and policy for West Germany. On July 1, with the blockade one week old, the three Allied military governors took brief time away from the city to fly down the air corridor to Frankfurt to meet with the state presidents of the eleven Länder of West Germany. They informed the German leaders formally of the decisions of the London Conference, now approved by the Allied government, and invited the state presidents to set in motion the machinery to organize a Constitutional Assembly to begin drafting a new democratic constitution for a Federal Republic. The Soviet blockade would not be allowed to stop the emergence of a West German state. After brief discussions and mutual exchanges of support and congratulations all around, the Allied generals flew back to Berlin immediately.

Action also came at last from Washington on the stalled Atlantic security talks. On June 23 – the day the Soviet High Command gave the orders for the Berlin blockade – John Hickerson asked the minister at the British Embassy, Sir John Balfour, to call at the State Department. Balfour was told, to his great satisfaction and relief, that the United States was now ready to open formal talks on an Atlantic security arrangement. A Senate resolution, drafted by Vandenberg with the guiding hand of the State Department, had now been passed, giving congressional sanction to some form of association or alliance with Europe, but Hickerson remained very cautious as to exactly what kind of an arrangement the United States yet envisaged. That would have to await the talks. He proposed that they start within a week. Washington suddenly seemed to be in a hurry after nearly three months of delay. The date of July 6, 1948, was soon agreed for the opening of a seven-power meeting of the United States, Britain, France, Canada and the three Benelux states that would carry America into the first "entangling alliance" in its history.

In those dramatic, history-filled last ten days of June 1948, the hinge of fate turned for the West in postwar Europe. In West Berlin the seemingly irresistible force of Stalinist Communist expansion into Europe met head on with an immovable Western determination, whatever the actuality of Western power at that time might have been. But this determination in Berlin could never have been mustered without the launching of the Marshall Plan, without growing American involvement in the Greek civil fighting, without the American naval buildup in the Mediterranean, without the signing of the Western Union Treaty in Brussels, without the democratic election victory in Italy, without the diplomatic drive to set a new political and economic course for West Germany, without this gathering sense that the West was moving forward together with a revival of will to restore strength and security. All of this catalyzed in those last days of June around the focal determination: We stay in Berlin. After that the hinge turned.

Berlin was the high point of Stalin's postwar challenge to the West. What would have happened if there *had* been a retreat from Berlin? Could further Communist inroads into Western Europe have been checked or halted? Could a European Recovery Program have gone forward against rising Communist opposition in the Western democracies, let alone been approved by an American Congress? Could governments have survived in France, Italy or elsewhere against internal and external pressures creating uncertainty, intimidation and fear? Could a West German Republic have been created under Soviet threat if Berlin had gone the way of Prague? What use would a North Atlantic Treaty be without a viable Europe?

But by the end of July, as the airlift planes thundered into Tempelhof and Gatow and Tegel airfields, the landings increasing by the hour, the West had already won. It would take nearly a full year of danger and tension before Stalin called it quits. By the time the blockade was lifted, West Germany had its federal constitution and the North Atlantic Treaty had been signed.

EIGHT

The Vandenberg Resolution

Undersecretary of State Robert Abercrombie Lovett and Senator Arthur Hendrick Vandenberg, Republican of Michigan, formed a close and genuine working friendship in 1947 and 1948 that fit like an executive hand in a congressional glove, and proved to be of lasting benefit as the nation inched and tiptoed into the Atlantic Alliance.

Vandenberg, who served in the Senate from 1928 until his death in 1951, was a prewar leader, symbol and embodiment of American isolationism. He remained an isolationist, fighting President Roosevelt's preparedness measures, right up to Pearl Harbor. He then abruptly closed his own book on his past and wrote: "That day ended isolationism for any realist." His conversion was genuine and wholehearted, although it took him some years to work his way out from under that cloud of his past. But he was completely unlike his Republican colleague, Senator Robert A. Taft, who remained an isolationist at heart to the end of his days, oscillating between grudging support and unreconstructed obstruction for the war effort and America's postwar power role in the world.

Vandenberg had all the cliché attributes of a United States senator – a large balding head, a bulky torso that overflowed deep leather armchairs, a love of attention, an air of self-importance, a pompous manner, a constant cloud of cigar smoke, a mellifluous speaking style of loud and florid phrases such as "our merific inheritance" or "these marcescent monarchies of the world." But behind this senatorial mien he had a good mind, he was an honest man, he wanted his country to do the right things for the good of the world, and he had a deep love of the Senate, its political workings and the stage that it gave him on which to display power.

Vandenberg also had an unending parade of tutors and guides in his role as a statesman: Walter Lippmann, James Reston, Joseph Alsop, Dean Acheson, General Marshall and ultimately Robert A. Lovett were only a few of those who helped direct his pen and thoughts. Marshall did not like the business of special courtship of senators, assuming that they ought to be motivated by an understanding of national interests just as he was. But he did devote extra time to Vandenberg, to a point where he once remarked: "We could not have gotten much closer unless I sat in his lap or he sat in mine."

Dean Acheson later wrote of his Vandenberg experience: "His mind was not original; but it was open. He was not a creator of the ideas which he was eminently capable of receiving and using. He had the capacity to learn and the capacity for action – rare gifts in themselves. He did not furnish the ideas, the leadership or the drive to chart the new course or to move the nation into it. But he made the result possible. Without Vandenberg in the Senate from 1943 to 1951 the history of the postwar period might have been very different."

When Lovett succeeded Acheson as undersecretary in June of 1947, immediately after the Marshall Plan speech, he also inherited the delicate and necessary task of handling Senator Vandenberg. In 1946 the Republicans had won control of both the House and Senate after the long Roosevelt years, and Vandenberg had taken over as chairman of the powerful Senate Foreign Relations Committee. He had made himself the arbiter and embodiment of bipartisan foreign policy. Acheson had worked diligently and effectively with Vandenberg, but they were far from any natural personality mix. Acheson had a quick and powerful intellect but he scarcely could conceal – usually did not bother to conceal – an attitude of condescension toward his fellow man. He had a wit that was sharp, barbed and acerbic along with being very funny.

Lovett was fully Acheson's intellectual equal, and the two men were lifelong close friends from college days together at Yale. But Lovett was altogether more reserved in personality, cautious, a little bland, self-deprecating and with a sense of shyness. Lovett would show deference where Acheson would show superiority. Lovett's wit would amuse while

Acheson's would often wound. Moreover, Acheson was a committed and combative Harry Truman Democrat, while Lovett was much more apolitical in his attitudes. For Lovett the task of "stroking" senators was more natural than it was for Acheson.

When Acheson took Lovett to meet Vandenberg for the first time there was a kind of hand-over ceremony. "I've known Bob since Yale and I hope you will be agreeable to accept his services," Acheson said with a flourish. Vandenberg, who had a rather ponderous sense of humor, responded: "I welcome you to the job of Undersecretary of State, and may God have mercy on your soul." Lovett liked that, and from then on he and Vandenberg never looked back, forming a warm and confident relationship and genuine enjoyment of their mutual company.

Together they plunged at once into the yearlong task of pushing, pulling, prodding and steering the Marshall Plan and subsequent appropriation bills through Congress – a process that Acheson described as "applying the trademark of determining the price by either stamping a proposal with a Vandenberg brand, or exacting from the administration a concession which Vandenberg thought politically important." By the first week of April 1948, the European Recovery Act had passed the Senate and final consideration began in the House of Representatives. It was at this delicate political moment that the Pentagon proposals to launch yet another major foreign-policy initiative and open negotiations with the Europeans on a North Atlantic security pact reached Lovett's desk, with Secretary Marshall away in Bogotá.

Lovett was completely in accord with President Truman's decision that the first priority was bipartisanship – which in effect meant "applying the trademark or determining the price" with Senator Vandenberg. Lovett was innately cautious anyway, and he had immediately formed considerable doubts about the wisdom, the scope and the timing of the Pentagon proposals. He saw "terrible difficulties" on Capital Hill if word leaked out that the idea of a military alliance with Europe was even being discussed in the State Department. In fact, the whole episode of the Pentagon talks and the resulting proposals remained one of Washington's best-kept secrets for many months, although when Vandenberg was brought into the picture both Joe Alsop and Scotty Reston soon picked up the scent of an alliance in the air.

Meanwhile Lovett's own reservations about the wisdom or necessity of a treaty of alliance with Europe had been reinforced when Belgian Prime Minister Paul-Henri Spaak arrived in Washington on April 5 and called at the State Department for a review of the outlook in Europe following the signing of the Brussels Treaty. Spaak knew nothing at all of the tripartite Pentagon talks that had been concluded only the week before. Unknowingly and unwittingly, the Belgian now proceeded to undermine much of the diplomatic pressure and maneuver that Bevin had been applying to involve the United States in a treaty with Europe. Meeting with Lovett, Spaak said (much to the silent consternation of Jack Hickerson and Ted Achilles, the pro-treaty advocates in the department who were present with the acting secretary):

> He believed the Soviet government was acting on the assumption that any overt act in Europe would mean war with the United States, regardless of whether or not the United States entered into formal treaty relations for the defense of Western Europe. If the United States was prepared to enter into formal guarantees of Western Europe, such commitments would be universally welcomed, particularly in France, but *formal commitments were not the essential need.* [Italics added] The real need was for maximum military coordination at the earliest possible moment.

This, of course, was precisely what Kennan and Bohlen were also preaching in the State Department. But four days later, Ernest Bevin dispatched from London his formal endorsement of the Pentagon proposals, in which he forcefully declared to Lovett and the State Department:

> One of my great anxieties in this business is whether, if trouble did come, we should be left waiting as in 1940 in a state of uncertainty. . . . To sum up, *we do not believe that there is any substitute for a treaty if something effective is to be done.* [Italics added] A real defense system worked out by the United States, Canada, the United Kingdom and the Western European States would affect the whole approach of the world to the peace problems and be a first great step towards what ultimately would become a real world collective security system in accordance with the principles of the United Nations.

Against this background of conflicting opinion within the State Department and conflicting opinion from the Europeans, Lovett held his first meeting to broach the subject with Vandenberg in the privacy of the senator's apartment in the Wardman Park Hotel on April 11. The two men frequently had a quiet bipartisan drink together at the Wardman Park at the end of the day, but this was one of the more important occasions.

Lovett found Vandenberg not at all hostile to the idea of American military *backing* for Europe, saying that he "recognized fully" the necessity for some kind of military assurances and aid. But he told Lovett that it would be "doubtful and dangerous" to attempt to carry this into some kind of a treaty guarantee for Europe which would require a two-thirds vote for Senate approval.

When Lovett then sounded out the senator on the idea of a unilateral declaration by the President that "the United States would regard an attack upon the Brussels Treaty powers as an attack against the United States," as had been recommended in the secret Pentagon proposals, Vandenberg's response was "Why should Truman get all the credit?"

The 1948 presidential election was barely six months away, and Vandenberg was naturally as preoccupied with politics as he was with policy. So, he proposed to Lovett, why not have the Senate take the initiative instead of the President? According to Lovett's memorandum of the conversation in the State Department papers, he had in mind "a resolution which might refer to the importance of making the United Nations an effective instrument for the maintenance of international peace, urging the President to give attention to the perfection of certain steps, and dealing with the problem of security in general terms." Vandenberg was particularly proud of Article 51 of the United Nations Charter, which he had helped to draft as a member of the U.S. delegation at the San Francisco Conference in 1945. The article declares that nothing in the Charter "shall impair the inherent right of individual and collective self-defense if an armed attack occurs." So the senator now suggested that a Senate resolution to strengthen the interpretation of this article would furnish the President with a vehicle or framework for action to strengthen European security.

From Lovett's standpoint, Vandenberg's suggestion was not only good bipartisan politics but also good diplomacy. It would enable him to fend off pressures from London and the Brussels Treaty powers to plunge into immediate negotiations on an alliance. It would keep the whole subject on the back burner while vital ERP appropriations were wheedled out of Congress. And in any case the State Department still had to get its act together over the wisdom of having a treaty at all, or whether some action short of a treaty would be enough. This would largely turn on what the Vandenberg Resolution would actually say, and the vote by which it would be endorsed.

Lovett then discussed Vandenberg's idea with President Truman, who was perfectly happy to have the Senate take the initiative. So Lovett set up a drafting committee in the State Department to prepare "suggestions" for Vandenberg. He assigned the work to Hickerson and Achilles, the strong advocates of an Atlantic treaty, along with Dean Rusk, who was then an assistant secretary looking after United Nations affairs. Working with them was the clerk of Vandenberg's Senate Foreign Relations Committee, Frances Wilcox.

Given the normally cumbersome process by which this kind of policy document is produced in the American government, the Vandenberg Resolution took shape in the fairly rapid time of one month from that first discussion at the Wardman Park Hotel. It was ready for consideration by the Foreign Relations Committee on May 11, and was adopted by the Senate exactly one month later.

There were three further formal meetings with Vandenberg at the State Department to discuss the form and text of the resolution, with General Marshall in charge when he returned from Bogotá, and John Foster Dulles also sitting in. Truman of course gave his approval to the final text from behind the scenes, making sure that it would be Vandenberg's show.

Vandenberg was verbose in speechmaking but had an admirable fetish for brevity of written proposals. He was known in the Senate as "one page Vandenberg." Achilles later recalled that "the Senator insisted on typing up the final draft himself, although he had to use very narrow margins and almost ran off the bottom of the page" to get it all on one sheet. In fact, the three key paragraphs of the resolution were drafted by Achilles, with only one change written in by Vandenberg.

The resolution made no mention of "treaty" or "alliance" or even any mention of Europe at all. Nevertheless, the text drafted by Achilles was elastic enough to cover almost any action in the field of security cooperation that the State Department might ultimately decide to endorse. In unadorned and straightforward language, the resolution began by advising the President that it was the "sense of the Senate" that he should "particularly pursue" within the United Nations Charter a first objective of removing the veto over admission of new members, and removing the veto as well from all questions of peaceful settlement of disputes to come before the Security Council.

Then, at the heart of the matter, it recommended that the President also pursue:

> Progressive development of regional and other collective arrangements for individual and collective self-defense in accordance with the purposes, principles and provisions of the Charter.
>
> Association of the United States by constitutional process with such regional and other collective arrangements as are based on continuous and effective self-help and mutual aid, and as affect its national security.
>
> Contribution to the maintenance of peace by making clear its determination to exercise the right of individual or collective self-defense under Article 51 should any armed attack occur affecting its national security.

According to Achilles, Vandenberg added the words "by constitutional process" in the second paragraph. Of course "collective arrangements . . . based on continuous and effective self-help and mutual aid" could well mean a treaty, but it was still for the President to decide how to implement the resolution and what would be possible and acceptable in the Senate under its generalized terms. A treaty was still a quantum leap away.

Vandenberg decided not to hold public hearings in the Foreign Relations Committee on his resolution. He felt quite rightly that it would not only be a waste of time but would attract a lot of pressure groups with crackpot ideas about how to "strengthen" the United Nations. Already there had been a variety of proposals in both the House and Senate that would have torn the organization apart in the name of improving it.

Moreover, Vandenberg was in a hurry to get the resolution through the Senate in advance of the Republican Party National Convention that was due to open in Philadelphia on June 20 to chose a presidential nominee.

He wanted it on the books in order to influence the campaign platform on which the Republican candidate would be running.

Of course there was thorough discussion in the Foreign Relations Committee behind closed doors before the historic resolution was duly given unanimous approval and sent to the floor of the Senate for action on June 11, 1948. The debate lasted about eight hours, and the resolution passed by a vote of 64 to 6.

The Vandenberg Resolution was certainly a high point of that successful era of bipartisanship, and the senator from Michigan set off for the Philadelphia convention a happy man at the apex of his influence and power. He was widely expected to be a candidate for the nomination, but in fact he made no move at all in that direction and his diaries and private papers subsequently made clear that he really had no driving ambition for the presidency at all. Of course, he did not publicly withdraw or disavow such ambitions. Instead he used that potential strength to ensure that the Republican party adopted his kind of foreign-policy plank in its platform – not Senator Taft's.

Vandenberg's one chance for the nomination – if he had a chance or interest – would have been a deadlock between Taft and Thomas E. Dewey. But he made no move to mix into floor politics and did not even visit Convention Hall until after Dewey had been nominated.

It takes two to make a bipartisan policy – and Harry Truman's political statesmanship at this time was every bit as shining as Arthur Vandenberg's. As the political campaign got into high gear Truman kept in regular secret personal contact with Vandenberg, by telephone and messages and occasional visits through a White House side door. In particular, Truman called Vandenberg to thank him at one point for a foreign-policy speech at a key moment in the campaign. Vandenberg was bitter, however, about Truman's campaign tactic against "the do-nothing Eightieth Congress," when he rightly felt that he had done so much. But across the noise of politics, they still could talk about bipartisan objectives. Harry Truman was far from the lame duck, or dead duck, everybody thought he was in the summer of 1948.

As the Vandenberg Resolution moved from the drafting stage to the Senate floor, the argument over the need for a treaty of alliance sharpened in the State Department with the return of George Kennan from an extended tour of the Far East, followed by a couple of weeks in the hospital with a duodenal ulcer. But at the end of April, Kennan was back in action with a memorandum for Secretary Marshall (now back from Bogotá) and Lovett, which, he wrote, had been discussed with Bohlen "and may be taken as substantially his views as well as my own":

> I believe that the appeals from Bevin and Bidault spring primarily not from a worry about whether we would be on their side in the event they are attacked by Russia, but from their feeling that we do not have any agreed concept between ourselves and themselves as to what we would do in the event of a Russian attack, and particularly what steps, if any, could be taken to save the continental members of the Brussels Union from the dual catastrophe of Russian invasion and subsequent military liberation. If this analysis is correct, what Western Europeans require from us is not so much a public political and military alliance (since the presence of our troops between Western Europe and the Russians is an adequate guarantee that we will be at war if they are attacked) but rather realistic staff talks to see what can be done about their defense.

Kennan and Bohlen next met jointly with Sir John Balfour at the British Embassy to press this view directly. According to the British record, they reiterated that "it was unthinkable that the U.S. would stand idly by and see Western European countries engulfed by the Soviet Army." They argued further that "in the present political setting, would not an Atlantic Pact cause undue provocation to the Soviets, and was it not too much to expect Congress to be willing to undertake so far-reaching a commitment in an election year?"

However, strong public support for an Atlantic pact now came from Canada, whose diplomats and political leaders played a very active role throughout that year of negotiations. It was precisely with this in mind that Bevin had pressed for Canadian participation from the outset.

On April 29, the Canadian external affairs minister and future prime minister, Louis St. Laurent, decided at the urging of Lester Pearson, his undersecretary of state, to go public and come out firmly for a treaty. Addressing the House of Commons in Ottawa, St. Laurent said:

Canada and the United States need the assistance of the Western European democracies just as they need ours. Our foreign policy today must be based on a recognition of the fact that totalitarian Communist aggression endangers the freedom and peace of every democratic country, including Canada. On this basis we should be willing to associate ourselves with other free states in any appropriate collective security arrangements which may be worked out under Article 51 or 52 of the U.N. Charter.

St. Laurent did not actually use the word "treaty," but it was self-evident that a "collective security arrangement" would not be the same thing as a unilateral declaration of support. At that time, no other government leader on either side of the Atlantic had yet gone as far in publicly declaring for a North Atlantic pact. Bevin responded at once with a statement to his House of Commons welcoming and supporting the Canadian stance. If the Canadians could perceive the need for North America to join an Atlantic pact, could the Americans lag behind?

The Canadians then went further. In Washington, the Canadian ambassador, Hume Wrong, decided to tackle George Kennan head on over the issue of a treaty. A career diplomat with long experience in Washington, Wrong was highly regarded and had known both Hickerson and Dean Acheson since the 1920s. He invited Kennan to lunch on May 19, to argue with him face to face that the presence of U.S. troops in Germany along with some unilateral declaration of American support for Europe simply would not be enough.

He told Kennan that even if the countries of Western Europe already had as much practical assurance of U.S. support as they would have under a treaty of alliance, "plenty of people would not think that this was the case, and would therefore refrain from running risks which in our interests they should run."

In the case of Canada, Wrong pointed out to Kennan:

It would be far more difficult for Canada to collaborate in planning defense against Soviet aggression on the basis of a unilateral U.S. assurance than it would be if both countries were parties to an Atlantic agreement. Under such an agreement, the joint planning of the defense of the North Atlantic would fall into place as part of a larger whole, and would diminish difficulties arising from fears of invasion of Canadian sovereignty by the U.S. An Atlantic pact would go a long way towards curing Canada's split personality in defense matters by bringing the U.S., the U.K. and Canada into a regular partnership.

Kennan was then invited to visit Ottawa for further discussions. Escott Reid, the senior career official in the External Affairs Ministry and a key player behind the scenes in the NATO negotiations, had prepared a two-thousand-word memorandum for Kennan on the case for a treaty versus a unilateral declaration. One of its telling argument was:

> If the United States military support for Western Europe is to be effective, the United States Chiefs of Staff must know where they can operate in the event of war or in an emergency. They must know the bases from which they can undertake a quick and effective offensive. They must be sure in advance of the territories which they can employ. They must, if necessary, establish bases immediately. All this will be much easier to do under a treaty.

And Reid's memorandum repeated the argument that in the case of Canada, as well as Denmark, Iceland and Norway, "it would be politically easier to grant defense facilities to a North Atlantic Alliance than to the United States."

All this seemed to have a cumulative effect, for Wrong reported to Ottawa at the end of June: "I think that Lovett is inclined to be sympathetic but not fully satisfied on the treaty proposal. Bohlen still tends to oppose it, while Kennan appears to be converted."

Kennan's "conversion," however, was more of a case of bowing to the inevitable rather than any change of conviction, for he writes in his *Memoirs*:

> In June I wrote a memorandum to put on the brakes. Here, I accepted (there was no alternative) the situation created by the Vandenberg Resolution, but urged that military aid be granted only on the Marshall Plan principles (namely, that the Europeans must first draw up their own program and take responsibility for it) and that we should not discuss any further American political commitment along this line unless further conversations convinced us that this was necessary in order to bolster

public confidence in Western Europe. But by this time, of course, the
Senators had the bit in their teeth, and no words of this sort on my part
could have any effect.

Kennan remained largely oblivious to the genuine anxieties of a
defenseless Western Europe as the Berlin situation began to heat up in
May and June following the Soviet walkout from the Allied Control
Council. Bevin, in a mood of growing frustration at the delay in getting
talks started in Washington, dispatched another plea to Marshall on May
14 – but it was not delivered. Ted Achilles recorded this twist in a State
Department memorandum:

> Donald Maclean came in yesterday afternoon. He said that the Embassy
> had received another message from Bevin to the Secretary but had
> discretion as to whether or not to present it. The message again urged the
> desirability of negotiating a treaty for the security of the North Atlantic
> area. Since Chip and George Kennan had indicated strongly to Balfour
> their belief that a treaty was not desirable, the Embassy was inclined not to
> present the message, since it might merely produce a reply indicating
> United States unwillingness to conclude such a treaty. I said I thought a
> further message would produce such a reply, and that the Embassy's
> judgment seemed sound and that there would be ample opportunity as and
> when talks started to present Bevin's ideas on a treaty.

The three months' wait during April, May and June, from the conclusion of the Pentagon talks to the passage of the Vandenberg Resolution
and start of the seven-power talks, was indeed a period of impatience
and frustration in Europe and irritation in Washington at constantly
having to fend off European pressures for action. But it was not all
wasted time.

One productive meeting took place between Lovett and the British
ambassador, Lord Inverchapel, who was about to retire in late April.
Lovett told Inverchapel that congressional leaders so far were "mainly
sympathetic" and were definitely in favor of "something more affirmative
than a presidential declaration, although not yet favoring an actual treaty."
But, he continued, they were "realistic in the sense that they needed to be

convinced that the five Brussels Treaty allies were working on arrangements of their own." He therefore proposed to Inverchapel that the Brussels Treaty powers should provide the State Department with an information memorandum about their actual military situation, size of forces, supply situation, potential sources for increased armament, their military plans and the forces that would be needed to carry out the plans.

This put the ball back in the European court. Bevin and the British swung into action. A meeting of the five European defense ministers was called to consider Lovett's request, and on April 30 a Brussels Treaty Military Committee was formed to get to work at once preparing an answer for the Americans. The British then took things another step further by shrewdly proposing to the United States that it send "military observers" to London to work with the Military Committee on military plans and supply problems. This was agreed in Washington, and in June a first group of U.S. staff officers began turning up in London. By the end of the summer, the senior American was Major General Lyman L. Lemnitzer, later a NATO Supreme Allied Commander. Even without a treaty, Bevin had succeeded in creating a first organic military link between the United States and Europe.

Meanwhile, a preliminary military report was hammered out by the Brussels Treaty committee in the rush time of only two weeks. It was only a general appraisal of the situation in Europe, with details to follow, but it contained one striking and important basic passage on strategy for defense of Western Europe:

> In the event of an attack by Russia, the five powers are determined to fight as far east in Germany as possible. Their preparations are aimed at holding the Russians on the best positions in Germany covering the territory of the five powers in such a way that sufficient time for American military power to intervene decisively can be assured. . . . They recognize that their plans must be very closely linked to the American strategic concept and the development of such forces as they are prepared to provide for the defense of Europe from the outset.

This was a bold assessment and a brave expression of determination by the Brussels Treaty powers – particularly since they had nothing like the

necessary military power to carry it out. But it was an important declaration of political will, which also amounted to an irrefutable case for
American support if such a forward defense strategy in Europe was to be
made effective. Moreover, that general strategic statement in that first
military appraisal by the Brussels Treaty Military Committee remains the
basic NATO defense doctrine today.

Meanwhile diplomatic activity began to pick up in Scandinavia, where a
threat of Soviet pressure against Norway in mid-March had triggered the
original Pentagon talks. Now, in mid-May, the Norwegian foreign minister, Halvard Lange, disclosed to the American ambassador in Oslo,
Ulrich Bay, that the Swedes were pressing Norway and Denmark to join a
Nordic defense pact which would be based on Sweden's traditional policy
of neutrality. As a precondition for such a Scandinavian alliance, Sweden
was insisting that Norway and Denmark first declare that they would not
join any other outside pact or bloc. Lange reported that the Danes were
giving general support to the idea, but he told the American ambassador
that he had referred the matter to the Norwegian Cabinet, which had
promptly refused. Lange stoutly asserted that it would mean "forsaking
basic principles of freedom of future action and would commit the nation
to the well-known principle of Swedish neutrality, and this Norway would
never do."

Lange served as his country's foreign minister from 1945 for more than
twenty years, and was the dominant Scandinavian figure on the international scene. A stalwart Labor party man of intelligence and skill, he was
fluent in four or five languages and had worked at one period in the old
League of Nations secretariat in Geneva before the war. During the war
he was imprisoned by the Nazis for months in solitary confinement in
Norway and then shipped to a concentration camp in Germany. He was
barely alive when British troops liberated the camp and sped him to a
hospital. Neutrality had done his country no good at all in the face of the
Nazis in 1940, and Lange would have no truck with neutrality in 1948
with the Soviet Union now sharing a common border with northern
Norway.

The Swedes mistakenly believed that Scandinavian solidarity would
prevail. According to Lange, Swedish Foreign Minister Östen Undén

was arguing that neutrality would be more likely to be respected if all the Scandinavian countries adopted a common policy, and he was also blandly assuming that, in any case, "if an emergency arose the U.S. and the U.K. would rush all possible aid in the event of a violation of Scandinavian neutrality by the Soviets." But at the same time, the Swedish defense minister had publicly declared that even if northern Norway were occupied by the Russians, Sweden would refuse to fight or go to Norway's aid unless Sweden itself was subsequently attacked.

This was scarcely the kind of talk to encourage the Norwegians to go neutral and rely on Sweden after the experiences of World War II. But Lange was a very careful man politically as well as diplomatically. He told the American ambassador that talks with the Swedes would probably be kept going for the rest of the year because "important sections of the Norwegian Labor Party" would want to be satisfied that every avenue of Nordic cooperation had been explored.

But Lange also volunteered that he would not allow the talks with Sweden to drag on indefinitely, and if the negotiations failed, as he fully seemed to expect, then "he would recommend to his government and the Norwegian people that Sweden be left to herself and he would recommend a declaration of Norway's affiliation with the west through whatever channel might be open at that time." With seven-power talks at last about to open in Washington, this was welcome news. Both the United States and Britain regarded Norwegian participation in whatever Atlantic security arrangement finally emerged to be of vital strategic and political importance.

At last the Great Day arrived in Washington – a hot and muggy July 6, 1948, when formal seven-power negotiations finally opened to explore a security arrangement between the United States and Europe. But the State Department's official statement on this historic meeting was deliberately contrived to convey about as much news interest and excitement as the posting of a notice of an interesting afternoon of two tables at a local bridge club. All that the State Department would say was that talks had begun "on measures to give implementation to the Vandenberg Resolution on support of the United Nations," and as these would be purely exploratory discussions to be referred back to governments, no further information would be released. There was not a whisper or hint that an Atlantic Alliance might be in the making.

In fact, Lovett opened the meeting with an impassioned warning to the ambassadors of Britain, France, Canada, Belgium, Holland and Luxembourg that "a leak, particularly during the political campaign in the United States, might throw the whole enterprise into jeopardy – political heat in this country will increase up to election day and scars will be left over afterwards and any leak might cast a cloud over the whole plan." During these opening discussions, which lasted five days, not only did nothing leak. Nothing very much happened either.

It quickly became clear that despite passage of the Vandenberg Resolution, Lovett was still not ready to commit the United States to *any* particular course of action on European security. It was all neatly summarized in the British Foreign Office official history of the negotiations, written at the time by Nicholas Henderson, then a young second secretary, who attended every one of the meetings from July 6 on, and later returned to Washington in 1979 as a very successful British ambassador during the period of the Falklands War. As well as being an incisive and effective diplomat, Henderson was a facile and amusing stylist on paper.

> The American attitude [he wrote] as revealed in the course of the first five meetings of the Ambassadors' Committee was that of some modern Minerva, ready to lend its shield to the good cause of European democracy, but not prepared to promise to descend into the earthly European arena and become involved itself should trouble occur. It became depressingly clear in the course of those first five meetings that the State Department, in calling the conference, had no intention of making any proposals itself.

Lovett, Henderson wrote, "was always frank and courteous but he also was consistently cautious and a master of circumlocution. As master of ceremonies, he belonged to the *laissez-faire* school, and far from leading discussions he was apt to let them ramble on in circles, probably deliberately."

Moreover, the agenda for that first round of ambassadorial discussions was not at all the still-secret Pentagon proposals – but simply a list of generalized topics that were put forward by Lovett and the State Department almost to avoid getting down to anything specific. The topics taken up in order over the five days were:

- The situation in Europe as it affects security, including estimates of Soviet intentions
- Security measures taken and to be taken in Europe by the five Brussels Treaty powers
- Security relations with other Western European countries
- Nature of the U.S. association under the Vandenberg Resolution with European security arrangements

So how *did* the talks go in those first five days in the Ambassadors' Committee? Well, they talked a lot about what the Europeans were doing for themselves under the Brussels Treaty. They talked about whether that treaty membership should be enlarged. They talked about whether it could then become a hard core around which some transatlantic arrangement could be built. They talked about "graded membership" in an alliance. They talked about the "dumbbell concept" of a separate North American guarantee for a European pact. There was a lot of generalization about common interests, democratic values, Atlantic civilization and the threat of Communism. Kennan, in an intervention that disclosed his reservations about a North Atlantic Treaty, talked about a future situation emerging where the countries of Eastern Europe might come out from under the Iron Curtain and "be able to come into the European family," and how the United States "would not wish to do anything that might hinder the ultimate unification of Europe." The French talked a great deal about the need for immediate American military assistance for the Brussels Treaty powers – a theme that they harped on so incessantly over the next weeks that they came close to sinking the North Atlantic Treaty in the process.

Of course, the ambassadors chased around these circles on a high plateau of polite generalities, rather like a Viennese minuet with the dancers approaching each other, bowing, touching hands, retreating, turning, circling and then approaching to bow again and prepare to start the dance. Only Lovett had an elusive technique of avoiding the dance. If anyone sought to press him to be more specific as to what the American position would be on this or that, he would politely and enthusiastically respond to the effect that it was precisely to determine the American position that these very valuable and important exchanges were taking place.*

Finally, on the last day of that first round, July 9, they reached the nub of the problem with the agenda item "Nature of the U.S. association under the Vandenberg Resolution with European security arrangements." The able, experienced, precise, no-nonsense Dutch ambassador to Washington, Eelco van Kleffens, led off. It was his "personal hope," Kleffens said, that "the ultimate outcome would be some North Atlantic Pact." He did not think that the Brussels pact was any suitable basis for a response to the Vandenberg Resolution. Nor could he conceive of the United States adhering to it, so in his view it was necessary to find a new formula, a new treaty.

Next the new British ambassador waded in – Sir Oliver Franks, youthful at forty-three, a brilliant academic drafted into the British civil service during the war, and the man who had presided so successfully over the European preparatory work in Paris on the Marshall Plan. Skilled in the art of "committee tactics," knowing how to intervene without imposing himself on any meeting, Franks joined in calling for "a new pact to deal with the problems of the whole area of the North Atlantic rather than simply some enlargement of membership in the Brussels pact."

Lester Pearson of Canada then completed this effort of polite encirclement of Lovett by asserting that he, too, wanted to see "the creation of a new system." Even without the Brussels Treaty, he said, Canada would still want an Atlantic security system "with members associating themselves with the security of each and all." The Canadian government, he underscored firmly, "could not make any contribution to the collective security of the area by any unilateral guarantee." In other words, as far as Canada was concerned, there had to be a treaty.

At this point the State Department record shows that Lovett did move very slightly when he interjected to express agreement with Pearson – but only to the extent of saying that he "could not contemplate" that a

---

*Years later I once asked a Foreign Office friend the possible consequences of the fact that Donald Maclean had been able to report all these discussions to Moscow. He laughed and said, "Oh, I suppose someone in Moscow was saying – here's another one of those dreary reports from that fellow Maclean in Washington that I have to read."

unilateral guarantee on security would be sufficient. This was as close as Lovett came in five days of talks to moving the United States in the direction of a treaty.

But at the end all was still vague and elliptical. The windup comment came from the Belgian ambassador, Baron Robert Silvercruys, experienced in the ways of Washington, who always liked to try and come to the point. The State Department record reads:

> There had been a most useful exchange of views and exploration [Silvercruys said]. He did not, however, as yet have a very clear picture of the sort of association which the United States and Canada were prepared to contemplate. Mr. Lovett responded that an effort had been made to find the form of organization and method of association to bring the United States into some form of collective security enterprise as a member. This might be an association between separate groups, an enlargement of the Brussels Pact, or a wholly new North Atlantic arrangement.

On this groping and inconclusive final remark from its chairman, the Ambassadors' Committee ended its first round of meetings. The only real progress was simply the fact that they had met at all. A process, in other words, had finally begun.

The only decision taken by the Ambassadors' Committee was to establish immediately a Working Group of diplomatic technicians from the staffs of the seven participants in Washington. Their mandate was simply to get on with the job – go over all of the circumlocutions, try to boil it all into agreed objectives, and come up with specific recommendations and proposals for some kind of an agreement on Atlantic security. The ambassadors would continue to meet from time to time to "guide" the Working Group, and when a report was ready they would give it approval before sending it on to governments for decision and action. Everyone was fully aware, of course, that the American government would not commit itself to anything final and definitive until after the presidential election.

But the Working Group got down to business promptly on July 14. There was a long way to go, and nobody yet knew where it was all going. There was a diplomatic and political consensus to be built out of generalities and vague ideas. History was not standing still, and time was not to be wasted.

NINE

"The French Are in Our Hair."

"We met almost every working day to the beginning of September. That was before the days of air-conditioning, and we all worked with our coats off in shirt-sleeves. Most of us were already on a first-name basis, and we all were by the third day. We became life-long friends in the process. The 'NATO spirit' was born in that Working Group."

So Ted Achilles wrote in later years, and it is certainly the case that the birth of the NATO Treaty was one of the most collegiately successful diplomatic negotiations in the history of free nations. From the outset the Working Group meetings were completely informal. While notes, of course, were taken, no formal agreed records were kept. Everyone was free to speak his mind, and it was automatically understood that nothing anyone said informally could be taken as a position or commitment of any government. As a result there was a good deal of rambling discussion, but this also meant that all of the problems were probed frankly and candidly and thoroughly, with a great deal more penetration and humor than was possible in the more formal stilted exchanges at ambassadorial level. Achilles also relates:

"One day Sir Derick Hoyer-Millar made a proposal which was obviously nonsense. Several of us told him so in no uncertain terms, and a much better formulation emerged from the discussion. Derick said: 'Those were my instructions. All right. I'll tell the Foreign Office I made my pitch and was shot down and try to get my instructions changed.' He did. From then on we all followed the same system. If our instructions were sound and agreement could be reached, fine. If not, we'd work out something, and whoever had instructions that did not fit would undertake to get them changed. It always worked, although it sometimes took time."

On the American side, Jack Hickerson was dominant in the Working Group throughout, with Achilles alongside handling the load in the drafting committees. Hickerson of course had been a staunch advocate of a treaty of alliance from the first moment that the subject was broached by Bevin. Achilles declares – and Dean Acheson later said more or less the same – that "more than any other human being Jack was responsible for the nature, content and form of the NATO Treaty and for its acceptance by the Senate – it was Jack's treaty." Kennan says in his *Memoirs* that he had been appointed by Lovett to chair the Working Group, but Achilles refutes this. He says that "aside from occasionally seeing memoranda and drafts, George had nothing to do with the negotiations and was never on the Working Group." This is not entirely accurate either, but Kennan's role overall was marginal. On the other hand, Bohlen did chair some of the Working Group meetings during the summer, but he was mainly preoccupied with the Berlin situation, and in September he shifted out of the picture to go to Paris with the U.S. delegation to the United Nations General Assembly, meeting in the French capital in order to be well away from the American election campaign. Although Kennan dropped his stiff opposition to a treaty, Achilles says, "Chip more or less fought a rear-guard action all the way through – his opposition was due to his belief, pretty much a conviction, that the Senate would never consent to ratification of a military alliance." Bohlen in his memoirs glosses over all this by saying merely that he was not "directly involved" in negotiation of the treaty (which was narrowly true) and that "NATO was a simple necessity" (which he did not feel at the time).*

Of this part of the story, Nicholas Henderson wrote:

It would be misleading if any impression were given that Bohlen and Kennan were deliberately trying to sabotage the negotiations. From the

---

*I first met Bohlen in London in December 1947, at the time of the Big Four foreign ministers meeting, and came to know him well across the years with many an evening at the poker table. But I was unaware of his opposition to the NATO Treaty until I began preparations for this book, and hence was never able to question him about it. Chip died on January 1, 1974, of cancer at the age of seventy.

moment the talks began they were all for making a success of them. But for many months they were not sure in their own minds what the most desirable outcome should be. It was a measure of their extraordinary skill and of the enormous appeal of their personalities that, although they had so frequently to strike so negative a note, they never aroused the least personal resentment on the part of the representatives of the other powers.

The most active participant in the Working Group, apart from Hickerson and Hoyer-Millar, was the Canadian minister in Washington, Thomas Stone. The French and Belgian delegates remained largely and uncharacteristically inarticulate during those first weeks, apparently because of lack of clear instructions and uncertainty as to what their governments actually wanted. Stone sent a sputtering message to Ottawa at the end of July after seven meetings of the Working Group that "contributions of the French and Belgian members so far have been exactly zero – they have come forward with no positive or constructive ideas whatsoever, nor have they had anything to say about ideas that have been put forward by other people that in any way contributed to their development." Later this changed, certainly on the part of the French representative, Armand Bérard, and not always for the smoother or better.

Originally it was not the intention of the State Department to include Luxembourg in the talks, but this was then left tactfully for the Benelux states to decide, and they decided that Luxembourg should be present. Hughes Le Gallais, who was a one-man legation in Washington for the little duchy, sat on both the Ambassadors' Committee and the Working Group. But his presence was certainly no hindrance to the proceedings, as Henderson amusingly recorded.

Hughes Le Gallais was not obsessed by his burden, and did not allow his presence at the long afternoon meetings to interfere with the regular siesta habit which he had acquired during long residence in the East. With his gift for repose and his wistful air of ineffable melancholy he resembled nothing so much as the dormouse in *Alice in Wonderland*. But he was much more tactful than the dormouse. It would sometimes happen at the Working Group that the Dutch and Belgians would take up different viewpoints on a particular question. Le Gallais would then be asked for his opinion. With infinite sagacity and solemnity he would reply: "I agree with the views of my Benelux colleagues."

As the Working Group settled down to a long hot summer trying to produce clarity out of confusion, the foreign ministers of the five Brussels pact countries met in The Hague on July 19–20 to discuss the results – or rather lack of results – from the Ambassadors' Committee, and to try to coordinate the next moves they might make. It was a discussion of some asperity. Irritation and frustration were running high at the lack of any clear proposals from the American side, and at Lovett's deliberate tactics of caution, evasion and circumlocution. Tensions were high even without this disappointing start in Washington. The airlift into Berlin was barely beginning to get into effective operational gear, with the blockade now in its fourth week, and it was far from certain yet that air deliveries could sustain the city. The B-29 bombers of the U.S. Air Force had only begun to arrive in England. There was the hourly danger that if the Russians downed a single Allied aircraft, even accidentally, they might be lighting the fuse on another war. The condition of the French Army in 1948 to meet an attack by the Red Army was weak to the point of being pitiful. The British were better off, and they at least had the security of the English Channel as breathing space. But only the Americans could really assure any forward defense for Western Europe.

Georges Bidault was an emotional man even in quiet times, and there was much to be emotional about. He lashed out to the other foreign ministers that the Americans had already "abandoned" the Brussels pact which had been signed by the Europeans at great risk, and now the United States "was trying to get out of its obligations on the cheap by a general declaration involving no real obligations at all." Spaak of Belgium waded in to say that he saw the Atlantic pact idea emerging from the Washington talks as no more than a paper scheme which the United States could not make militarily effective and which would add nothing to security. The Americans were after another Rio Treaty, he said, which would be "cumbersome, lacking any automatic commitment and not corresponding to the actual dangers." Bidault returned to the attack, declaring that "the Americans have no consistent policy, the Atlantic Pact is a fabulous monster like the unicorn – no one knows what it amounts to. Treaties and alliances create risks and these ought to be compensated by guarantees." Bevin tried to apply British reason to cool down the argument, urging that they all look to the advantages of an Atlantic pact with the Americans and in the meantime press on with making their own treaty as effective as possible to show the Americans they were making progress. But in the middle of the two-day meeting, the French government fell in Paris, and Bidault lost his post as foreign minister. So the discussion ended without any agreed decisions, except that Bevin would take the diplomatic lead in dealing with the Americans over next moves.

Part of the problem with Bidault and the French at this juncture of the NATO story was a fundamental misunderstanding as to what the purpose of those Washington exploratory talks really was, what they were really all about and what they were supposed to accomplish. It was a misunderstanding for which the Americans and the British were at least partially responsible.

The French had been excluded from the secret tripartite Pentagon talks at the end of March, and they knew nothing at all of the "working level" agreement recommending negotiations for some kind of a North Atlantic security arrangement. At the time that the Brussels Treaty was signed on March 17, Bevin had informed Robert Schuman secretly and personally in a one-to-one conversation that security talks with the Americans were about to take place, but the French had been told nothing further about the results.

As far as the French were aware, therefore, the purpose of the Washington talks was ostensibly to discuss tangible American help for the Brussels pact. On the day that treaty had been signed, President Truman had declared: "I am confident that the U.S. will by appropriate means extend to the free nations the support which the situation requires." And General Marshall had twice followed this up with messages promising talks "on the part the United States should play" in support of the new treaty.

Then in mid-May there had been an exchange of messages between Lovett and Bidault in which Lovett informed the French that when talks began their aim would be "practical measures to increase Western European security." There had been no mention of any consideration of ideas about some new Atlantic security arrangement, and Bidault had replied that "what the French Government desires is not a spectacular system of guarantees, but an effective and concrete system of assistance." This, of course, was precisely what Kennan and Bohlen were also urging at the time, in opposition to the idea of a new treaty.

It is understandable, therefore, that the French went into the Ambassadors' Committee expecting to talk primarily about military assistance to bolster the Brussels Treaty forces, while the British and the Canadians went with the primary purpose of implementing the secret Pentagon proposals and involving the United States in an entirely new Atlantic pact.

There is plenty of history in this century and longer to show that it is easy to get at cross-purposes with the French and seldom easy to disentangle the snarls when they occur. This fundamental misunderstanding persisted through much of the summer, with Armand Bérard, minister at the French Embassy, telling the Working Group in August after more than two weeks of discussions that "his government had thought the present conversations were to be concerned with military aid to the Brussels powers rather than with formation of a larger association."

In fact, in mid-July the French had received secret support in their bid for American military assistance from Averell Harriman, who had arrived in Paris to head the European office of the Marshall Plan. In an eyes-only cable for Marshall and Defense Secretary James Forrestal, Harriman said:

It appears to me that maintaining and strengthening the will to resist in Europe should be fundamental in our policy through the coming months. By this I do not mean immediate commitments on a comprehensive and integrated armament program, but adoption of an attitude toward the Brussels Pact countries which will give them a greater feeling of assurances that we really mean business when we say their security is our security. I feel strongly that there is a need for tangible evidence of this in the form of token shipments of equipment in the near future. These might be a limited number of aircraft to equip selected units of the French Air Force or some ground equipment for army units. The military value of these token shipments is not important, but the effect on public opinion will be inspiring. You will recall the psychological effect of our shipment of one million rifles to Britain in 1940 which, though of negligible military importance, had an incalculable morale effect.

But the French now began to press for immediate military help from Washington with that reckless indignation they are so capable of showing, to a point where on this occasion they came close to sinking the whole project of an Atlantic Alliance. Moreover, the government crisis in Paris was a long one, and it was not until September that Robert Schuman began his remarkable four-year tenure at the Quai d'Orsay.

On August 17, Ambassador Bonnet called at the State Department on instructions from Paris to deliver a message to Secretary Marshall. The meeting was close to a diplomatic disaster.

Bonnet had a harmless egotism, loved being ambassador to Washington and thought that he played successfully the *bonhomie* role of everybody's friend. He was a Hollywood casting director's dream of the old-fashioned French diplomat – a handsome head, a quizzical face, a Maurice Chevalier accent, a talking style in which the flow of gestures matched the flow of words, neither particularly economical nor concise. He was on the whole tedious and tactless and he pursued his points with tenacity, oblivious to the effect that he might be having on others. He was out to state the French case and nothing but the French case, no matter what damage he might be doing to the French cause in the process.

When he saw Marshall, he proceeded to lay down three "conditions" that the French government would attach to entering into any North Atlantic security arrangement. First, he asked for immediate U.S. assistance in equipping French forces. Second, he said that France would want assurances that in the event of war with the Soviet Union the United States would send reinforcements of ground forces to Europe immediately to help in the defense of France. Finally, he asked that France immediately become a member of the Anglo-American Combined Chiefs of Staff organization that had been set up in World War II.

The flat, dry, official memorandum of this discussion that Marshall dictated does nothing to convey the exasperation that he felt. He at once replied on the question of the Combined Chiefs of Staff – having been its dominant American member throughout the war. Marshall told Bonnet that the Chiefs had not met for more than two years, and had been allowed to lapse because "it complicated our relations with other countries," but he would check to make sure "that no meeting was contemplated."

Bonnet said that the French understood that a report being prepared by the commanders in Germany – Clay, Robertson and Koenig – on Allied contingency plans in the event of a Soviet attack would be submitted by the Americans and the British to the Combined Chiefs. Marshall coldly replied that the report "might well be considered" by the Chiefs of Staff of all three countries, or by the Military Committee of the Brussels Treaty in London, since "it would be impossible properly to plan dispositions east of the Rhine in Germany except in connection with plans for dispositions west of the Rhine in France." But he rejected the idea of Anglo-Saxon collusion behind the backs of the French. Next day Marshall sent further word to the ambassador that although never officially disbanded, the Combined Chiefs had last met in 1946 to consider Anglo-American operations in Trieste "and are to all intents and purposes completely inoperative at the present time." At the end of 1945 when all the other wartime Anglo-American boards had been dissolved, the Combined Chiefs of Staff had been kept in suspended animation pending conclusion of peace treaties with Germany and other wartime enemies. But Marshall's assurances still did not allay French suspicions about the Anglo-Saxons – as General Charles de Gaulle would continually demonstrate for the next twenty years.

This meeting with the French ambassador "had such an irritating effect on General Marshall that he felt like calling off the Atlantic Pact negotiations at once," Lovett subsequently told Lester Pearson. In a report to Ottawa, Pearson quoted Lovett as saying that Marshall found it an "effrontery" that the French would try to lay down "conditions" for joining a North Atlantic security pact. The British Embassy reported to London that Kennan's reaction was: "Well, if the French do not want a treaty we had better drop the idea after all."

Nor was this the end of Bonnet's ignominious diplomatic Charge of the Light Brigade. He now asked for a formal meeting of the Ambassadors' Committee to make a statement of the French position on a North Atlantic Treaty.

When the Belgian ambassador, Baron Silvercruys, heard of this request and its purpose, he called Lovett and the other ambassadors to urge that instead of a full-dress formal meeting they arrange a purely informal gathering to allow Bonnet to blow off steam. Silvercruys was afraid – and rightly so – of the effect that it would have on the Americans and the Canadians if Bonnet began pounding the table about French "conditions" and making demands in a meeting where it might suddenly become necessary for some formal response.

So they gathered at Lovett's Washington residence on Kalorama Road, near the French Embassy, on August 20, for some pretty blunt and open informal discussion that lasted two hours and a half. Perhaps by some prearrangement the other ambassadors took up all of the first hour or so, and when Bonnet finally took the floor it quickly became apparent that he was simply off on a familiar canter around the track about immediate military aid for France, and was ill informed by his own government as to what was now going on in the Brussels pact Military Committee, where the United States was already participating to shape some European military assistance program. Lovett recorded:

> I asked him if his request had been cleared through the Military Committee in London. He said he did not know. I asked him then how he thought this country could possibly deal with requests from everybody in Europe if we went at it piecemeal and I reminded him that I thought one of the original purposes of the Western European Union was to coordinate the rearmament program. The others sailed into Bonnet at this point, and he said he would revert to it later.

Lovett bluntly told Bonnet that "while long-term arrangements are being worked out, the United States is doing everything it possibly can do to help meet the short-term emergency, with planning in Germany and discussions in the Military Committee in London – what more can we do in present circumstances?"

Bonnet took up a recurring French theme that an immediate military-assistance program for France was essential because the signing of a military pact with the United States would be provocative to the Soviet Union. Lester Pearson proceeded to turn this French logic on its head by replying:

The real act of provocation would be *not* to sign a pact, but increase the military strengths of potential members of that pact. Those who are most worried about the provocative effect of a pact also seem to be the most insistent on increasing their own military power. On this logic, the only way to avoid provocation would be for everybody to remain weak – which would be the greatest provocation of all, and which nobody wants.

After this two hours and a half at Lovett's residence, Pearson returned to the Canadian Embassy to report to Ottawa that "the attitude of the French is causing increasing impatience and irritation here and is incomprehensible to everybody." Later he sent a further cable: "These discussions demonstrated that the Americans are becoming profoundly impatient with the negative attitude of the French. There is, I think, a real danger of the whole project being wrecked."

Pearson was not exaggerating. Lovett in the wake of the meeting with Bonnet dispatched a personal letter on the situation to Ambassador Jefferson Caffery in Paris on August 24, that began with the notable opener: "Dear Jeff: The French are in our hair."

With an irritation that he would probably not show in any formal instructions, Lovett listed to Caffery all the demands that the French had been making. He rejected them all as "impossible," and told the ambassador that he was to make it clear to the French government that it was "fantastic" for the French to be trying to attach conditions to joining a future North Atlantic pact since it was the United States that was "doing the favors." But in Washington, Bonnet went on irrepressibly talking about "conditions" all the way to the very end of the negotiations.

In alarm at this deterioration since The Hague meeting, Ernest Bevin swung into action and sent Sir Gladwyn Jebb from London to Paris to confer with Jean Chauvel, the secretary-general of the French Foreign Ministry, who was the best man to talk to in the hiatus while the French were still sorting out a new government. At first Chauvel was defensive of the position that France had been taking, telling Jebb that the idea of a North Atlantic pact "had come as a surprise, as we had not been informed prior to the conversations in Washington that a pact of this nature was under contemplation." For that reason, he said, France had "perhaps been suspicious that instead of getting concrete United States aid which it had hoped for, we were being put off with proposals of a vague and general character."

Jebb, with all his air of Anglo-Saxon superiority, was also the match of any Frenchman in diplomatic debate and logic. He argued with Chauvel that it was utterly essential for Europe to involve the United States in an alliance, and France should not mix up short-term assistance with long-term assurance.

Pearson then instructed the Canadian ambassador to Paris, Georges Vanier, to see Chauvel and stress that if France was so worried about getting a commitment out of the Americans to send reinforcements to Europe, then it should realize that "establishment under a North Atlantic Treaty of agencies for joint planning would make it extremely difficult, if not impossible, for the United States to refuse to give assurances that they will have certain ground forces available to send immediately to Europe to defend France in an emergency."

The effect of all this – particularly after Robert Schuman was finally installed at the Quai d'Orsay and could exercise a grip on instructions – was that the French at last got their priorities sorted out, and by the time the Working Group report was ready in early September, France was ready to give full support to a North Atlantic Treaty.

In August, Lovett also sent an exasperated message to Caffery about repeated French requests for arms:

> To their demands we have patiently told them that the necessary equipment does not exist, that it will not be produced until someone is ready to pay for it, that lend-lease is not a popular word in this country, and that appropriations will require legislation which will not be enacted except on a basis of commitments on the part of recipients to exert their own maximum efforts to increase their own and each other's security and that of the United States.

But the equipment *did* exist and the State Department had not really tried very hard for the French. Partly it was general irritation with the way the French were pressing their case, but it was also because the State Department was determined to shape a military-aid program for Europe in the same fashion that economic aid was being handled under the

Marshall Plan. First get together and decide collectively on your needs, the Europeans were being told. Use the Brussels pact Military Committee in the same way that the European Recovery Program was being managed through the Organization for European Economic Cooperation (OEEC). The American crusade for European unity tended to infuse almost every action that Washington took in that postwar period.

However, the French appear to have outmaneuvered the State Department by pressing their case direct to the Pentagon. The French commander in Germany, General Pierre Koenig, turned to General Clay to ask if American surplus equipment and spare parts could not be found in Germany, left over from wartime stocks, to bring three French divisions in the occupation forces up to combat readiness. Clay referred the request favorably to the Pentagon, where Forrestal and the new Army Chief of Staff, General Omar Bradley, felt that there was plenty of reason to be more forthcoming about arms for the French than the State Department had been showing.

Possibly Averell Harriman's earlier urgings to Marshall and Forrestal for a quick morale-boosting token aid program for the French had something to do with this. But certainly there was every urgent military reason to give help to bring the French forces in Germany up to fighting condition – given the gravity of the Berlin situation. A Pentagon review of stores left behind in Germany in the postwar run-down of U.S. Forces showed that about one third of what the French needed was available right on the spot, and the rest could be shipped from surplus stocks in the United States. The total cost would be around $400 million. On September 13, the Joint Chiefs of Staff recommended presidential action. Their memorandum read:

> Even though the deficient condition of those three French divisions would be corrected eventually by the Western European Union process, it is felt that our current relations with the USSR would not justify our failure to correct, within our capabilities, known weaknesses in the French forces. The condition of the French forces in occupied Germany is a matter which affects U.S. national security.

Truman wasted no time, giving his approval on September 16. Without appropriation, authorization or congressional approval, he used his powers as Commander in Chief of the Armed Forces to order the equipment transfer, just as President Roosevelt had transferred old guns and old destroyers to the British during World War II. Caffery carried this welcome news to Robert Shuman, who was now firmly installed for a long and important tenure at the Quai d'Orsay.

Further action to bolster the military picture in Europe followed on October 3, 1948, when it was announced that the governments of the five Western Union powers had approved the appointment of Field Marshal Viscount Montgomery of Alamein to be Chairman of the Commanders-in-Chief Committee of Brussels Treaty forces, and established a new Allied Combined Headquarters at Fontainebleau, south of Paris.

Montgomery would be giving up his post as Chief of the Imperial General Staff, and in fact the prime minister and the rest of the British government were glad to be rid of him. He had treated ministers and his fellow Chiefs of Staff contemptuously, and his tour as CIGS had been an egotistical disaster. Whatever his success in war, he was regarded almost without exception by his British military contemporaries as "the worst CIGS in fifty years," and in his own diary he noted that he received only *one* message of good wishes on his departure.

Until he was practically forced to take the European job himself, Monty had been adamantly opposed to the somewhat insipid concept of appointing a Chairman of the Commanders-in-Chief Committee instead of a Supreme Allied Commander who could give orders. Moreover, acting completely on his own, without consulting the prime minister or any responsible Cabinet ministers, Montgomery had made a private approach to the Americans to see if they could be persuaded to name a commander for Europe, long before the North Atlantic Treaty was even heard of.

In March of 1948, soon after the Brussels Treaty had been signed, Montgomery wrote personally to General Omar Bradley, who had just taken over from General Eisenhower as Army Chief of Staff in Washington. He sent Bradley a copy of his own staff paper on holding the Russians on the line of the Rhine, and told him that "the forces in Western Europe need an American Supreme Commander." His letter to Bradley continued: "I personally told Ike that I would back you for the job, but that was before you took up your present appointment." Although acknowledging that it would be "politically impossible" to appoint a Supreme Commander "at the present time," he went on to suggest General Joseph L. "Lightning Joe" Collins for the job, and proposed that he be "selected and come over here to study the problem."

In May, as the Berlin crisis began to heat up, Bradley replied to Montgomery that if the Western Union powers wanted an American commander, that could be considered, but he proposed General Lucius D. Clay in Germany. Monty was contemptuous of Clay (he was contemptuous of practically everyone but himself), and he told Bradley simply that it would not work to have a Supreme Commander who was also responsible for the American occupation zone.

All of this had gone on, apparently, without the knowledge of President Truman or Secretary Marshall. It seems almost certain that neither of them would have been prepared at that juncture to send an American Supreme Commander to Europe, since it could well have been interpreted by Stalin and the Soviets as an escalation of preparations to go to war. Nevertheless, the need for some kind of a unified command structure in Europe was a major concern for the Pentagon and the U.S. government.

On August 23, 1948, Marshall met with Forrestal, Bradley and Army Secretary Kenneth Royall to discuss the situation at length. They drafted a memorandum that went immediately to the White House, proposing that the United States urge the Europeans to proceed with "immediate establishment of a Land and Air HQ" under the Brussels Treaty, and inform the British that they would support the selection of either Montgomery, Field Marshal Viscount Alexander of Tunis, who was Monty's wartime rival, or French General Alphonse Juin to take charge. They further recommended that "no American representative be formally included on the staff at this time, but a place reserved for an American deputy supreme commander." Marshall informed the President:

> We do not want without advising you to commit ourselves to the support of the appointment of a supreme commander of the Western Union forces who would automatically become the supreme commander of the Western front, and as such would be exercising command over the American troops now in Germany. We are all in agreement at the present time that during the preliminary phase of hostilities, should they occur, it would not be

advisable to have an American commander. Incidentally the British are very insistent that there should be an American commander.

Truman okayed Marshall's memorandum that same afternoon, sending it back with a handwritten comment: "I have approved your memo. It is my opinion, however, that we must be very careful not to allow a foreign commander to use up our men before he goes into action *in toto*. H.S.T."

So a few weeks later Montgomery agreed to become a "chairman" – a job he had denounced and vowed he would never accept. The French promptly made a *Kaserne* in Fontainebleau available for the new European command – the first such peacetime establishment in European history. But the field marshal could not get along with French generals any better than he could get along with the British or Americans. Under his "chairmanship," the commander in chief of land forces would be General Jean de Lattre de Tassigny, a soldier with an ego and a temperament every bit as supreme and vindictive and didactic as Monty's. Within a matter of weeks, feuding had broken out between these two prima donnas over conflicting concepts and responsibilities and theories as to how the rather fuzzy command setup was supposed to operate and who was *really* in charge. This played like a peacetime rerun of the famous feuding between Montgomery and Eisenhower during the war. Nevertheless, an Allied Military Headquarters was being established under experienced and successful World War II soldiers, and this simple fact in October of 1948 was of greater importance than the internecine warfare between two impossible men.

Moreover, the Americans *were* there discreetly in the background. The military was making faster progress toward an Atlantic Alliance than the diplomats.

From the outset in the Working Group, it became more and more clear day by day that the common objective and logical outcome in the end would have to be a North Atlantic Treaty. It was slow going, but in due course even the French were swept along by a feeling among intelligent and experienced career diplomats that a great common cause was in their hands and they were on their way to making history.

Of course the men in the Working Group were constantly reminded of the political shoals that the State Department was navigating both on Capitol Hill and within the department itself. Hickerson made this point in "a solemn and serious statement" at one of the early meetings in that hot summer:

> Hickerson said that the fact that these talks were taking place in Washington was indicative of the most radical change in United States foreign policy which had ever taken place, and he wanted the representatives of the countries present to appreciate this fully. Insofar as the State Department was concerned, its officials were *unwilling to risk failure in implementing this new United States foreign policy.* (Italics added) It would be disastrous if they were to put forward to the Senate an unacceptable pact or treaty. It would be almost equally disastrous if a pact or treaty were to be ratified with a series of hampering reservations after protracted debate. We will therefore maintain the closest possible contact with political leaders in both Houses to take their advice and counsel as to the phraseology and content of a pact or treaty which would be acceptable to Congress.

There would be no risk of a repeat of the political debacle over the League of Nations Treaty following World War I – that was the fixed determination of the entire administration from President Truman on down. Everyone involved in the negotiations knew from the outset, therefore, that in a sense the parameters would be fixed by the United States Senate. Hickerson simply believed that with care and common sense and careful political education these parameters could be stretched much farther than Bohlen, for example, believed would be possible. Nor was Lovett yet convinced or sure what the outcome should be. This difference of opinion in the State Department continued to plague the summer Working Group discussions, extending, as Nicholas Henderson recorded, "not only to the basic question of the wisdom of having a treaty, but to matters of detail such as the idea of different categories of membership in the treaty – all adding to the difficulties of other representatives."

But on a more positive note, Henderson also commented in his final report on the negotiations:

> There were, however, very great advantages to the other representatives in the methods adopted by the Americans. By washing their dirty linen in

front of the Working Group, the Americans concealed nothing. The other representatives always knew what the troubles were on the American side, and who was in favor of this or that. In consequence, Americans avoided any possibility of arousing suspicions. Another great virtue was the complete absence of false professional pride on the part of the American representatives. They did not take offense merely because their arguments were on occasion treated rather summarily by others; they did not persist in arguing for their draft when, as frequently happened, others preferred some alternative. And they never adopted a take-it-or-leave-it attitude or tried to browbeat the others. They were ready to push on before they had really agreed on anything among themselves.

This very American, open display of basic tactical and strategic differences was of course in marked contrast to British diplomatic practice, where it is rigorous tradition and discipline always to go into any negotiation with an agreed position, and never to display any internal difficulties or differences of opinion at the negotiating table.

Yet the more the Working Group circled and argued the treaty problem, the more every other alternative solution fell away and the more inevitable a North Atlantic Treaty became. The Working Group started off with an examination of the Soviet threat, on which Kennan and Bohlen were of course on home ground. A consensus was reached fairly rapidly that "to restore confidence among the peoples of Western Europe, the association of the United States and Canada in some North Atlantic security arrangement would be a major contribution." So far so good – but having accepted that basic premise, what kind of a "security arrangement"? Much of the time in August was then spent going in and out and round and round about a "two-pillar concept" and "graded membership" of limited commitments for peripheral or fainthearted states.

The Americans were sticking to a familiar theme that the Europeans should first build up the Brussels Treaty by taking in members such as Norway, Denmark, Eire, Portugal and perhaps Italy. The United States and Canada would form a second pillar by offering a North Atlantic guarantee to the Europeans. Initially this had the support of Kennan, who thought that the two-pillar concept "would establish group responsibility between the parties on each side of the Atlantic." In the Working Group, Hickerson then went along because, as the Canadians reported to Ottawa, "it would increase the influence of the United States in promoting a closer political relationship among the Western European countries leading to the establishment of a European federation." The British gave their backing politely but without conviction, simply because the proposal at least moved things further down the road to a treaty commitment on the part of the Americans. But the French were against trying to enlarge the Brussels Treaty because it would mean "spreading the butter too thin" when it came to sharing out anticipated American military supplies. The Canadians were opposed because they wanted to join a wider North Atlantic Treaty and not just to be an American appendage in a two-pillar arrangement with Europe.

In the end it became like an argument over whether a woman can be half pregnant. Since there was no unanimity, the Working Group turned to the Ambassadors' Committee for guidance. At this point, the two-pillar and limited membership treaty concept suddenly disappeared into a diplomatic wastebasket. It fell apart simply because on realistic examination it became clear that it was unlikely to meet a basic American requirement for a pact that would include the "stepping-stones" of Iceland, Denmark (because of Greenland), Portugal (because of the Azores) and Norway – all of which would be essential to any security link between North America and Europe.

What interest would any of these smaller states have had in first joining the Brussels pact in order to obtain a "two-pillar guarantee" from North America? What assurances could the Brussels Treaty offer Norway if the Soviet Union attacked in the far north, and conversely, what would Norway be expected to do if the Soviet Union attacked in West Germany? What sense would there be in trying to devise "limited membership" along with "limited commitment." Security, like pregnancy, could not be parceled out in limited packages.

When the Ambassadors' Committee met on September 2 to discuss progress in the Working Group, it was, surprisingly, Robert Lovett who took the lead in shooting down the two-pillar proposal. Norway had always been pivotal in American thinking about any Atlantic security arrangement, and Lovett now simply stated his view that "it ought to be possible for Norway and such countries to become full members of a North Atlantic pact without having to ratify the Brussels Treaty." By this simple acknowledgment of the obvious, Lovett moved the American position decisively in the direction of a straightforward North Atlantic Treaty of equal membership for all on both sides of the ocean. With some relief, the Canadian ambassador, Hume Wrong, and Sir Oliver Franks for Britain expressed agreement at once with Lovett. The French had always opposed any enlargement of the Brussels Treaty anyway. Thus, after a month or more of argument and discussion in the Working Group, the idea of a two-pillar treaty arrangement simply disappeared without a trace.

There was now only one way to go, and it took only one more week for the Working Group to produce a final report. In the State Department, Ted Achilles had already prepared a "set of proposals" for a North Atlantic Treaty largely following the lines of the Rio Treaty, adapted in language and objectives for the security problems of Europe and North America. This became the basis for the Working Group's final report.

On September 9, 1948, the Ambassadors' Committee met to give its approval to the report and send it off to the seven governments. It was an admirably concise and well-written document of eleven printed pages in the State Department papers that summarized the close examination of the political and security considerations on which the case for a North Atlantic Treaty was now firmly based. The outlines of the form such a treaty might take were included in an annex. After months of uncertainty on the part of the Americans in particular, the Working Group came out unanimously and unequivocally for *"a treaty containing unmistakeable clear provisions binding the parties to come to each other's defense in case of attack,"* and added just as flatly that *"no alternative to a treaty appears to meet the essential requirements"* of North Atlantic security.

A treaty text, of course, was still to be negotiated, and that would be the next and final stage. But at last the die was cast.

A long and useful pause now set in until the American election, while the Berlin airlift thundered on into the graying days and long nights of winter; while Secretary Marshall settled down in Paris for a lengthy session of the United Nations General Assembly; while Field Marshal Montgomery feuded in secret with General de Lattre de Tassigny over how to plan and organize the defense of Western Europe; while West German political leaders got down to work in Bonn on a constitution for a new Federal Republic; while France fought off another wave of Communist strikes – and while Marshall Plan aid began flowing to Europe like a blood transfusion for a weakened heart.

In London, Ernest Bevin now had the great central objective of his foreign policy within grasp – a treaty of alliance joining the United States and Europe. In Washington, great was the relief at the State Department at having come so far and above all at having kept it almost entirely secret. How could the Atlantic Alliance ever have been born if headlines in the spring and summer of 1948 had proclaimed:

EUROPEAN PACT PROPOSED IN SECRET PENTAGON TALKS
BEVIN ASKS SECRET U.S. PLEDGE ON WAR
STATE DEPT. ADVISERS SPLIT ON ATLANTIC PACT
FRANCE DEMANDS ARMS BEFORE PACT
SPAAK TELLS LOVETT EUROPEAN PACT NOT NECESSARY
BRITISH SEEK AMERICAN COMMANDER FOR EUROPE
FRANCE ASKS ALLIES TO DEFEND ALGERIA
LOVETT: "THE FRENCH ARE IN OUR HAIR"

As the Canadian Lester Pearson once remarked about the need and the problem of diplomatic secrecy: "There is nothing more difficult for a democratic government to abandon than a headline."

Fortunately the Vandenberg Resolution had in effect "legitimized" the election-year debate in the United States on American support for Europe. But only the insiders knew how far the secret discussions had already taken America in the direction of a North Atlantic Treaty. Since there had been no big headline leaks, politicians on the campaign trail did not have to take sides on something the Truman administration had not yet even proposed. So they were able to campaign ever more loudly about standing up to the Soviet Union, firmness in Berlin, America shouldering its responsibilities for peace, firmness behind Allies in Europe and all the rest. By the time election day rolled around, public opinion had gotten out ahead of the silent State Department on the question of America's duty to Europe and peace. No longer was it farfetched, unthinkable, impossible to consider entering into an entangling alliance. It was now the next logical step for America to take to meet the Soviet challenge, to consolidate the success that was flowing from the Marshall Plan, to ensure the Berlin airlift, to establish fully America's commitment and role as a world power.

Then on November 2, 1948, came Harry Truman's astounding, lonely election victory.

TEN

Full Speed Ahead

President Harry S Truman set out by train from Independence, Missouri, on Thursday, November 4, for a triumphal return to Washington after one of the most astounding election victories in American political history. The train paused in St. Louis, where Union Station was jammed with jubilant Democrats who laughed and cheered when Truman greeted them from the rear platform of the presidential Pullman car, holding up a copy of the previous day's first edition of the arch-Republican *Chicago Tribune* with the memorable banner headline: DEWEY DEFEATS TRUMAN. The train sped on through the night, and when Truman reached the capital on Friday more than half a million people – two thirds of the entire population of the city at that time – turned out to line the route from Union Station up Pennsylvania Avenue and cheer the buoyant President as he drove home to the White House.

In the Oval Office next day, November 6, as the first major act after election to office in his own right, Truman signed a National Security Council directive formally instructing the State Department to open negotiations for a North Atlantic Treaty.

Harry Truman had no doubt at all that the first goal and focal point of foreign policy for his second term of office was to be a collective-defense alliance with Europe. Through the Marshall Plan, Europe was on its way to achieving freedom from want. But the Berlin blockade was at its height, the Soviet menace was growing, and freedom from fear was far from attained. Truman had his weaknesses and his foibles and he made his mistakes. But he knew his history, and he was clear and sound in his decisions to meet the postwar challenges as America took up its role as a world power. In Dean Acheson's phrase, he was "the captain with the mighty heart."

There was no need for Truman to read up on the records or schedule any briefings to review how things stood in the discussions on an Atlantic pact before deciding what to do, what America's position should now be. He was one of the most thorough and conscientious presidents ever to occupy the White House. From the outset of the Pentagon talks in March, he had followed it all closely through Lovett and Marshall. He had read all the summary reports, and he was fully briefed on the issues and progress. He had also made bipartisanship a priority in his conduct of foreign policy, and it was of course for this reason that Lovett had deliberately imposed caution, hesitation, political prudence and even strong doubts about the wisdom of a treaty during the preliminary talks, often to the frustration of the Europeans. But this had enabled bipartisanship to prevail, so that the question of an alliance with Europe had never become a political issue during the election campaign.

During the preliminary discussions, Truman for his part had rigorously refrained from taking any position or presidential action which would have committed the next President in any way to any particular course of action on such a fundamental historic change in traditional American foreign policy. Talks had been detailed and recommendations had been made but no decision or commitment had been taken. Truman was careful to leave it entirely for the newly elected President to take that great decision and carry it out after the American people had made their choice. Now that he was back in the White House, there was no reason for hesitation or delay any longer. He was clear where America's duty lay, and the clear order came: Full speed ahead. It was the start of another stormy and turbulent four years of history for Harry Truman.

The Canadian government had informed Washington in mid-October that it was ready to negotiate a North Atlantic Treaty. On October 25, foreign ministers of the five Brussels Treaty powers began a two-day meeting in Paris to take the same decision. Presiding over the Paris meeting was Robert Schuman, and this was a marked and welcome change for calm discussions after the prickly, excitable and often caustic and near-hysterical Georges Bidault. The ministers, with Ernest Bevin weightily in the lead, quickly agreed to press ahead as soon as the Americans were ready, and then decided to go one step further. On the proposal of Paul-Henri Spaak of Belgium, who by now had become a firm supporter of an alliance with the United States, they instructed their Permanent Commission of Ambassadors in London to prepare a European draft of a North Atlantic Treaty to be proposed when the talks resumed. Of course this would follow the guidelines of the Working Group report of September 9. But the Europeans were particularly anxious to go into the negotiations with their own united front on the wording of the vital "commitment clause" for mutual assistance in the event of armed attack, which would be at the heart of a treaty to bind America to the defense of Western Europe.

It had long been clear that this probably would be the main sticking point with the State Department and the United States Senate. The Europeans wanted a commitment considerably stronger and more specific than the Americans had yet shown much willingness to consider. So work began at once in London on a first draft of a treaty – undertaken in fact by virtually the same British, French and Benelux diplomats who had drafted the Brussels Treaty of Western Union only nine months earlier. But the European draft was not completed until late November, and accordingly, it was not until December 10 that the "full speed" negotiations resumed.

Meanwhile, important changes in Washington were under way in the wake of the Truman election victory that would affect the conduct of the negotiations. General Marshall returned to the capital in late November after an absence of nearly three months in Paris at the United Nations General Assembly. Almost at once he entered Walter Reed Hospital for a major kidney operation. Marshall was then sixty-eight, and he had delayed the operation for nearly five months because of the Berlin crisis. He had carried on with such soldierly discipline that few were aware how ill he was. But he knew that the operation would involve lengthy recuperation, and he told Truman that he must give up office. In great secrecy, the President asked Dean Acheson to prepare to take over as secretary of state. Lovett meanwhile continued as acting secretary for the next two months. Marshall returned to his office only briefly for a few days before stepping down when Truman was inaugurated for his second term on January 20, 1949.

For two vital years, General Marshall had shaped the strategy and taken the decisions that transformed United States foreign policy into the active exercise of power in a world role. Under Marshall, clarity replaced confusion. But such was the self-effacing character of this great man that achievement was left largely to speak for itself. Marshall never concerned himself about publicity or recognition. He was sparing of press conferences or speechmaking, and in those more refined and civilized times a secretary of state could get on with his business without microphones and television cameras thrust into his face almost every working day of his life. Marshall left a mark of his eminence on history and on the State Department that few secretaries will ever attain.

On Capitol Hill another big change was under way, with control of both houses of Congress back in the hands of the Democrats and Senator Tom Connally of Texas replacing the redoubtable Senator Vandenberg as chairman of the powerful Foreign Relations Committee.

Connally of course was a loyal Democrat who could be counted on to do his duty and back the President fully. But he lacked the stature and intellectual qualities of statesmanship that Vandenberg had cultivated. He had displayed no great depth of interest in the details or the broad historic issues posed by a North Atlantic Treaty. Age had added to his limitations, not his virtues. During the period when Lovett was so assiduously concentrating on briefing and educating Vandenberg to solidify bipartisanship with the Republicans, Connally had more or less been taken for granted. But now that he was elevated to the committee chairmanship in place of Vandenberg, he would play the leading role between the State Department and the Senate in the delicate negotiations over an acceptable treaty text. This was to have its problems, and would require political repair work on the Hill. If there is one thing that a senator always does understand, it is senatorial protocol and his own prerogatives.

The most important postelection change of all in Washington was, very simply, the political atmosphere that now surrounded the project of a North Atlantic Treaty. It had become an accepted public fact that the United States was well on its way to joining some kind of an entangling defense alliance with Europe, and this was generating remarkably little editorial opposition or heated rumblings of isolationist denunciation. In part this was because the right wing of the Republican party, where the only real opposition still lay, was now beginning the descent into what eventually became that black paroxysm of the McCarthy period. Whatever these witch-hunters would eventually do to American political morality, civil rights and human dignity, they could not very well wage a hysterical fight against Communism at home and then oppose at the same time a North Atlantic Treaty whose basic purpose would be to halt Communist aggression far from America's shores.

With the election over, there was no longer any serious doubt that a treaty of alliance with Europe was acceptable to the American people, and that the votes were now there on a broad bipartisan basis for ratification by the Senate. This was a considerable political evolution in the twelve months since Ernest Bevin had first broached the treaty idea with a sympathetic but most skeptical and cautious George Marshall in London in December 1947. Of course public opinion had been constantly propelled by the relentless aggressions of the Soviet Union in Europe, culminating in the blockade of Berlin. But the political evolution had also been nurtured with sound intuition by President Truman, first of all, together with Marshall, Lovett and the essential support of Vandenberg. Often it takes great leadership to *wait* for events instead of charging out in front. What these four men sought, instinctively and collectively, was national consensus – not an act driven by fear, not personal success or political capital out of promoting a treaty of such fundamental far-reaching historic importance to the future of the nation. During 1948, through the heat of the election campaign, Truman, Marshall and Lovett carefully avoided making any public speeches or press conference statements calling on America to form an alliance with Europe. Public opinion was allowed to form around events, not appeals. Senator Vandenberg's declarations were largely exhortations that America forget its isolationism and face up to fulfilling its new responsibilities to the world. It was not Harry Truman's treaty. It was not Arthur Vandenberg's treaty. In this great period of American leadership, these men knew that their role had to be simply to wait and encourage a political current to gather swiftness and watch for the winds to change. America was not driven into the North

Atlantic Treaty by fear, or cajoled into it by politics. It joined by national consensus under exceptional men.

The consensus was there, the Senate votes were there. But what kind of a treaty – how strong a treaty? There were still many crucial questions when the negotiations resumed on December 10.

When the ambassadors of the seven nations gathered at the State Department to get down to serious negotiations, "the most striking feature was the changed attitude of Robert Lovett," according to the notetaker and historian of the Foreign Office for these events, Nicholas Henderson. Hesitation and caution were suddenly swept away as Lovett welcomed the ambassadors with a statement that the United States now wished to make rapid progress to take full advantage of the big election change in Congress, and he would like to see a treaty concluded by February. This indeed was breathtaking speed after the diplomatic plodding of the summer. Lovett then sprang another surprise.

In advance of the meeting, when the British had informed the State Department that the Brussels Treaty powers would have their draft of a North Atlantic Treaty to present, both Jack Hickerson and Ted Achilles strongly advised against such a move. They told the British minister, Sir Derek Hoyer-Millar, that in their opinion it would be unwise for the Europeans to offer a treaty draft that might look like "ganging up" on the Americans with a take-it-or-leave-it proposal. This was the last thing the Europeans had in mind or would risk doing, so they quickly consulted and agreed to keep their treaty draft in their briefcases. Hickerson and Achilles had offered their advice in good faith, in line with the cautious approach that Lovett had consistently imposed on the negotiations in the past.

But in the meantime, President Truman let his acting secretary know that he now wanted to make an announcement of the North Atlantic Treaty in his inaugural address on January 20 – little more than a month away. The president had dropped caution and shifted to Admiral Farragut's famous order: "Damn the torpedoes." The European ambassadors were taken completely by surprise when Lovett now told the meeting that he understood they had prepared a draft text, and the quickest way to get down to work would be if they would distribute it as a basis for discussion.

"The Ambassadors first flayed the ground wildly like characters in a Mickey Mouse film who have been chasing something and are suddenly called upon to change direction," Nicholas Henderson recorded. But the last thing that Robert Lovett could be accused of would be impetuousness or irresponsibility. He always knew what he was doing. So at the end of that first meeting the Europeans agreed to submit their handiwork not as a "draft treaty" but as a "summary of suggestions" for a treaty. They were still anxious to be able to disavow any accusations or connotation that they were handing the Americans something on a take-it-or-leave-it basis.

When the ambassadors next met on December 13, it quickly became clear that this was not the forum in which to make rapid negotiating progress. The discussion went round and round, circling the problems in generalities instead of getting down to practicalities. In particular, the tedious interventions of the Frenchman, Henri Bonnet, were again having an irritating effect on Lovett, which Bonnet was quite incapable of detecting. So the cool and incisive Sir Oliver Franks finally stepped in to suggest that the ambassadors had perhaps talked enough about the treaty and should consign the drafting work immediately to the lower-level experts of the Working Group to get on with the job. With some relief, this was at once agreed.

Now at last it really was "full speed ahead." Along with the "suggestions" for a treaty draft from the Europeans came a flow of similar proposals from Hickerson, Achilles and George Kennan, with crucial input also from the Canadians. A treaty text began to fall into place rapidly. In the remarkable time of a mere ten days, the Working Group handed the Ambassadors' Committee an agreed first draft of ten articles for a North Atlantic Treaty on December 24, in time for Christmas.

It was, to be sure, a rough draft and an incomplete draft, but it was a text that governments could now seriously consider and discuss, and this was a major breakthrough. The Working Group was not supposed to solve every problem – simply to push things forward as rapidly as possible to focus the final issues for decisions that governments would have to take.

Accordingly, their ten-article draft did not include any preamble. They decided to leave this to the last for the political leaders to shape and determine – in Jack Hickerson's phrase, "No applesauce until we've finished with the meat and potatoes." They also set aside three very contentious political issues of the treaty. The first was a definition of the geographical area the treaty would cover. This was bedeviled by a French demand that the treaty cover all of the then-French North African possessions – Algeria, Tunisia and Morocco – as well as France itself. This brought a Belgian response: "Well, in that case what about the Belgian Congo?" so the Working Group quickly decided not to waste time trying to resolve that one. Geography and membership of the treaty of course went hand in hand. Here the argument centered largely on whether Italy should be invited to join, with the French strongly backing the Italians (after earlier having opposed them) but the British and the Americans generally reluctant to see Italy included. So the membership question was set aside. Finally, there was the question of the duration of the treaty. Here again the French were taking a "maximum position" and demanding a fifty-year treaty, while the Americans were wondering if they could get a ten-year treaty through the Senate.

Nevertheless, the first draft of ten articles was done. (The final version of the North Atlantic Treaty contains fourteen articles.) By far the most important breakthrough in that ten days of labor was the drafting of an agreed text for the vital Article Five – the "commitment clause" at the heart of the treaty, on which all else turned.

Article Five of the North Atlantic Treaty in its key paragraph contains exactly ninety-nine words. It is safe to say that not since the ratification of the Constitution of the United States have so many men spent so much time drafting and debating so few words. This of course is as it should have been, for Article Five involved the most far-reaching Senate decision on United States foreign policy since the founding of the Republic.

Discussions about a "commitment clause" began in the Pentagon talks in March of 1948, and went on more or less continuously either in secret negotiations, political talks or open debate until final Senate ratification of the treaty in July of 1949. Of course the wording of Article Five was a matter of high concern not only to the American government, its diplomats and legislature, but to the governments and diplomats and legislatures of all the other original eleven signatory powers as well. Countless people were involved in devising Article Five, if only to "read and comment."

At the outset in the super-secret Pentagon talks, the very first memorandum of understanding by the British, Canadians and Americans specified that the security commitment in any North Atlantic arrangement "should follow the lines of the Rio Treaty." Six months later in the final report of the seven-power Working Group and the Ambassadors' Committee on September 9, it was again reiterated that "approval of any treaty by the United States Senate would be greatly facilitated if the Rio text were adhered to as closely as possible." In short, there had not been much shift in the American position after six months of preliminary discussions about a North Atlantic Treaty. However, the Americans were certainly fully aware of the European view that the wording of the Rio Treaty fell considerably short of what was needed, wanted and expected in any Atlantic pact.

Nevertheless, when the final stage of the negotiations began in the Working Group in December, things had scarcely moved from two basic models on the table:

> The Rio Treaty model: An armed attack by any state against a Party shall be considered as an attack against all the Parties, and, consequently, each Party undertakes to assist in meeting the attack in the exercise of the inherent right of individual or collective self-defense recognized by Article 51 of the Charter.
>
> The Brussels Treaty model: If any Party should be the object of an armed attack in the area covered by the Treaty, the other Parties will, in accordance with the provision of Article 51 of the Charter, afford the Party so attacked all the military and other aid and assistance in their power.

It is scarcely necessary to go to a dictionary to appreciate the considerable difference between the Rio pact undertaking to "assist in meeting the attack," without even using the word "military," and the Brussels Treaty pledge to "afford the party so attacked all the military and other aid and assistance in their power." But how far could the United States go – how far would the United States Senate be willing to go – in the wording of a commitment to go to war as the price of collective defense?

If the Rio Treaty did not go far enough, the Brussels Treaty pledge raised a rather different problem, which was cited at the outset in the Pentagon talks by Major General Alfred M. Gruenther, later a NATO Supreme Allied Commander. Speaking on behalf of the American Joint Chiefs of Staff, Gruenther told the Pentagon group early on that "it was necessary to be entirely clear that no commitment to aid a state, victim of attack, should require that the aid should be delivered locally – we should retain freedom to carry out action against the aggressor in accordance with strategic concepts." In other words, the correct strategic response to an attack might not be at all where the attack occurred. Gruenther did not think that the Brussels Treaty wording was satisfactory on this point.

When the Working Group turned to the problem of Article Five, the Europeans heard with great relief an announcement by George Kennan of an important change in the American position. The State Department now accepted, Kennan said, that the pledge in a North Atlantic Treaty had to be more specific than the wording of the Rio pact. At the same time, however, Kennan said that it would be a mistake to specify in the treaty that all countries should be expected to give military aid in the event of an attack. Iceland, for example, has no military forces, but offered a very valuable base. Kennan also echoed General Gruenther's earlier strictures about the language of the Brussels pact, and said that they should avoid any treaty wording that might seem to limit their action merely to "meeting the attack" and should find a broader and more inclusive form of words.

Kennan therefore proposed that the heart of the collective commitment should read: "Take such action as may be necessary to restore and maintain the security of the North Atlantic area." This language would leave it open to the Atlantic Allies to respond to any attack by any means they chose, anywhere they chose, to maintain their security. This opened the way to quick agreement. The Europeans pressed, and Kennan agreed, that the pledge should be strengthened to read "military or other action." They did not like the phrase "as may be necessary," arguing that this might simply open the way for needless debate at a moment of crisis, and might be seen as a way out of taking any action at all. Kennan countered that it was important that the treaty be written to give governments clear flexibility in deciding how to respond to a situation and to be able to differentiate between minor incidents and all-out war. However, to strengthen this point it was agreed to add the word "forthwith" to the pledge of individual and collective action.

So the Working Group draft of Article Five fell rapidly into place:

> The Parties agree that an armed attack against one or more of them shall be considered an attack against them all; and consequently that, if such an armed attack occurs, each of them, in exercise of the right of individual or collective self-defense recognized by Article 51 of the Charter of the United Nations, will assist the Party or Parties so attacked by taking forthwith such military or other action, individually and in concert with the other Parties, as may be necessary to restore and assure the security of the North Atlantic area.

The most important article of the North Atlantic Treaty was in place – but Kennan warned the Working Group that there had been no prior consultations on this with anyone in the Senate. In fact, few senators were even in Washington that postelection Christmas, and there was again a hiatus after the Working Group draft went off to governments. Lovett held only one more meeting with the ambassadors in mid-January, at which each reported the formal acceptance by his government of the Working Group draft, subject to final negotiations. After that, Lovett prepared for his departure from the State Department with General Marshall.

President Truman then told the nation in his inaugural address on January 20:

> If we can make it sufficiently clear, in advance, that any armed attack affecting our national security would be met with overwhelming force, the armed attack might never occur. I hope soon to send to the Senate a Treaty respecting the North Atlantic Security plan. In addition, we will provide military advice and equipment to free nations which will cooperate with us in the maintenance of peace and security.

Truman's words certainly heartened the Europeans as an endorsement of a treaty commitment that would provide clearly and unequivocally for the use of military force in the new defense alliance.

Dean Acheson had been through an overly long and less than sympathetic Senate committee hearing to determine whether he was fit to be secretary of state – a sign of the harassing troubles he would be facing for the next four years. He had survived perfectly well, but not without leaving the marks of his barbed wit and intellectual superiority here and there. It was not until February 3 that he could turn to the major business at hand at the State Department.

Taking with him Chip Bohlen, still the counselor of the department, Acheson went to the Hill to confer for the first time with Senators Connally and Vandenberg, and discuss for the first time the ten-article draft of the North Atlantic Treaty. Acheson had barely had time to skim through the background of a whole year of diplomatic and political negotiations surrounding the treaty. He did not have much political feel for the situation, and neither the suavity nor the careful personality of Lovett in dealing with senators. Bohlen, who accompanied him, had always been skeptical of how much the U.S. Senate would swallow in the way of a treaty commitment. Connally was anxious to put his mark on things now that he was elevated to the committee chairmanship. Vandenberg was clearly in a mood of sour postelection disappointment. After the hostility of the confirmation hearings, Acheson was anxious to try to get off to a good working start with the two high priests of the Foreign Relations Committee. But the political and diplomatic chemistry for a successful first meeting were simply not there, and the result was close to disastrous for the treaty.

At once the two senators pounced on Article Five, taking strong objection to its carefully constructed wording, with the added pique that they had not been consulted in advance, whatever the practical reasons of their availability might have been.

They demanded the deletion of the words "military and other" before the word "action," since "military" did not appear in the Rio Treaty. They wanted the word "forthwith" taken out, because it read to them like an attempt to stampede the United States Senate. They wanted to remove the clause "as may be necessary" and they wanted to insert a clause about "constitutional process," to make clear the right of Congress to declare war. All of this would have reduced or emasculated the text to nothing more than a pledge "to assist the Party or Parties so attacked by taking action, in accordance with due constitutional process, to restore and assure the security of the North Atlantic area." Gone would have been any sense of immediacy in response to an aggression. Such a pledge would have been as weak as, if not even weaker and fuzzier than, the wording of the Rio Treaty.

It was not until five days later, on February 8, that Acheson met for the first time with the Ambassadors' Committee to inform the other six governments of his consultations on the Hill. Things went from bad to worse. Acheson made an arrogant and sour first impression and left the ambassadors in a state of indignant shock. Escott Reid of the Canadian External Affairs Ministry recorded of that first meeting: "He was the new boy at the negotiating table, this was his first appearance with the Ambassadors, it was only ten days since he had been able to look at any of the papers on the discussions that had been going on for eleven months – yet he spoke to the Ambassadors not as a neophyte but as a teacher lecturing not very intelligent students." Reid goes to to add with almost sputtering indignation:

> Acheson may, of course, have decided that the more arrogant the language that he used in presenting to the Ambassadors the demands of the Senators for watering down the pledge, the more likely he was to break down the opposition of the Ambassadors and their governments.

If that was Acheson's tactic or intention, it certainly did not work. The ambassadors were there under instructions from their governments to get a sound and solid treaty.

Yet here was the secretary of state supporting the demands of the senators across the board instead of supporting the treaty draft they had been working on for eleven months, which had been endorsed by Lovett, the State Department and the other six governments.

Acheson now told them that their draft "perhaps overstated the problem," particularly because it seemed to imply that "the United States would be rushed into some kind of automatic commitment." He sought to minimize the importance of including the word "military" in the pledge of mutual assistance, contending that this would be "an unnecessary embellishment" because the word "action" by itself would still cover any kind of action – military, diplomatic or otherwise. In particular he riled the ambassadors by suggesting that they had been too hasty in their work – after eleven months.

This brought a sputtering retort from Henri Bonnet that the draft "had been unanimously approved after much thought and protracted negotiations and talks," with Baron Silvercruys of Belgium adding: "I do not think we have been precipitous or that there has been an absence of thoroughness in dealing with the problem." Sir Oliver Franks simply said with finality that to water down the agreed text now would be "disastrous."

So ended Acheson's first encounter as secretary of state with his principal Allies, and he retired to try to figure out what to do next to stave off a virtual collapse of a major foreign-policy initiative on which the President had now publicly staked his authority.

The following week the crisis worsened. There had been an increasing amount of press leakage about the treaty – not surprising with so many men now involved and the general political atmosphere about what was going on now much more relaxed and positive. Some of the leakage had been quite deliberate on the part of the State Department through Ted Achilles with the specific aim of gradually educating public opinion as to what was afoot.

But inevitably there were also distorted interpretations of what all this amounted to. On February 12, such a distortion appeared in the *Kansas City Times*, which quoted Acheson as telling Norwegian Foreign Minister Halvard Lange, then in Washington for consultations on the treaty, that "it would be interpreted as a moral commitment to fight" even though only Congress could declare war. This stirred up the Missouri isolationist die-hard, Senator Forrest C. Donnell, who had fought against even joining the United Nations. He took the Senate floor on February 14 to express his fears and doubts about the meaning of reported pledges in an Atlantic pact and the sacred right of the Congress to declare war. If Donnell had been left alone with his doubts, which were permanent anyway, all would have been well. But Senator Connally could not resist the opportunity to intervene in his new role as chairman of the Foreign Relations Committee. Always florid in language, Connally was in his best *opéra bouffe* form when he rose to reassure Senator Donnell:

I do not believe in giving carte blanche assurances – telling them do everything you want to do, you need not worry, as soon as anything happens we will come over and fight your quarrel for you. We should not blindfold ourselves and make a commitment now to enter every war that may occur in the next ten years, and send our boys and resources to Europe to fight. We cannot be Sir Galahads, and every time we hear a gun fired plunge into war and take sides without knowing what we are doing and without knowing the issues involved.

This was the simplistic claptrap of prewar isolationism of the 1930s, and showed how little Senator Connally really knew about the purpose of the North Atlantic Treaty. Vandenberg rose manfully to try to correct the damage, declaring that an Atlantic Treaty was necessary to prevent a third world war, and pledging that nothing would be signed or ratified that went beyond the resolution he had sponsored and the Senate had approved, and there would be "nothing which is not written within the four corners of the United Nations Charter."

Later that same day, following this eruption on the Senate floor, Acheson and Bohlen met again with Connally and Vandenberg, and again things worsened. Both the senators were now demanding that Article Five had to make clear that there was no obligation on the United States, "moral or otherwise," to go to war. Connally asked for a further weakening of the pledge that "an armed attack against one or more of them shall be considered an attack against them all." He wanted this simply to read "an attack on one would be regarded as a threat to the peace of all." By now it began to look as if the whole treaty was likely to come unraveled in the final stage of negotiations.

Alarm bells were ringing in Europe. Ernest Bevin circulated a memorandum to the entire British Cabinet which began: "My colleagues will have read in the press of the deplorable debate which took place in the American Senate on 14 February." After reviewing several gloomy reports from Sir Oliver Franks, Bevin ended by counseling: "Mr. Acheson is no doubt doing his best to wrestle with the Senators and we shall know the results of his efforts in a few days time when the Ambassadors' Committee reassembles."

In Paris, Robert Schuman told the Canadian ambassador that the language being proposed by Connally "was meaningless and unacceptable and as for himself he would not sign any treaty which was not *sérieux et complet.*" Schuman went on to say that it was "the worst possible thing that could happen" to have the American senators bandying the still-secret North Atlantic Treaty about in public.

Mr. Acheson was doing his best, for he was now fully aware that he had a major political-diplomatic crisis on his hands. The President wanted a strong treaty. The Europeans looked on what was happening as an emasculation, not just cosmetic changes. Acheson decided to take the problem to Harry Truman. But first he held a crucial meeting with Sir Oliver Franks.

In advance of Acheson's meeting with Franks, on February 16 Bohlen presided over a crisis session at the State Department to review the tangle and make recommendations to the secretary. Present were Hickerson and Dean Rusk (later secretary of state under Presidents Kennedy and Johnson). They drafted four different versions of Article Five, one of which left out the word "military" entirely and was recommended as the "minimum acceptable." Meanwhile Senator Vandenberg had reentered the discussions with a proposal for new language to alter the phrase "as may be necessary," instead of eliminating it as the senators had earlier demanded. He suggested that it should read "as it deems necessary," which carried the implication of specific consideration of particular action instead of any automatic commitment.

By now the feverish consideration of the possible and proper wording of Article Five was beginning to resemble an exercise in Talmudic scholarship. In this atmosphere, Acheson met with Sir Oliver Franks alone, away from the State Department, for a completely personal and private talk. No record was published by the State Department, but the general outlines of the talk are known from the British side.

They first took up the Vandenberg rewording of the "necessity" phrase, and Franks said he would have no great objection to the change provided that it was made clear that the wording "as it deems necessary" in the treaty would in no way preclude advance military planning or staff talks among the parties to the pact. When they then turned to the more fundamental question of dropping the word "military" from the action phrase, Franks said he would be completely opposed to any such change in the agreed draft.

The British ambassador acknowledged that it could be argued that the word "action" would certainly imply and presumably include military action, but that was no longer the point, he said. It was now common knowledge on both sides of the Atlantic that discussions were virtually completed on a treaty that would provide for American military backing for Europe. The treaty should make plain beyond any misunderstanding what would happen if trouble occurred. It would be "most unfortunate" if there was any retreat from this now. It was precisely the sober mention in a treaty undertaking of possible military action that would contribute to the political, moral and economic recovery of Western Europe. They also had to consider the effect it would produce in the Soviet Union if there were now to be a retreat and the commitment to use of military force were dropped from the treaty.

Sobered and stiffened by this conversation with the clear-thinking and intellectually elegant Englishman, Acheson went to see President Truman in the Oval Office on February 17. Together they went over the four alternative drafts that had been prepared by Bohlen and the State Department team, and Acheson recounted fully the position of the British, America's strongest ally in Europe and the principal protagonist of a North Atlantic Treaty.

At the end, Truman not only took a firm decision. He worked out with Acheson yet another form of words to carry it out. He told Acheson that in his judgment it was absolutely essential to include a commitment to military action in the treaty. No doubt he had his own inaugural address in mind. He assured Acheson that he would not give up "without a stout fight" in the Senate. But instead of the simple, stark word "military," they devised the alternative wording "including the use of armed forces," which would be separated by commas from the words "such action." By this change of punctuation and semantics, the new phrasing would enable senatorial minds to conclude that there was no automatic commitment to the use of force that would usurp senatorial or constitutional practice.

With this decision taken, Truman told Acheson he would telephone Senator Connally personally and have him come to the Blair House that evening. (Truman was then living in the Blair House while the White House was undergoing a complete interior reconstruction.) He said he would tell Connally that Acheson would present the new wording with the full backing and authority of the President.

Truman's intervention was kept entirely secret. Acheson's short official memorandum on the meeting came to light only when the State Department papers were published twenty-five years later in 1974. It was marked "Top Secret – Very Limited Distribution." There is no record of the President's subsequent talk with Connally. Whatever he did say to the windy senator, however he chose to say it, Truman kept it all private so that Connally would not have to be seen bending or bowing to some presidential rebuke or arm-twisting. Truman was well aware of Senate sensibilities. But the result of this prudent intervention by the President is clear. Harry Truman's leadership preserved a viable North Atlantic Treaty.

Armed with presidential authority, Acheson went back to the Senate. Connally had calmed down, and Vandenberg, who had a far better understanding of what was at stake, was ready to throw his considerable weight back on the scales. By the end of the month, the key phrasing of Article Five had been successfully honed and polished into new final form:

> The Parties agree that an armed attack against one or more of them in Europe or North America shall be considered an attack against them all; and consequently they agree that if such an armed attack occurs, each of them ... will assist the Party or Parties so attacked by taking forthwith, individually and in concert with other Parties, such action as it deems necessary, including the use of armed force, to restore and maintain international peace and security.

Forty years later, this pledge is still valid, and the historic proof of its effectiveness is simply the fact that it has never been put to the ultimate test.

While the struggle over Article Five was being played out in Washington, the long Scandinavian diplomatic dance over Sweden's efforts to line up a Nordic neutral alliance finally petered out. The Swedish contention that "collective neutrality" would offer Scandinavia greater security than collective defense was not a proposition that Norweigian Foreign Minister Halvard Lange was prepared to swallow. But he was a prudent politician and a skilled and intelligent diplomat. It was Lange's leadership and political education of the Norwegian Labor party that brought this rather isolated and sprawling little country of barely three million people (at the time) to set aside its traditional Nordic outlook in favor of joining the Atlantic Alliance.

From the time the Swedes initiated their efforts in May 1948 to bring Norway and Denmark into a neutral alliance, Lange had kept in close but very discreet contact with both the British and American governments. He had forecast at the outset to the American ambassador in Oslo that the Swedish effort would fail because Norway would never give up its freedom of action by submerging in some neutrality pledge. Lange had also said that when Sweden's effort did fail, Norway would be ready to consider an Atlantic alternative. Both Britain and the United States always regarded Norway's membership in any Atlantic Alliance to be essential for strategic as well as political-diplomatic reasons, but they had left it to Lange to play his own hand and take his time.

However, in the first days of January after the Working Group had completed the first draft of a treaty, the State Department under Lovett decided that the time had come to make the first diplomatic moves to bring other states into the alliance along with the original seven. Every capital in Europe was aware that a North Atlantic Treaty was being negotiated, and some were more interested than others.

The initial approaches were made to the Washington embassies of Norway, Denmark, Portugal and Eire. The ambassadors were asked orally and informally by the State Department to sound out their governments as to their willingness to consider participating as original signatories of a North Atlantic Treaty. There was no approach to Sweden. The able American ambassador to Stockholm, H. Freeman "Doc" Matthews, a career diplomat, had cabled Washington:

> I consider it extremely important from a tactical point of view that no invitation to the Swedes to join the North Atlantic Pact be made at this time. I see many signs of effectiveness of our tactics of showing indifference to Swedish policy, all of which could be undone if we made any approach at this time. Let the Norwegians or the Danes tell the Swedes about the North Atlantic Pact if and when the time seems proper.

The Swedes of course were quickly apprised of the American approach by their neighbors, and they responded by immediately calling one last round of meetings to press again for a Nordic neutral alliance. Scandinavian foreign ministers met first in Karlstad, Sweden, on January 5. They followed this with meetings in Copenhagen and then at Oslo at the end of the month. The Danes were far more susceptible to the Swedish blandishments and arguments than the Norwegians under Lange. Finally, at the Oslo meeting Lange brought it all to an end with a firm "No" to neutrality. He then headed almost at once for Washington for crucial discussions with Acheson about the terms and conditions for entering the Atlantic pact.

With the breakdown of the Nordic negotiations, the Soviet Union unleashed a furious propaganda attack against Norway, referring ominously to their common northern border and fiercely warning about "a North Atlantic union with an openly aggressive political course, the ultimate aim of which is forcible establishment of Anglo-American world domination and unleashing a new war." In a formal note that followed, the Soviet Union proposed instead that the two countries sign a non-aggression pact.

Before Lange left for Washington, he sent a studiously calm but firm reply to Moscow, pointing out that both countries had already signed a pledge of nonaggression when they joined the United Nations. But, the note continued, the UN had not succeeded in becoming strong enough to maintain peace and security. Norway now proposed to find out more about the North Atlantic pact, but it would never permit Norwegian territory to be used for aggression, nor would it permit any foreign bases on Norwegian territory in peacetime. This simply produced another violent rebuke from Moscow, and was the beginning of an unending record of such exchanges that continued between the two capitals for most of the next four decades.

When Lange saw Acheson on February 7, he laid great stress on Norway's need for prompt military assistance from the United States as a reassurance against this growing barrage of Soviet threats and domestic Communist agitation as the government neared its final decision to join the Atlantic pact. The best Acheson could offer at this point was sympathy. He told Lange that no arms program for Europe would even be considered in Washington until after the treaty was in place. He said no pressure would be put on Norway in its decision, but he did then go public by stating the simple fact that future demands for American military help would exceed supplies, and in general there obviously would have to be priorities "where the U.S. has commitments or interests." In other words, the chances of military help were much better inside the treaty than outside.

Finally, on February 24, word came from Oslo that Lange had cleared the last hurdles with the Cabinet and the Storting. Moreover, Norway wanted to enter the Washington talks as quickly as possible and take part in the final stages of the treaty negotiations in order to confront the Soviet Union with a fait accompli, without waiting until the treaty was ready for signature. Lange was a skilled diplomat and a strong man.

Meanwhile, in contrast to this robust Norwegian stance, Denmark was dithering about what to do. Iceland responded to Washington with cautious readiness to join. Portugal asked whether Spain would also be invited to join. The Irish government, as had been expected, replied that an end to the partition of Ireland would be a precondition for Irish membership in any North Atlantic Treaty, and that was the end of that.

This left the contentious problem of Italy. A strong faction in the State Department led by Hickerson favored Italian membership, but there was Senate opposition to extending a North Atlantic Alliance into the Mediterranean. Moreover, Acheson foresaw difficulties with Greece and Turkey if Italy was asked to join. The British were also opposed to Italian membership for reasons similar to the American objections, along with the fact that Italy was an ex-enemy state and the problem of Trieste might be dragged in to add confusion to the purposes of the new alliance. France had originally opposed including Italy, largely because it meant "spreading the butter too thin," but then changed its mind for both strategic and political reasons and had become Italy's most vociferous supporter.

For all these conflicting reasons, Italy had not been included in the initial State Department approach to other potential members, but on January 12 the Italian government – to the irritation of the department – forced the issue by formally declaring its desire to join the Atlantic pact. Acheson, with much else on his platter, continued to delay any decision. On March 1, the seven-member Ambassadors' Committee met to review the treaty's progression, and Acheson opened by asking for agreement to an immediate invitation to Norway to join the talks, as desired by Lange. The irritating and irrepressible Henri Bonnet leaped in at once to declare that France would be unable to agree to an invitation to Norway unless Italy was also asked to join. He had thrown fat into a fire.

One after another, the other ambassadors proceeded to rebuke Bonnet for attempting to link two entirely separate questions, and his constant habit of stating "conditions" for agreement – when everyone knew perfectly well that the French were practically on their knees praying for a treaty to sign. Sir Oliver Franks turned on Bonnet coldly and told him "it would be greatly appreciated if the French position could be put, not in the language of conditions, but in the language of views strongly held by the French Government."

> Although it might be a defect of national temperament on his part [Franks continued], it made it more difficult to reach an agreed solution if, using the natural metaphor, a pistol was put at his head. His natural instinct was to react against it and he did not wish to be put in that position.

To which Bonnet unabashedly replied that "his natural reaction was the same when he was engaged in a negotiation and had the impression of talking to a wall." Bonnet then went on to say that he was not making conditions, but "merely asked that thought be given to the consequences which could result if the French position were rejected."

Acheson was in something of a cold fury with the Frenchman – the more so because he had come to the meeting prepared to tell Bonnet that he was working with the Senate to meet France's insistence that the guarantees of the Atlantic pact would also cover the Algerian "department" of France. After everybody at the table had told Bonnet what they thought of his diplomatic tactics, Acheson turned to the Algerian question. This mollified Bonnet sufficiently to agree to an immediate invitation to Norway, and Acheson gave assurances that the question of Italy "would be taken at an early occasion." But Bonnet went right on posing "conditions" and haggling with everyone right up to the time the treaty was ready to be signed.

Next day Acheson took the Italian question to President Truman, going over Senate objections and reporting that it now boiled down to either accepting or rejecting a European desire to have Italy in. Truman in the end said he would prefer a pact without Italy, but under the circumstances he instructed that Italy be admitted.

On March 4 the Ambassadors' Committee was enlarged to include Wilhelm Morgenstierne of Norway – described by Acheson as "a solemn man, wholly lacking in humor with an expression of having been weaned on Ibsen." What Morgenstierne lacked in humor he made up for in solid ability and a firm belief in the course that Norway was taking. He joined the talks almost exactly one year after that morning in Oslo in March 1948 when Lange called in the American and British ambassadors to tell them that Norway was coming under pressure from the Soviet Union and would fight if her territory was invaded – and what help could she then expect from the great powers outside? It was entirely fitting that Norway should now be present at the conclusion.

The end was very near. The original seven had decided early on that they would complete the treaty draft among themselves before formally inviting other governments to become original signatories. Norway's admission while the negotiations were still going on was the only exception. Italy smoothed her final passage to signing by giving assurances that she would not involve her new treaty allies in the Trieste question or other problems left over from World War II such as the former Italian colonies. The Portuguese came on board after Generalissimo Francisco Franco assured his fellow dictator, Antonio Salazar, that Spain had no objection to Portugal's joining an Atlantic Alliance. This was regarded as essential by the United States because of mid-Atlantic basing facilities in the Azores. Iceland had to overcome some brief problems with the local Communist party before asking to sign. Denmark finally swallowed hard and decided that it could not afford to shiver alone in neutrality. Danish adherence was strategically vital not only because of control of the Baltic Straits but also because of American base facilities in what was then Danish Greenland.

The geography of the treaty area to be covered by the vital pledge in Article Five was of course largely determined by the geography of the twelve original member states. But this did not include West Germany. Article Six of the treaty was therefore added with the specific declaration that "an armed attack on one or more of the Parties is deemed to include an armed attack on the occupation forces of any Party in Europe." This same article also extended the treaty guarantees to "the Algerian Departments of France," but the French had to forget about any guarantees for Morocco or Tunisia. The provision lapsed when Algeria became independent in 1962.

To put senatorial sensibilities completely at rest, Article Eleven specified that "the Treaty shall be ratified and its provisions carried out by the Parties in accordance with their respective constitutional processes."

As for the northern boundary of the treaty, Dean Acheson told a Senate committee hearing almost off the cuff that "it extended all the way to the North Pole" – well beyond the Norwegian-controlled island of Spitsbergen and beyond the Northwest Territories of Canada. As for the southern boundary, it was Ted Achilles who came up with the idea of fixing the North Atlantic Treaty area on the Tropic of Cancer, which conveniently runs between Florida and Cuba and thereby offered a clear delineation for the United States between the NATO Treaty and the Rio Treaty. However, this did cause a momentary alliance problem during the Cuban missile crisis in 1963 when naval forces earmarked for NATO were moved south of the Tropic of Cancer to prepare a blockade of Cuba.

It was primarily at Canadian insistence that Article Two was written into the treaty pledging "development of peaceful and friendly international relations" and elimination of "conflict in international economic policies." The Canadians did not get the strong language they would have liked, largely because the Europeans felt economics was already well taken care of by the Marshall Plan and the Organization for European Economic Cooperation, as it was then called.

The North Atlantic Treaty is totally vague about what has become the North Atlantic Treaty Organization of today. Article Nine simply states that "the Parties hereby establish a Council on which each of them shall be represented to consider matters concerning the implementation of this Treaty." It merely adds that this council "shall be so organized as to be able to meet promptly at any time," and that it shall set up subsidiary bodies as may be necessary – "in particular a defense committee which shall recommend measures for implementation of Article Five." There is no mention at all of a civilian organization, a secretariat, a unified military command, a military headquarters or a Supreme Allied Commander. Nevertheless, Article Nine was an acorn from which a very considerable oak tree has since grown.

It was the Canadians who suggested as a counter to the extravagant French demand for a fifty-year treaty that after the treaty had been in force for ten years it should be reviewed at the request of any party, and after twenty years any party might withdraw on one year's notice. General Charles de Gaulle was the only "party" who has ever shown any signs of exercising this option.

On March 15, the Ambassadors' Committee met to put the seal of approval on the treaty draft, after one last semantical debate lead by Henri Bonnet over whether in Article Five it would be preferable to use the words "armed aggression" instead of the agreed wording "armed attack against one or more of the Parties." At last it was done, and it was agreed to make the text public in a flurry of press conferences and speechmaking in every capital on March 18. The signing ceremony was fixed to take place in Washington on April 4, 1949.

One week after the NATO Treaty was unveiled, the State Department received from Moscow the first direct word from Stalin that he was ready to discuss calling off the Berlin blockade.

ELEVEN

1949–1950: Alliance Born

The signing of the North Atlantic Treaty in the Inter-Departmental Auditorium on Constitution Avenue in Washington on April 4, 1949, was a simple low-key businesslike affair, dignified and purposeful but scarcely dramatic or memorable. There were short speeches from each of the twelve foreign ministers, and special applause for Ernest Bevin when he lumbered up to the podium. President Truman delivered a brisk address declaring the hope that the treaty "would create a shield against aggression and fear of aggression – a bulwark which will permit us to get on with the real business of government and society, the business of achieving a fuller and happier life for all of our citizens." It was a hope that has been continuously fulfilled. But to the wry amusement of Dean Acheson, the United States Marine Band launched into an insouciant medley from the opera *Porgy and Bess* that included "I Got Plenty of Nothin'" and "It Ain't Necessarily So," along with "Bess, You Is My Woman Now," presumably for Mrs. Truman, who was sitting in the front row.

All in all the ceremony was appropriate to the launching of a ship that now had to be towed away to a fitting-out yard to sit while builders and welders got to work to get it ready to put out to sea. It would be another two years before the superstructure of the North Atlantic Treaty Organization was finally in place on top of the North Atlantic Treaty. In the words of General André Beaufre, one of the foremost French military thinkers and writers of that period:

Such as it is, the treaty does no more than express very broad and – it must be admitted – very vague principles of cooperation. The architecture of the Alliance, then, will have to be filled in gradually – in the application of the treaty and in its practice rather than its theory.

But immediately the Europeans found themselves up against the same problem that had attended the negotiation of the treaty itself – a reluctance on the part of the United States to commit itself, no longer about whether to have a treaty at all, but now on the question of implementation of the treaty. The next step, of course, would be military aid for Europe, but nothing could be put up to Congress until ratification of the treaty was completed, which meant a hiatus in building that "shield against aggression" of at least six months. In Norway and Denmark, Belgium and Holland, Britain and above all in France a new sense of frustration was soon rising from governments that felt they had taken a decisive step in signing the North Atlantic Treaty and now had little or nothing to show for it in the way of concrete help and practical steps from America to build up a meaningful common defense against the Red Army.

The Berlin blockade had ended in May, a month after the treaty was signed, and in Washington this produced a definite atmosphere of a crisis past and a risk of war receding. The blockade was followed by a long and totally useless Big Four foreign ministers meeting in Paris, but superficially, at least, it appeared that confrontation had been replaced by conference. The end of the blockade had been a definite success for a policy of limited containment on the part of the United States and its Western Allies. During the blockade there had been no increase in the actual combat strength of U.S. forces in Germany. The B-29 bombers had been sent to Britain, and U.S. Air Force personnel had poured into Germany to operate the Berlin airlift. But the United States deliberately avoided any buildup of its ground forces in West Germany that might have looked like a direct military challenge to the Soviet Union. While the airlift did its job, the size and deployment of occupation forces in West Germany remained virtually unchanged – and this limited response to the Soviet threat had worked: The blockade was called off.

But with the blockade ended, the military facts remained the same, and they belied any relaxation of the threat posed to the new Atlantic Alliance.

At that time it was estimated that the Red Army had about thirty-five divisions in East Germany and Eastern Europe, close to a potential attack line against the West. The military deployment in Western Europe was all but pitiful. United States forces totaled approximately 140,000 soldiers and airmen. Supposedly this meant at least three combat divisions. But in fact these troops were so widely scattered across southern Germany, bivouacked to perform police and occupation duties and keep alert for some revival of Nazism, that only two divisions could be fielded and these scarcely rated as a quality fighting force at all. The British Army of the Rhine in northern Germany was more closely deployed in fighting formations, but it amounted to only about two and a half divisions. France had three underequipped divisions in Germany, with its military reserves scattered all the way from Morocco to Indochina. There were a couple of low-quality Belgian and Dutch divisions doing occupation duty – and that was it for the defense of Western Europe when the North Atlantic Treaty came into force.

Moreover, President Truman was determined on a major squeeze in defense spending, with the airlift now over. The Joint Chiefs had recommended a $23.6 billion budget for the 1950 fiscal year, and this had been cut by Secretary Forrestal to $16.9 billion. But Truman firmly ordered that defense spending be held to a mere $14.4 billion. Louis Johnson had then replaced Forrestal in the Pentagon, determined to swing the ax to meet the Truman target.

The signing of the North Atlantic Treaty, the success of the Berlin airlift and resumption of talks with the Russians had produced a certain lull in Washington, but not in Europe, which was living with the military reality. The supposition that the United States was rushing in those days to create some military hegemony over a reluctant Europe is simply not the way it all happened.

It was the Europeans who were pushing and pleading for a reluctant America to move in, take over and dominate. But the United States was trying – or at least thought it was trying – to get the Europe back on its own feet to look after its own economic and security problems. This had been the whole purpose of the Marshall Plan, a self-liquidating program which the United States had determinedly sought to make a catalyst for a new era of European unity. This was why General Marshall had urged

Bevin to launch a security arrangement in Europe with the Brussels Treaty before turning to the United States. This was why George Kennan and Chip Bohlen had opposed the North Atlantic Treaty idea, and contended instead that the United States should confine itself to a unilateral guarantee of support for Europe if it were attacked but should not become more deeply involved. This was why the United States was insisting that the Europeans use the Brussels Treaty machinery to work out their needs for American military assistance long before the North Atlantic Treaty came into force.

Of course it was clear and accepted in Washington that American military help for Europe was utterly essential if the new treaty was indeed to be "a shield against aggression." But nowhere in the State Department or the Pentagon or in the minds of American leaders when the treaty was signed was there any "master plan" to proceed forthwith to build a NATO political organization and military command structure under an American Supreme Allied Commander. Events would soon propel the United States in this perhaps inevitable direction. But as the Senate neared a final vote on ratification of the treaty, the new alliance was viewed rather like a military Marshall Plan, to help the Europeans pull up their own socks and take the future in their own hands.

In the ratification debate, Senator Vandenberg – seeking, of course, to round up every vote he could – even told the Senate:

I think a man can vote for this treaty and not vote for a nickel to implement it, because as far as I am concerned, the opening sentence of the treaty is a notification to Mr. Stalin which puts him in exactly the contrary position to that which Mr. Hitler was in, because Mr. Hitler saw us with a Neutrality Act. Mr. Stalin now sees us with a pact of cooperative action.

While this was true, the Europeans counted on a great deal more than waving a piece of paper at the Russians. Acheson, in testimony before the Foreign Relations Committee in advance of the ratification vote, had done what he could "to oppose attempting to win votes for the treaty by denigrating its commitments," but this was already a major problem. Acheson told the senators:

The judgment of the executive branch is that the United States can and should provide military assistance to other countries in the pact to maintain their collective security. The pact does not bind the Congress to reach the same conclusion, for it does not dictate the conclusion of honest judgment. It does preclude repudiation of the principle, or of the obligation of making that judgment. There is an obligation to help, but the extent, the manner and the timing is up to the honest judgment of the parties.

Then, however, Acheson allowed himself to be caught out rather badly when Senator Bourke B. Hickenlooper, a Republican from Iowa of the isolationist wing, asked whether Americans were going to be expected "to send substantial numbers of troops over there as a more or less permanent contribution to the development of those countries' capacity to resist." Acheson's unfortunate reply was: "The answer to that question, Senator, is a clear and absolute No."

This was almost like President Roosevelt's famous pledge in his 1940 third-term election campaign, when Europe had already been at war for more than a year: "I say to you again and again and again – your boys are not going to be sent to fight in foreign wars." Acheson later acknowledged that his quick reply to Hickenlooper had been "deplorably wrong and almost equally stupid" even as a short-range prediction. But he said it was not intended to deceive, and he had a certain justification for such an off-the-cuff remark at that time.

In the summer of 1949, the Pentagon had no intention or plans at all to assign more troops to Europe. Earlier, while the 1949 defense budget was being prepared and the treaty was being negotiated, General Marshall had firmly informed Forrestal: "Our policy should be to build up Western European ground forces. . . . We should not, at this stage, proceed to build up U.S. ground forces for the express purpose of employing them in Europe." Now with an even tighter 1950 budget, this was more true than ever for the Pentagon.

Louis Johnson, swinging the ax for Truman, began by ordering a halt to the construction of the first of a new generation of supercarriers for the navy. This promptly precipitated a famous "revolt of the Admirals" in September of 1949, and the resignation of the chief of naval operations, Admiral Louis Denfield. Priority spending, such as it was, would go to development of the new B-36 strategic bomber for the Air Force to increase America's nuclear capability against the Soviet Union. The Army was ordered to complete in June of 1949 what turned out to be a fatal withdrawal of U.S. combat forces from Korea, leaving behind only a military assistance group of about five-hundred officers and men.

In this situation there was neither room nor inclination to consider any increase in American forces in Germany. Both the administration and the Congress saw the American role in the new alliance as limited to aid to the Europeans to enable them to defend themselves, backed up by the ultimate power of the American nuclear bomb. This was scarcely what the Europeans wanted, expected and believed they needed. But it was American policy and certainly the prevailing American attitude when the United States Senate voted overwhelmingly on July 21, 1949, after twelve days of debate, to ratify the North Atlantic Treaty by 82 votes to 13.

Four days after the ratification vote, President Truman sent to Congress a request for legislation authorizing a military-aid program for the North Atlantic Treaty Allies totaling $1.4 billion – a very sizable sum at that time, which in fact amounted to about another 10 per cent of spending on top of Truman's budget for America's own defense that year. If the United States was not going to commit any more of its own forces to Europe, it certainly was not indifferent to building up Europe's defenses. But would $1.4 billion be enough even to prime the pump on European rearmament? Paul H. Nitze, then deputy head of the Policy Planning Staff, had spent several weeks in Europe while the treaty was still being negotiated, surveying the military picture, and he had returned with the conclusion that $40 to $50 billion would be necessary to build up forces capable of holding a Soviet attack. But with Truman cutting America's own defense spending, $1.4 billion for the Allies staggered Congress. A tremendous battle broke out immediately on Capitol Hill – in the words of Senator Connally, it was "the most difficult piece of legislation to get through Congress since the Lend-Lease Act in 1940."

While this struggle was at its height, the twelve foreign ministers of the new alliance gathered in Washington in mid-September for the first organizational meeting of the new North Atlantic Council. It was brief and routine rather than any inspired or notable launch of a new organization, and its only result was further disappointment for the Europeans. An organizational chart for the alliance had been prepared for approval by the foreign ministers – if a loose collection of uncoordinated committees could be called an "organization." There was to be no headquarters, no secretariat, no international budget, and no one particularly in charge. All would be informal and ad hoc.

Only a Military Standing Group of senior officers from the United States, Britain and France was to be "so organized as to function continuously" in the strategic direction of military planning for the alliance. These officers would soon be tucked away in the Pentagon. But to the dismay of the British and the French, apart from the Standing Group the United States was excluding itself from direct participation in military planning for the defense of Europe.

That first organizational chart for NATO established five geographical planning groups under the Standing Group, to cover Western Europe, Northern Europe, Southern Europe including the Western Mediterranean, the North Atlantic Ocean area and finally Canada–United States defense planning. But the U.S. Joint Chiefs of Staff ruled that direct participation of the United States in these groups would be limited to the North Atlantic and Canada–United States planning. Europe would be left to the Europeans, and the United States would participate in this work only with observers. Once again the United States was displaying its reluctance to get involved with any new commitment to Europe beyond its limited and weak occupation forces in Germany. All that could be said for this inauspicious first meeting of the new North Atlantic Council, which lasted only one day, was that at least it was a beginning.

On Capitol Hill, before the alliance foreign ministers left Washington, the House of Representatives voted by a sizable majority to slash Truman's military-aid request for Europe in half. But the President led a strong fight in the Senate with the help of loyal Democrats and enough bipartisan support from Vandenberg and John Foster Dulles during his brief senatorial career. The lines barely held, but in the end the Senate approved a bill with its own amendments and conditions attached and the money authorization intact. The Senate voted on September 22, and the bill then went to a joint conference with the House of Representatives for a final battle over the amount to be authorized.

At this crucial juncture, history intervened. On September 23, 1949, the White House issued a laconic statement that launched a complete reappraisal of United States defense policies, its long-term strategic thinking about the Soviet Union, its outlook on problems of global security and relations and obligations with its Allies. The White House announcement simply said:

"We have evidence that within recent weeks an atomic explosion occurred in the U.S.S.R."

A four-year American monopoly of the atomic bomb was over, and it had ended at least one if not two years before U.S. experts had believed would be possible. Espionage had been a major contribution to the speed of Soviet atomic development, but this part of the story was yet to unfold. The announcement produced no "panic" or "crisis" headlines. The reaction was far more profound – as Senator Vandenberg wrote in his diary: "This is now a different world."

There was an immediate response on Capitol Hill. Dean Acheson dryly recorded:

Once again the Russians had come to the aid of an imperiled non-partisan foreign policy, binding its wounds and rallying the divided Congress into accepting the Senate version of the Mutual Defense Assistance program. On October 16, 1949, the President signed the bill into law.

From the time of that first Soviet test explosion of an atomic bomb, a major shift rapidly took hold in the American response to the Soviet threat. No longer could this prudently be seen as primarily an economic-political challenge of Soviet Communism to Western democracy, with a relatively low risk of military hostilities. No longer would it be enough to rely on containment of Soviet power through assistance programs such as the Marshall Plan, or carefully restrained use of counterforce such as the Berlin airlift.

The Soviet Union, armed or soon to be armed with atomic weapons and already possessing enough conventional military power to overwhelm Western Europe, now had to be seen – whether rightly or wrongly – as an aggressive military threat to world stability and peace. This would mean a decisive shift away from the restraint of the original containment policy as conceived and to a large extent influenced by George Kennan, in which shoring up democracies with economic and political viability was to hold the line against Communism. The new phase of containment would be based on direct deployment of U.S. military power in confrontation with the Soviet Union. Distant backing of threatened Allies – whether their fears were justified or not – would no longer be enough. It was response to the Soviet nuclear explosion that turned the North Atlantic Treaty into *Pax Americana.*

Other events at the same period propelled the United States on to this decisive new course. In London on September 18 the British had been forced to declare a massive devaluation of the pound from its long wartime level of $4.20 down to $2.80. This sudden financial eclipse for *Pax Britannica* came as final notice in Washington that British power could no longer play any decisive role in the postwar strategic balance with the Soviet Union.

Meanwhile, West Germany held its first democratic election under its new constitution, and on September 15 Dr. Konrad Adenauer became the first chancellor of the new Bonn Republic. It was the beginning of a remarkable fourteen years in power for the courtly, resilient, conservative seventy-three-year-old Christian Democrat, who lasted longer as head of government than the entire *Götterdämmerung* history of Hitler's Third Reich. But with a new West German government now in being, the pivotal and unavoidable question of the role it would play in its own defense and the defense of Western Europe was automatically thrust into the forefront for the new Atlantic Alliance before it was even organized.

Then, in December 1949 in China, the Red Army of Mao Tse-tung entered Peking and Shanghai, and the rump remains of the Chinese Nationalist government decamped to Formosa. The Communist takeover of China had long been foreseen, like the Soviet nuclear bomb, but that did not minimize the political impact in the United States when it became a final reality. The China Lobby now unleashed all of its venomous fury on the Truman administration, and Senator Joseph McCarthy of Wisconsin began his malevolent domination of the American domestic scene.

President Truman was under heavy pressure from every direction at the end of 1949 to take action, to show some clear response to these onrushing events and the new phase of the Soviet challenge. The focal point clearly was America's declining defense posture, accentuated by the advent of the Soviet atomic bomb. Much heart-searching and technical debate and discussion took place in the closing months of 1949 among nuclear experts and politicians and political scientists. Finally, the President announced at the end of January that he had authorized "feasibility work" to begin on building a thermonuclear hydrogen bomb. In the end, Truman came to the simple conclusion that this was the only way that the United States could ensure that it would retain its nuclear lead over the Soviet Union, and to fail to keep the lead would be tantamount to strategic surrender.

But Truman then went further. When he gave the go-ahead on development of the hydrogen bomb, he also directed Acheson and Defense Secretary Johnson "to undertake a reexamination of our objectives in peace and war and of the effect of these objectives on our strategic plans, in the light of the probable fission bomb capability and possible thermonuclear bomb capability of the Soviet Union." The document that emerged from this study – known as NSC-68 – became a new blueprint for American postwar foreign policy.

George Kennan's famous Long Telegram of February 1946 had galvanized the State Department and the U.S. government into realistic recognition of the Soviet challenge. The NSC-68 study under Acheson now moved U.S. policy from restrained containment into the hyper-confrontational Cold War reflexes of the ensuing years.

There is an interesting similarity in the fashion in which Kennan and Acheson each came to view his own handiwork. On the Long Telegram, Kennan wrote in his *Memoirs* that the problem had been trying "to make them understand [in Washington] the nature of the phenomenon with which we in the Moscow Embassy were daily confronted and which our government and people had to learn to understand if they were to have any chance of coping successfully with the problems of the postwar world." Acheson in his memoirs wrote that the NSC-68 study four years later was "the most ponderous expression of elementary ideas, the purpose of which was to so bludgeon the mass mind of 'top government' that not only could the President make a decision, but that the decision would be carried out." Both were historically successful.

But at the time the NSC study was nearing completion, Kennan decided, not totally without coincidence, to take early retirement from the State Department and deploy his influence from the public fields of academia, which he continued to do with intellectual skill and literary eloquence for the next forty years. His departure, too, was part of the watershed in U.S. foreign policy, for he had found himself increasingly out of tune with the new hard line that was developing.

Kennan had one of the best and most stimulating minds ever enlisted by the U.S. Foreign Service. But penetrating as he was, he had a rather nineteenth-century concept of the future of Europe – a view, incidentally, that was shared by General Charles de Gaulle. It was to be a Europe standing on its own feet, sorting out its own affairs, its Iron Curtain divide gradually giving way to Pan-European understanding, with America intervening only from a distance to maintain peace and the balance of power, the kind of role that England had played for two centuries.

But the Soviet Union was much too powerful for that game, the stakes were now far too high and terrifying, and the European powers far too weak to play on their own. Kennan always held that war against Western Europe was never a real option or intention for the Soviet Union, and on this he was probably a better prophet than a policymaker. Forty years on, it can be said that containment has worked and Kennan was right. Kennan always backed a strong defense effort, but he was against seeking out military confrontation with the Soviet Union. In 1950 his voice of restraint had become like whistling into a wind. It was simply too big a risk to base a policy on the probability that the Soviet Union would not plunge into aggressive war, no matter how true this has turned out to be.

Paul Nitze had replaced Kennan as head of the Policy Planning Staff and he now headed the work of reexamination of strategic policy ordered by Truman. He and Acheson saw eye to eye on the central theme of the Soviet threat and the central objective of turning around completely the American defense effort to take up the challenge, in place of the insipid budget on which the United States was currently operating.

The NSC-68 document was not only ponderous, but massive and exhaustive, taking up fifty-seven closely printed pages in the published State Department records. Its dire apocalyptic tone was set in an opening passage that declared: "This Republic and its citizens, in the ascendancy of their strength, stand in their deepest peril." From this opener, it went on to warn that Soviet expansion was progressing "because the Kremlin is inescapably militant," and any further extension of its area of domination "would raise the possibility that no coalition adequate to confront the Soviet Union with greater strength could be assembled." The study then went into detail on the steady growth of Soviet military power against the decline in United States power, with American gross national product dropping rapidly for two years running from its wartime high.

Now the Kremlin's possession of atomic weapons would "put new power behind its design and increases the jeopardy to our own system," the study asserted. It had therefore become "imperative that this trend be reversed by a rapid and concerted buildup of the actual strength of both the United States and the free world."

Then, in a dismissal of the Kennan view of containment, the NSC document declared:

> One of the most important ingredients of power is military strength. Without superior aggregate military strength, in being and readily mobilizable, a policy of containment – which in effect is a policy of calculated and gradual coercion – is no more than a policy of bluff. In the face of obviously mounting Soviet military strength ours has declined relatively. We have failed to implement adequately the fundamental aspects of containment.

Instead of containment, the emphasis of American policy would now shift to "building up situations of strength":

> A rapid buildup of political, economic and military strength and thereby of confidence in the free world is the only course which is consistent with our fundamental purpose. Unless a decision has been made and action undertaken to build up strength in the broadest sense of the United States and the free world, an attempt to negotiate would be ineffective and probably long drawn out, and thereby might seriously delay the necessary measures to build up our strength.

After acknowledging that a buildup of strength "will place heavy demands on our courage and intelligence; it will be costly; it will be dangerous," the concluding passage of the study said: "The whole success hangs ultimately on recognition by this government, the

American people and all peoples that the Cold War is in fact a real war in which the survival of the world is at stake."

When the report reached Truman, he was in no doubt about its conclusions and the course he should take. His problem was political – how to engineer a gigantic turnaround for Congress and the country. Once again the Soviets came decisively to his help at a critical time.

In May of 1950, Secretary Acheson set out for Paris and London, and the second full-scale meeting of the North Atlantic Council, foreign ministers of the alliance. The treaty was already one year old – yet very little had emerged in tangible results. As an organization it was virtually nonexistent, and its *raison d'être* was far from clear to itself, its members or its public. The American military-assistance program had yet to make any real impact on the defense of Western Europe. So far the treaty had not been much more effective than if the United States had limited its involvement to the original idea of a unilateral declaration of support for Europe if it were attacked.

Yet the strategic balance was moving steadily against the West and in favor of the Soviet Union, and Western leaders all knew this. Acheson's deep preoccupation after completion of the NSC-68 study had been how to rouse the American people to accept the burdens and challenges that the American government would have to demand if there was to be a massive turnaround in U.S. defense spending. To this end he had already made a number of major speeches around the country, all hammering at the same basic theme:

> We cannot afford to wait and merely hope that Soviet policies will change. We must carry forward our own determination to create situations of strength in the free world, because this is the only basis on which lasting agreement with the Soviet Government is possible.

Acheson, unlike General Marshall, was a very articulate man in public and private. But as he crossed the Atlantic he had only more of this same exhortation for the Europeans. He was bringing no fresh ideas and certainly offering no fresh American commitments. Even when it came to improving the workings of the alliance, all that the State Department was proposing was the establishment of a "permanent commission" to co-ordinate studies and make policy recommendations. It was decisions, not recommendations, that were needed.

Hanging over all this, like a cloud gathering on the horizon, was the German question – West Germany's future relations with the alliance and its eventual role in Western defense. A major Western European defense effort without the involvement of West Germany was a palpable impossibility. But here again, Acheson knew that he had to wait, that the German issue was far too complex and emotional in postwar Europe to rush the fences or try to force a decision.

As the London meeting neared, others were brooding also about the state of the world, the future of the new alliance, and where all this drift was carrying. Kenneth Younger, minister of state at the Foreign Office and Bevin's principal political deputy, wrote in his private diary on the eve of the meeting:

The Americans are under a compulsion to "hot up the cold war" in every way on account of the state of American opinion, while the French, for a similar reason, are above all anxious not to seem to close the door against agreement with the Russians. The difference is only one of emphasis, but it is important.

We and the Americans want to start building up an Atlantic Community which includes but transcends Western Europe, while the French still hanker after a European solution in which the only American function is to produce military and other aid. The difference is important because it stems from two quite different conceptions. Bevin has no faith in the solidity or efficiency of France or Belgium, and believes Western Europe will be a broken reed, and will not even attract the loyalty of Europeans or impress the Russians, unless it is very solidly linked to North America. I think this is realistic though depressing.

Younger had put his finger on what might really be called the Great Dichotomy of the North Atlantic Alliance that has run through the first forty years of its history, and may well become even more pronounced in the future. At the time Younger was putting these thoughts in his diary, that great Frenchman Jean Monnet was pondering a very different view of the near and distant future. Rather than a diary, it was Monnet's habit to write out notes and reflections, to order his own thoughts and ideas, and in April of 1949 he wrote:

> Men's minds are becoming focused on an object at once simple and dangerous – the cold war. All proposals and actions are interpreted by public opinion as a contribution to the cold war. It creates a rigidity of mind which is characteristic of the pursuit of a single objective. The search for solutions to problems ceases.
>
> The German situation is rapidly turning into a cancer that will be dangerous to peace in the near future, and immediately to France unless its development is directed towards hope for the Germans and collaboration with free peoples. *We must not try to solve the German problem in its present context. We must change the context by transforming the basic facts.* [Italics added]
>
> If France fails to speak and act now, what will happen? A group will form around the United States, but in order to wage the cold war with greater zeal. Countries of Europe are afraid and seeking help. Britain will draw ever closer to the United States; Germany will develop rapidly, and we shall not be able to prevent her being armed. France will be trapped once more, and this will inevitably lead to her eclipse.

From these and other musings Jean Monnet produced in May of 1950 the most imaginative and far-reaching act of French foreign policy in this century, if not in all its history: the creation of the European Coal and Steel Community. By proposing to place the coal and steel industries of France and West Germany – and any other European nations that might wish to join – under the control and direction of a single supranational High Authority, Monnet at a stroke "transformed the basic facts" of the German problem and laid the basis for the economic strength and political unity of Western Europe that has become the European Community of today.

Monnet never held a government Cabinet office and was never elected to anything in his life, but he was one of the truly great men of this century – a Frenchman of international vision with the rare gift of turning ideas into workable proposals, dreams into reality. He was a man of influence, who always left it to men of power to take his ideas and carry them out. In this case, it was French Foreign Minister Robert Schuman who provided the political skill and wisdom and above all the conviction to carry Monnet's concept and plan into historic success.

Acheson flew in to Paris on his way to London on the morning of Sunday, May 7, to be greeted by Ambassador David K. E. Bruce at the airport with word that Schuman wished unexpectedly to call on him at the American Embassy residence for an informal talk that same afternoon. In strictest secrecy – not even the French Cabinet had yet been informed and only nine men in the French bureaucracy had been involved in Monnet's discussions and drafting of the plan – Schuman disclosed to Acheson and Bruce what France would be proposing to Europe two days later. Acheson's initial uncertainties quickly gave way to relief and enthusiasm, as he grasped the broad implications of a concept both simple and far-reaching to transform the German problem. As he later put it: "Once the small restricting frame is broken, thought rapidly expands and accommodates to a wider setting, and after that the effect is most unlikely to be undone."

Bearing the French secret, Acheson traveled on to London for meetings with Bevin. When the big news then broke from Paris, Bevin was in indignant fury at what he regarded as double-dealing behind his back, and it took patient and forceful reasoning for Acheson to explain and calm him down. Meanwhile Schuman had also secretly contacted Chancellor Konrad Adenauer in advance, and had received his immediate and unequivocal and fervent assurances that West Germany would accept the plan wholeheartedly as soon as it was announced. Apart from anything else, it would be a major step back to full sovereignty and the end of the occupation for the Federal Republic.

But the British refused even to contemplate the idea of placing their coal and steel industries in the same pool under the control of some remote Continental High Authority – and thereby began a self-exclusion from the construction of Europe that was to last twenty-three years, one of the biggest misjudgments and mistakes in the history of British foreign policy.

In launching the Schuman Plan, the French at a stroke moved the German problem, for the time being at least, out of the context of Germany's place in the Atlantic Alliance and placed it in the context of its place in Europe. But the North Atlantic Treaty had been a necessary prerequisite to the French offer to pool its own coal and steel industry with that of West Germany. Without this security guarantee from the United States, the French could never have contemplated such an offer to the Germans. It now became equally true that consideration of German rearmament could not be contemplated by the French until the success of the Schuman Plan submerged Germany's ominous heavy industry in a new relationship with its European neighbors.

The French move was decisive, therefore, in developing the European element within the Atlantic Alliance. But at the same time in that successful May in London, the French also moved adroitly and success-fully to lay the groundwork for today's North Atlantic Treaty Organi-zation. Schuman proposed to the meeting of foreign ministers that in place of the plethora of ad hoc committees and study groups, "each government shall name a deputy to its present representative, able to devote all the time necessary and as continuously as required to the exercise of the Council's responsibilities, to ensure that the activities of the organization shall have a permanent character."

At first Acheson was hesitant, apparently at the prospect of such a delegation of authority as the French proposal seemed to imply. A "permanent commission" to study problems was one thing, but a North Atlantic Council of permanent deputies able to exercise responsibilities that hitherto had rested with foreign ministers seemed to be a quantum jump into commitments the United States had been avoiding. Yet if Acheson was going to rally the new alliance into a forward role in the Cold War, and press those aims of the NSC-68 study, then he had to accept the French proposal to activate the NATO organization on a permanent and not just an ad hoc basis.

So, after some intensive redrafting of the original French proposals on the functions and responsibilities of the new permanent deputies, the twelve foreign ministers agreed to set up a NATO political headquarters in London, with a staff of "highly qualified persons contributed by member governments." The deputies would then select their own chair-man to organize and direct the conduct of the affairs of the alliance on a continuous daily basis.

It was therefore on French initiative that the North Atlantic Treaty Organization came into being – but this of course did not prevent General

Charles de Gaulle from heaping scorn on "integration" and rancorously pulling France out of the NATO military command structure sixteen years later.

Acheson returned to Washington well satisfied at "the most important steps yet to be taken to move from mere agreement to do something in case of trouble toward the creation of a new factor in international relations to prevent trouble." But the secretary of state was slow to respond to the London agreement to name a permanent deputy and set up a NATO headquarters. The delay probably centered on Averell Harriman, who was then serving as European director of the Marshall Plan in Paris. The Europeans were expecting and hoping that Harriman would move to London to energize the new NATO headquarters, and they were prepared to send men of an equal caliber of experience and authority to serve on the new Permanent Council – men who had held ministerial posts and who could speak with authority for their governments. Harriman, however, was anxious to get back to the center of power in Washington, and on June 16 it was announced that he would soon be joining the White House staff as special assistant to the president – in effect the post of national security adviser, which did not formally exist at that time.

On June 19, Ernest Bevin sent a personal message to Acheson saying that he was "much concerned about the delays" in setting up the new NATO headquarters and "we are awaiting a lead from you and nothing effective can be done until your deputy is nominated and has taken up his duties."

After this prodding, Acheson's selection for the new NATO post was a low-key disappointment to the Europeans. The assumption must be that the secretary of state simply did not want a high-profile public figure in the NATO assignment, for there was a considerable pool of strong talent to choose from in Washington in those days. Instead he turned to a relatively unknown New York lawyer, Charles M. Spofford, who was vigorous, intelligent and competent, even if he was without experience in diplomacy or international affairs and did not bring to the new organization the kind of identity and leadership the Europeans hoped for. Spofford's appointment was announced in Washington on Saturday, June 24.

That Saturday, Dean Acheson drove out to his modest country retreat, Harewood Farm in Maryland, for a quiet weekend with some time off for his two avocations, gardening and woodcrafting, furniture making. He was in bed reading himself to sleep at 10:00 P.M. that evening when the telephone rang with a call from the White House switchboard, with John Hickerson on the line from the State Department.

North Korean forces had invaded South Korea.

The only "inside story" from the Soviet side on the launching of the Korean War has come from Nikita S. Khrushchev, in a book titled *Khrushchev Remembers*, which was smuggled out of the Soviet Union and printed only in the West in 1970, seven years after he had been deposed from the Kremlin leadership. Although self-serving and suspect, the book does have a plausible and truthful ring to it in the account of events in Korea.

According to Khrushchev, the North Korean Communist puppet leader, Kim Il Sung, first proposed an attack on South Korea when he visited Stalin at the end of 1949. By this time both Soviet and American occupation troops had been withdrawn from the peninsula, and Kim told Stalin that he "wanted to prod South Korea with the point of a bayonet." The South, he asserted, would then "explode and the power of the people would prevail." Khrushchev says that Stalin did not oppose the idea, particularly because "the struggle would be an internal matter which the Koreans would be settling themselves." But he was cautious, and told Kim to consider it more carefully and come back with a plan.

Mao Tse-tung then made an extended visit to Moscow early in 1950 after his armies had completed their takeover of China. According to Khrushchev, when Stalin raised with him the possibility of an attack on South Korea by Kim Il Sung's forces, Mao gave his assent. Kim then returned to Moscow with detailed plans for his attack. Khrushchev says that Stalin "was worried that the Americans would jump in, but we were inclined to think that if the war was fought swiftly – and Kim Il Sung was sure that it could be won swiftly – then intervention by the U.S.A. could be avoided." So Stalin sat back and allowed the North Korean attack to go forward.

It was only by the narrowest of military margins that the war was not "won swiftly," when American forces rushed into Korea from Japan and managed to hold a thumbnail enclave around the southern port city of Pusan, after Communist forces had overrun everything else on the peninsula. Then came General Douglas MacArthur's sensational end-run landing of American forces in the rear of the Communists at Inchon, the retaking of the capital at Seoul, and the pellmell withdrawal and retreat of the enemy back to the north. But MacArthur next launched the tragic and ill-fated American denouement of the costly advance to the Yalu River, which brought the Chinese into the war. After a long military stalemate, an armistice formally ended the war in July 1953.

In Washington, the Communist attack on South Korea came as an explosive confirmation of all the analysis and apocalyptic warnings contained in the two-month-old NSC-68 policy paper. Even the existence of the NSC document was a closely held secret at the time, but it had been seen and read by the top inner circle of Truman's Cabinet, and its conclusions and carrying out its recommendations were already the main preoccupations of the administration. NSC-68 in effect became the "action paper" that to a large degree had already laid the groundwork for the swiftness and decisiveness of the American response to the Korean attack. Moreover, in line with the NSC study, this became a global response and not just a local response in Korea. It was a response that soon turned the North Atlantic Treaty Organization from an object of American help and assistance into a chosen instrument of United States foreign policy in the waging of the Cold War. When Stalin gave his tacit approval to Kim Il Sung's little proposal "to prod South Korea with the point of a bayonet," he provided the Truman administration with the prod that it needed and was looking for to galvanize the NSC-68 recommendations into money, arms, men and reality.

The first vital flurry of response in Washington was directed to pushing through a condemnation of the North Korean attack in the United Nations Council, which would then be the basis for a multinational military intervention by the NATO Allies and others. The Soviet delegate to the UN, Yakov Malik, had conveniently been boycotting all Security Council sessions ever since January, in protest against the refusal of the General Assembly to seat Red China in place of Chiang Kai-shek's defeated regime. Malik was still absent on Monday, June 26, and unable therefore to veto the resolution calling for UN action against the invasion. Meanwhile, Washington was also authorizing General MacArthur step by step to commit all the available American military forces in the area to halt the invaders.

But on July 8, a message went out from the State Department to U.S. missions in Europe:

> We must dispel feeling in Europe which followed initial relief over our vigorous action in Korea that we may now become overcommitted in the Far East and overlook the continued primary importance of Europe in the struggle against communism. With this in mind, you should take every step to indicate that as a result of the Korean situation U.S. leadership will be even more vigorous and confident. Keynote should be the need for greater effort by all. You should indicate that U.S. is ready to do its full part in a cooperative effort.

However, in an unusual Top Secret personal letter to Acheson from London on July 12, the astute and influential Ambassador Lewis W. Douglas drove to the core of the problem of energizing the NATO Alliance. After noting that European reaction to American actions in Korea "continues to be excellent," Douglas wrote:

> There are two areas for action in which we had been slow in facing the issues and moving. They concern the establishment of specific command relationships in Europe, and the question of commitments of U.S. forces planned to be made available in case of an emergency. *Until we are prepared to state our intentions more completely in regard to these two matters, there will continue to be slowness and hesitation on the part of NATO to move forward.* [Italics added]
>
> If we join up to the hilt, which implies a preparedness to make commitments regarding command and furnishing troops, then we can provide the basis for tackling the delicate problem of the French. If we can persuade the French to put their military house in order – and they do so – we then will have got the framework in which real Western European military strength can be developed. When that has been substantially achieved – and not until then – we will be in a position to consider rearming of Western Germany.
>
> We must recognize that entering actively into the military planning and command arrangements of Western Europe means ultimately placing a U.S. officer in a position of command here. Both the French and the

British have repeatedly stated this as a prerequisite to successful military planning in Western Europe. Our Joint Chiefs of Staff have been somewhat loath to face this issue. I feel that they can no longer delay in taking a cold and objective look at the apparent need for us to accept our appropriate role militarily in NATO.

Douglas chose to use a personal letter to Acheson rather than an ambassadorial telegram that would receive general distribution. His letter really constituted the basic "NATO agenda" for the remaining months of 1950, to complete the military structure of the alliance. From Paris, the equally respected and influential Ambassador Bruce, in a lengthy dispatch on July 28, added this appraisal:

> It would be ridiculous for other European nations to make substantial additional military efforts and cut back normal consumption and production while Germany was permitted to manufacture on a "peacetime basis." Nevertheless, it will be politically impossible to rearm German manpower or convert German industry to military production as long as European peoples see in such action the risk of a resurgence of German military might. A truly common effort is the only way out. If Germans are made soldiers in an Atlantic community army or even a European army, the question will then be viewed in a quite different light. Once the Schuman Plan is on the books, it should be much easier for the Atlantic community to call on the industrial strength of Germany to help rearm.

It has been a contention of revisionist historians that the buildup of United States forces in Europe, the creation of SHAPE Headquarters, the rearmament of West Germany and the intensification of the Cold War in Europe was an overreaction to the Korean War, because Stalin had no intention of risking military action against Western Europe. Korea, in other words, could have been safely treated as a local problem in Asia and not ballooned into a global challenge and response. But this was simply not the political reality of 1950. Well before the outbreak of hostilities in Korea, the French and the British were both already actively fighting Communist insurgencies – the French in Indochina and the British in Malaysia. If the "globalization" of the Communist threat was an exaggeration, it was both inevitable and justified from all that was happening. Europe was still living with strong historic memories of the step-by-step

Nazi aggressions against a background of appeasement that led to World War II. Even if the "Hitler parallel" might not accurately apply to a cautious chessplayer like Stalin, it could scarcely be ignored or dismissed by those who were making vital decisions for the West. "No more Munichs" became the watchword.

In Washington, strategic policy-making was firmly in the hands of leaders fresh from World War II, who remained determinedly focused on the security of Europe despite war in Korea – to the disdain and contempt of General MacArthur, who wanted to rout Communism on the ground in Asia.

Accordingly, despite all of the crowded and emotional decision-making of war in Korea in that summer of 1950, the central problem of Europe and the building of NATO remained in the forefront for Truman, Acheson, General Bradley and the American Joint Chiefs of Staff. It is fortunate for Europe and NATO that this was so.

Charles M. Spofford arrived in London on July 22, one month after the outbreak of the Korean War, to take up his post as America's first permanent representative on the North Atlantic Council. In a matter of days the new political headquarters of the alliance went into action under pressure of events, housed in a couple of graceful old Georgian townhouses on Belgrave Square provided by the British government. Spofford brought with him the news that President Truman would soon be sending to Congress a request for an additional $10 billion in defense spending – of which $4 to $6 billion would be earmarked for Europe. At the same time he urged the British and French in particular that America expected "the strongest possible evidence" that they would be beefing up their own defense spending. It was far from the last time that this appeal would be heard by the permanent deputies in the North Atlantic Council.

Two days later, the new French deputy, Hervé Alphand, sought a private meeting with Spofford on instructions from Paris to declare in some agitation that the French wanted a clear and prompt decision from the NATO Allies that "defense must be as far east as possible." He insisted to Spofford that "this meant additional American and British forces must be sent to Germany to be available along with additional French forces which would be raised." Alphand continued:

Defense of Western Europe could not be effected unless American and British troops were actually there to help meet initial shock. It would be to no avail if forces were sent after an initial attack because there would be nothing to defend. The lesson of Korea was clear in the minds of all Frenchmen, and Prime Minister Pleven felt it absolutely essential that he be able to give assurances to the French people with regard to these basic principles if he was to be justified in calling for additional effort and sacrifices that would be necessary.

There was a certain logic to the French case. But it was equally logical and self-evident that if the French wanted Europe to be defended along the Elbe River as far to the east as possible, then this inevitably raised the question of German rearmament and the West Germans contributing to their own defense. But this the French were far from ready to face. If it was ignored in Alphand's demarche and ignored in Paris, it scarcely could be ignored in Washington. So, for the next four or five months the question of how to begin beefing up NATO defenses in Western Europe bogged down in a chicken-or-egg argument about which came first – American assistance or German rearmament.

The United States was of course prepared to put billions into a European defense effort, but it expected the Europeans to produce immediate increases in forces and weapons on their own. The French were now saying that unless additional American troops were sent to West Germany first, it would be difficult to call on the French people for such sacrifices. The Pentagon at this stage was not prepared to send more troops across the Atlantic unless there was a start on German rearmament. The British and the French already agreed that there could be no effective defense of NATO unless an American Supreme Allied Commander arrived to take charge. But the American Joint Chiefs of Staff refused even to consider sending an American commander until it was clear what forces he would have to command – which took things back to the German question being blocked by the French. In short, everyone was chasing the problem in circles back and forth across the Atlantic.

Acheson quickly picked up on the European army idea put forward by Ambassador Bruce, as a key to unlock the deadlock. From West Germany, the influential high commissioner, John J. McCloy, added his weight, urging Acheson that a European army with a German contribution "is the only way to achieve effective defense, and any other course, even if vigorously followed, would not do." Then the redoubtable Winston Churchill, in one of his massive speeches at the Consultative Assembly of the fledgling Council of Europe in Strasbourg on August 11, blazed into headlines across Europe with a call for "immediate creation of a European army under a unified command in which we should all bear a worthy and honorable part."

In early August, Acheson proposed to Louis Johnson at the Pentagon that the United States should immediately commit additional American troops to Europe to "lay the groundwork" for creation of a European army and German rearmament. Acheson favored a step-by-step approach, realizing as he did that German rearmament was an explosive issue in Europe, whatever was happening in Korea. Johnson, however, rejected this out of hand. He was a bellicose and ambitious man, who was also running a political vendetta against Acheson behind his back. Instead of step by step, he insisted on a package deal. If the Europeans wanted more American troops and an American general to take over command of European defenses, then they should pay for it by agreeing at once to German rearmament. At the end of August, with another important NATO foreign ministers meeting ahead, Truman asked for an agreed recommendation from both secretaries. Acheson bowed to the Pentagon insistence on the package deal, in order to get from Johnson the commitments also to send troops and name an American supreme commander. Truman accordingly announced from the White House on September 9 that additional American ground forces would be sent to Europe. But he did not say how many would go or when they would go – nor did he disclose that the United States would also be seeking to link this with agreement from the Allies on German rearmament.

Truman, however, took another important decision. On September 12, as Acheson arrived in New York where the NATO foreign ministers would be meeting on the fringes of the United Nations General Assembly, it was announced from Washington that the President had fired the obstinate Louis Johnson and replaced him at the Defense Department with General Marshall, summoned once more out of retirement, whose rapport with Acheson was excellent. This quickly brought a new flexibility to the American position on the package deal.

From the outset, in Big Three meetings on the German question in advance of the NATO meeting, Acheson ran into a predictable roadblock from the French. Schuman politely but firmly refused to give any consideration at all to German rearmament. Bevin told Acheson: "You've got the right idea, me lad, but you're goin' at it the hard way." Fortunately, personal relations among these three remarkable men were far stronger than any of their differences. Schuman wondered "why the United States was in such a hurry" to rearm West Germany, and argued that they should first set up an integrated military command structure and build up American, British and French forces to lay the groundwork for an eventual German "contribution" to common defense. This was more or less the approach that Acheson had tried to sell to Louis Johnson, so the argument was back to square one.

General Marshall then arrived in New York for his first meeting with NATO defense ministers. After adding his calm and massive weight to the case for bringing the Germans into the Western defense buildup, Marshall also concluded – being a diplomat as well as a soldier – that agreement would take time, the package deal could not be sold in New York, and more argument would simply harden transatlantic difficulties. The two secretaries concluded, and Truman concurred, that they would have to pull back on the German question if they wanted the meeting to end in success – and success was highly important at this juncture of history.

Accordingly, at that New York meeting the United States took the most important step forward for the alliance since the signing of the treaty. A final communiqué announced that agreement had been reached "on establishment at the earliest possible date of an integrated force under centralized command in Europe." A Supreme Allied Commander would be appointed "as soon as there is assurance that forces will be made available to enable the latter to be reasonably capable of fulfilling command responsibilities." Clearly he would be an American.

The German question was then passed to NATO defense ministers to study "the nature, extent and timing of German participation in the buildup of the defense of Western Europe." In effect, this first round of NATO discussion on German rearmament ended with the French point of view essentially prevailing. The question had been finessed, although far from forgotten, and meanwhile the Americans had given vital public commitments on the dispatch of additional American divisions to Europe and the formation of an integrated NATO military high command. But in fact the pattern of that New York meeting in October of 1950 was repeated again and again in the diplomacy and politics of NATO for the first five years in the life of the alliance, with the French using dogged rearguard delaying tactics against putting Germans back into military uniforms. It was not until 1955 that creation of a new West German Bundeswehr finally began.

Meanwhile, as the NATO meeting ended, General Dwight D. Eisenhower called secretly at the White House at President Truman's request. Relations between the two men were then still passably cordial. Eisenhower had been president of Columbia University in New York for two and a half years, but with so much churning in the world he was more than ready for a change. He was of course well aware of the NATO decision to create an integrated military command in Europe, and of the fact that he was really the only candidate for the assignment.

He was scarcely surprised when Truman asked him if he would accept the job. But Eisenhower was a West Pointer to the end. His reply to Truman was: "I am a soldier and am ready to respond to whatever orders my superiors may care to issue to me."

So the Commander in Chief told the retired five-star general that at an appropriate time, when all the diplomatic negotiations had been completed with the Allies, and the suitable military commitments and arrangements were in place, orders would be issued for him to return to uniform and assume the new command.

The French were well aware that pressures for German rearmament would not go away, and the ubiquitous Jean Monnet now came up with his version of the European army idea. He proposed the creation of a European Defense Community, a supranational political institution along the lines of the European Coal and Steel Community. There would be a civilian High Authority at the top, with a unified command structure in charge of integrated units of French, Belgian, Dutch, Italian, Luxembourg and German soldiers. The largest such unit would be a brigade. All German forces would be placed under the Defense Community, but the other countries joining would continue to have national forces outside the integrated command. American reaction to what became known as the Pleven Plan, after Prime Minister René Pleven, was at first decidedly reserved. It was perceived quite rightly that this would delay, not facilitate, any quick reactivation of German military forces. It would mean a long negotiation and ratification process before anything could happen.

Nevertheless, there was now a French plan and it was a plan with the Monnet label that had immediate apeal to the American ideologues of the State Department, who in those days sought to weave and bend every policy they could lay hands on into the building of a united Europe. Accordingly, whatever the built-in delays and drawbacks, the United States had no choice but to swing behind the Pleven Plan.

But by November 1950, other difficulties were looming – not from the French but from the West Germans themselves. All the talk about German rearmament was not stirring any latent passions in German breasts to get back into uniform. In the fledgling Bonn Republic, there was determined reluctance and resistance to the idea of any rearmament at all. *Ohne mich* ("Without me") became the vocal political slogan of young Germans. Moreover, the adroit Chancellor Konrad Adenauer was telling the Allies quite determinedly and quite reasonably that if his government was going to be asked to raise German military forces for defense of the West, then the occupation had to be brought to an end swiftly and full sovereignty restored to the Bonn Republic to place it on an equal footing with the other states it would be helping to defend. This raised entirely different problems for the occupying powers that could not be avoided. In short, there would be no quick solution to German rearmament for either the Germans or the French, however impatient the Americans might be.

Then, with another meeting of NATO foreign ministers approaching in mid-December in Brussels, military disaster struck in Korea. General MacArthur's "victory by Thanksgiving" dash to the Yalu River brought China's Red Army into the war, pouring down in hordes on the badly dispersed American forces. Soon the Americans were reeling south in retreat under appalling winter conditions. British, French and other United Nations forces were fighting alongside the Americans as they were driven back across the 38th Parallel North-South border. Seoul again fell to the Communists, and there was serious talk of an "American Dunkirk" in the making – evacuation of United Nations forces from the south of the Korean peninsula.

The Korean military disaster had begun to stabilize by the time the NATO foreign ministers gathered on December 15. But the specter of the rout of the Americans had increased frantic fears among the Europeans about the security of their own continent if the Korean War was lost.

These fears were certainly recognized and shared in Washington. Many of the NATO Allies, after all, were also contributing to the Korean war effort. When Dean Acheson arrived in Brussels, he was fully determined that a major act of decisive support for Europe was as imperative for the United States as it was for the Europeans. A clear signal had to be sent not only to the peoples of Western Europe but to Stalin and the Soviet Union. Action could not be held up by further dithering over the German question.

As the NATO ministers convened, the Soviet Union opened up a massive propaganda barrage against the NATO Allies, warning of dire consequences if the alliance proceeded with its announced plans to create a unified European high command, and build up integrated defense forces. Stalin reinforced the propaganda with similar direct diplomatic notes to the NATO governments. But this only reinforced NATO determination that quick and decisive action had to be taken to set its own military house in order.

On December 17, Acheson announced that at the request of the NATO Council of Ministers, President Truman was appointing General Eisenhower as Supreme Allied Commander, with orders to proceed forthwith to Europe to establish a Supreme Headquarters Allied Powers Europe (SHAPE). On the first of January, 1951, General Eisenhower landed in Frankfurt with a small personal staff including his Chief of Staff designate, General Alfred M. Gruenther. They then began a quick initial round of the NATO capitals with plans for organizing the new command.

At last the NATO Alliance would become a visible reality.

TWELVE

The First Forty Years

From the moment that General Eisenhower charged down the gangway of his propeller-driven U.S. Air Force Constellation at Frankfurt's war-scarred Rhine-Main airfield to take command in Europe, the Atlantic Alliance began to breathe with a sense of purpose and mission, a confidence and vitality that had been quite beyond its political leaders to instill.

Indeed, for the brief eighteen months that Eisenhower served in Paris as the first Supreme Allied Commander, NATO's government leaders seemed to be more than pleased and ready to yield to him a role of leadership that he was uniquely qualified by experience and personality to fill. Political leadership of NATO, in any case, was dispersed in twelve capitals. But a military headquarters would be tangible and institutional, flags flying over it, officers in many uniforms assigned to it, communications with capitals flying back and forth, orders and instructions issuing from it. The fact that a NATO military command post was in being was a great deal more important in those distant days than any of the many gloomy assessments of its efficiency or readiness or the strength of the forces that it theoretically could command. General Eisenhower had all of the right political experience and prestige of success as a coalition commander in war to enable him in a short time to pull the new SHAPE Headquarters into operational visibility that no other military man on the horizon in 1951 could remotely have provided. The supposed weakness for which he was often wrongly criticized during World War II, of being more of a "political general" than a military commander, was in fact exactly the talent and experience needed to give Europe the sense that it yearned for – that it could and would now be defended.

Eisenhower began with a whirlwind tour of alliance capitals in gloomy January weather, in the main simply to tell anxious governments what he needed and what he intended to do. They were largely ready in those days to promise him anything he wanted. He returned to Frankfurt after eleven days for a final round of meetings with the American, British and French occupation commanders of the only real forces then available to defend Western Europe. Before heading back to Washington to deliver a major address to Congress, he showed his political deftness on the vital German question when he told a news conference that I attended:

"I bear no resentment whatsoever against Germany as a nation and I do not bear any against the German people. Of course I hope that some day the great German people are lined up with the rest of the free world because I believe in the essential freedom-loving quality of the German people. If they are, they must be on exactly the same status as all others. I would never consent to be in command of any unit whose soldiers were not there believing that they were serving their country and civilization and freedom."

It would be nearly five years before these sentiments were ultimately fulfilled, but in the meantime Eisenhower had reached out a hand that Chancellor Konrad Adenauer and the German people could grasp.

When he returned to Paris from Washington in the first week of February, the French government requisitioned the old Hotel Astoria, which then stood at the top of the Avenue des Champs-Élysées near the Arc de Triomphe, to serve as temporary headquarters for Eisenhower's new command. It is no hyperbole to say that the cream of the higher ranks of officers in national military establishments were ordered to Paris to serve under Eisenhower as he pulled SHAPE into being. It was agreed from the outset that the new NATO headquarters would supersede the Brussels Treaty headquarters at Fontainebleau. Indeed, if there was one thing that its squabbling commanders – Field Marshal Viscount Montgomery and General Jean de Lattre de Tassigny – could agree upon, it was the need for an American commander in Europe.

Whatever Monty's sour opinion of Eisenhower as a soldier, he was enough of a realist to know that Ike was the embodiment of an American commitment, of American military power and leadership, without which Europe could not be defended. So Monty could hardly wait to return to a role under Eisenhower, and become Deputy Supreme Allied Commander Europe at the new headquarters. De Lattre de Tassigny moved on eventually to command French forces in the ill-fated Indochina war.

By the end of March, the new command structure began to move into place. Under SHAPE there would be subordinate headquarters for Northern Europe at Oslo, Central Europe at Fontainebleau and Southern Europe at Naples, and later an Atlantic Naval Command at Norfolk, Virginia. A further proliferation of smaller commands then followed in the far north of Norway, the Baltic area from Denmark, the English Channel, the Eastern Mediterranean, the Western Mediterranean, Air Force commands all over the map of Europe, the Iberian Approaches, the Western Approaches, et cetera, et cetera. Eisenhower was like a postmaster general devising a kind of military post-office system to cover all of Europe. But it was of overriding political importance that the NATO command structure be seen to be reaching out to every corner of the alliance in order to fulfill the treaty pledge that "the Parties agree that an armed attack against one or more of them in Europe or North America shall be considered an attack against them all." It was this pledge, and not any considerations of military efficiency, that really determined the rather baroque command structure of the North Atlantic Treaty forces.

National governments gratefully and hastily provided Eisenhower with buildings and telephones and secretaries and cars and drivers for all of these burgeoning command posts. The French went to work on a crash program to build a low, sprawling main headquarters for SHAPE on the outskirts of Paris at an old military drill and training grounds of the French kings near Versailles. On April 2, 1951, General Eisenhower formally declared SHAPE Headquarters to be "operational."

With establishment of SHAPE Headquarters, the military buildup and political consolidation of the NATO Alliance rapidly took hold. The first of five United States Army divisions promised for reinforcement of Europe – the 4th Infantry – arrived at the north German port of Bremerhaven in a chilly spring rain a couple of weeks after SHAPE was activated. Although the Korean War was still costing men and resources, new American divisional and corps commanders were sent to Europe to reorganize, redeploy and improve the training of the rather ragged U.S. forces in Germany. Eisenhower traveled ceaselessly to NATO capitals to confer with prime ministers and defense ministers and push and prod the slow but determined buildup of European forces getting under way. If NATO never did and never has reached the targets set by the military planners in the last forty years, it has at least showed that Europe cannot be occupied without a fight, and that has kept the peace.

The fact that a NATO military headquarters was now alive and assuming such an active role in collective defense of Europe quickly spilled over into NATO's political sphere – if for no other reason than the necessity in democracies to exercise democratic political control over the military. Governments could not leave all the running to General Eisenhower, and it became more and more clear month by month that NATO's existing political machinery – the Council of Deputies sitting in London – was simply not adequate to cope effectively or coherently with the political decision-making required by the stream of recommendations, demands and requirements pouring out from SHAPE.

Throughout 1951, the Council of Deputies labored over political-military problems such as mutual-defense burden sharing, combined-force goals, and the inevitable and constant question of moving forward on Germany and the role of the Bonn Republic in European defense. The Council of Deputies also took two major decisions: first, to admit Greece and Turkey to the alliance, and second, to reorganize the political machinery with a new Permanent Council and a strong international secretariat under a secretary-general of high political standing and experience.

Foreign ministers of the alliance – now enlarged to fourteen member-states – gathered for a regular council meeting in Lisbon at the end of February 1952 that lasted five days. After dealing with a mass of important political decisions and directives to the military side of the alliance, they turned to the question of overhauling their civilian organization. A first choice for the new post of secretary-general was Sir Oliver Franks, widely known for his work on the Marshall Plan and as British ambassador to Washington. But Franks declined, wishing to return to academic life. The British then proposed Lord Ismay, at the time secretary of state for

Commonwealth relations in Winston Churchill's Conservative government, which had been formed only a few months before after a narrow
election victory over the Labour party. The choice, as in the case of
General Eisenhower, could scarcely have been better.

Patrick Lionel Hastings Ismay – known as "Pug" for reasons that
anyone who ever looked at his friendly pug-dog face would instantly
recognize – was one of the most remarkable subordinate soldier-
architects of victory in World War II. With extraordinary efficiency,
common sense, good humor and stamina, he served as personal Chief of
Staff to Churchill throughout the war – a buffer between Churchill and
his own Chiefs of Staff and the American Chiefs of Staff as well.
Throughout it all, he achieved the remarkable feat of personality and
intellect of never losing the respect or confidence of anyone.

Ismay began his military career in the First World War in the Camel
Corps in the Middle East. As a cavalry officer he moved on to serve for
years with the Indian Army. Returning to London in the 1930s he became
a staff officer on the Imperial Defense Committee, the coordinating body
within the Cabinet office responsible for military-political policy. By the
outbreak of World War II, Ismay was a major general when Churchill
moved him to the very center of military decision-making at the time of
the Battle of France. He was, in the words of a Cabinet minister, "the oil
in the can that kept the wheels of our bureaucracy turning."

Elevated to a peerage after the war, he came to NATO with greater
practical experience in administration and government, of the meshing of
military and civilian machinery, than any other one man on either side of
the Atlantic. Along with his instinctive feel for making bureaucracy work,
Pug Ismay had a wonderfully warm and friendly personality in his dealings
with everyone. He related to me that when Churchill sent for him to ask
him to give up his Cabinet post in London to take over the new job as
secretary-general of NATO, he said to him: "Pug, we are going to shend
you from sherving one government to sherving fourteen governments. I
hope that you will not always put ush at the bottom of the lisht."

Ismay was reluctant to accept the NATO post, but he could not and
would not refuse Churchill. And he would again be working with
Eisenhower, whom he knew well from the war years. As part of the
agreement by the French to accept a British secretary-general, the British

agreed to an urgent and fervent French plea to move the political headquarters of the Alliance from London to Paris. It was in any case a far more practical arrangement to have the political and military head-quarters within taxi distance of each other.

Under the new reorganization, the NATO secretary-general would preside over meetings of the Permanent Council of Ambassadors, who, almost without exception, have since come from the top diplomatic talent of each government. The secretary-general runs the NATO civilian bureaucracy and organizes and directs the whole complicated flow of NATO business and decision-making. Ever since Ismay, the post has always gone to a man who has served in a high Cabinet office with his own government, and is therefore able to deal as an "independent peer" with other foreign ministers or heads of government. Ismay set this high standard with easy effectiveness. Whatever his initial reluctance, he stayed on as secretary-general for five years. To him, as well as to Eisenhower, goes the credit for the solid organizational foundations on which NATO has rested and survived its own internal battles ever since.

In June of 1952, General Eisenhower gave up SHAPE command to return to the United States on a wave of primary election votes that would carry him with almost tidal force into the White House.

The era of the Founding Fathers of NATO was coming to an end. The great Ernest Bevin had died in April of 1951, worn out by his last turbulent five years. But he had lived to see the great strategic objective of his postwar diplomacy achieved – the United States tied firmly by alliance to the defense of Western Europe, and a Supreme Allied Headquarters established and operational only two weeks before his death. Senator Arthur Vandenberg died of cancer the same month as Bevin. General Marshall retired for the last time in September 1951 from the post of secretary of defense, to be succeeded for the remaining months of the Truman administration by the able and experienced Robert Lovett. By the time Lovett and Dean Acheson followed Harry Truman into retire-ment after the 1952 election, Robert Schuman was also gone, after a remarkable four years as the longest-lasting and most effective foreign minister of the Fourth Republic of France.

Eisenhower's choice as his new secretary of state was, of course, John

Foster Dulles, who had long been waiting in the wings as the Republican party's leading foreign-affairs specialist. Eisenhower and Dulles shared in a determination to keep the isolationist wing of the party at bay, and there was no question that a strong Atlantic Alliance would be in the forefront of their foreign policy.

Nevertheless, divergent trends in the application of that policy soon emerged in the Eisenhower years. On the one hand, Dulles embarked on an aggressive Cold War posture around the world – in particular with his efforts to encircle the Soviet Union and carry "containment" to the ultimate with projects on the NATO model like the Baghdad Pact in the Middle East and the Southeast Asia Treaty organization – CENTO and SEATO, neither of which exists any longer. Along with this were threats of "brinkmanship" and "rolling back" Communism.

On the other hand, Eisenhower, a fiscal conservative who had few illusions about the capacity of the military to discipline itself, and fewer inhibitions than most presidents about overruling military advice in defense matters, began to rein in military spending in the interests of combating inflation and maintaining a sound economy. In any case, the United States had been on an almost constant spending binge on behalf of itself and the free world from the launching of the Marshall Plan until the end of the Korean War. This of course had been of enormous benefit to America. But any period of national exertion almost always brings in its wake a period of rest and readjustment. The "Eisenhower pause" was politically popular in America after the Truman years.

But in order to back up Dulles's aggressive foreign policy while reining in military spending, the doctrine of "massive retaliation" was born, with its almost total reliance on the American nuclear superiority. For much-needed conventional forces in Europe, Dulles began to push with all the diplomatic muscle he could muster on the long-stalled question of West German rearmament.

For more than three years, the French had kept German rearmament completely tied up and bogged down in the endless diplomatic negotiations and political consideration of the Pleven Plan for creation of a European Defense Community. In December 1953, Dulles arrived in Paris for his second semiannual meeting with other NATO foreign ministers since taking office. He startled everyone when he gave vent at a press conference to his frustrations over the long political and diplomatic delay over the EDC treaty. He warned that there might have to be an "agonizing reappraisal" of America's commitment to NATO and the defense of Europe unless this was quickly resolved.

The Dutch, the Belgians, the Italians and Luxembourg were all ready to approve the treaty, but everything depended on the French.

In France, political opposition to the treaty, led by General Charles de Gaulle and the Communists, was so strong that no government had yet dared to ask for a National Assembly vote on ratification. Dulles had sent the veteran Ambassador David K. E. Bruce back to Paris on a special mission to push through approval of the treaty, but by 1954 the French government was concentrating totally on its diplomatic efforts to get out of the Indochina war. A conference to negotiate an end to the war convened in Geneva in April, and in May came the fall of Dien Bien Phu and the beginning of the end for the French Army. In June the government fell and Pierre Mendès-France came to power on an audacious pledge to get agreement on an armistice and withdrawal of French forces within one month.

To Dulles, any deal with the Communists was anathema, another Munich in the making, and he made his strong opposition to the French known by withdrawing from the Geneva negotiations. In the end, however, Mendès-France with determined diplomatic skill and the strong backing of British Foreign Secretary Anthony Eden negotiated a deal with the Soviet Union and the Red Chinese to partition Indochina on the 17th Parallel – Hanoi going to the Ho Chi Minh Communists with Saigon and South Vietnam remaining in democratic hands along with Cambodia and Laos at least for another two decades. It was a far better outcome than Dulles had believed possible.

Fresh from this diplomatic success, Mendès-France decided in August to dispose of the long-running issue of ratification of the European Defense Community treaty. He first asked for major revisions in the treaty to meet French political objections. When this was refused by the Dutch and the Belgians, Mendès-France announced that he would allow a free vote in the National Assembly to decide its fate. This clearly was tantamount to killing the treaty for good after almost four years of negotiation and politicking. He was impervious to fervent pleas from

Dulles, to whom he felt he owed no favors anyway. And so, in the last days of August 1954, the National Assembly held a final debate on the European army with Mendés-France sitting on the sidelines, and the treaty died when it failed to gain sufficient votes for passage.

The death of the European army treaty opened the first major diplomatic crisis in the Atlantic Alliance. Dulles and the European ideologues in the State Department were shattered. Both German rearmament and the forward march of European unity appeared to be going down the drain. Mendès-France had thwarted the secretary of state in Asia and Europe on two basic premises of his foreign policy, and the question now was, would "agonizing reappraisal" of the American commitment to Europe follow? Into this diplomatic breach stepped Anthony Eden.

While Dulles debated what he could possibly do to pick up the pieces, Eden set out from London a week after the National Assembly vote to tour European capitals with a bold and simple diplomatic solution to the German problem. Eden's proposal: Enlarge membership in the 1948 Brussels Treaty of Western Union to take in the two former enemies, West Germany and Italy, and at the same time admit the Bonn Republic to the Atlantic Alliance. Within the confines of these two treaties, the Germans would then be permitted to rearm with strict limitations (no ABC weapons – atomic, ballistic or chemical) and a condition that there be no re-creation of a German General Staff and that all German military forces would be totally integrated under the command and control of the NATO Supreme Allied Commander.

It is an interesting footnote to this history that the Eden solution to the crisis was in fact made possible by advice that the State Department's Jack Hickerson gave back in the early months of 1948. The Brussels Treaty, of course, was an enlargement of the original Franco-British Treaty of Dunkirk, signed by Ernest Bevin and Georges Bidault at the nadir of the postwar period in the awful winter of March 1947. But the Treaty of Dunkirk had been aimed solely at Germany, and possible revival of German aggression. When Bevin proposed in 1948 that Belgium, Holland and Luxembourg should be invited to join the Dunkirk Treaty, it was Hickerson who suggested that it should be rewritten into a general pledge against aggression instead of a specific pledge against Germany.

Hickerson pointed out in 1948 that one day the Europeans might want the Germans to join in a common European security agreement, and that time had certainly come. Accordingly, a further enlargement or expansion of the Brussels Treaty offered Eden an almost ready-made solution on how to proceed with the German question after the death of the EDC. As a fifty-year pact of alliance, the Brussels Treaty bound the Europeans even more closely than the NATO Treaty.

As Eden wound his way in early September of 1954 from London to Brussels, to The Hague, Bonn, Rome and finally Paris, he picked up fervent support for his solution at every stop along the way. By the time he reached Paris, the French were in a diplomatic corner – although the evidence was strong (I was then covering all this in Paris for the old *New York Herald Tribune*) that Mendès-France was relieved and ready to endorse the British initiative. In killing off the EDC treaty, he was not trying to kill dead the German rearmament question. He was too much of a realist for all that. Now on the diplomatic rebound, the French were much more amenable to a quick alternative solution to the crisis they had created than Dulles expected or believed possible.

Eden proposed and Mendès-France quickly agreed to a conference in London to draft a new version of the Brussels Treaty, taking in West Germany and Italy. The new treaty would also include a guarantee of the continued presence of the British Army of the Rhine in Germany. Canada and the United States joined in the London conference. The revised and renamed Western Union Treaty was signed in Paris on October 23, 1954.

In this sudden wave of success after failure, Mendès-France proved his statesmanship by going on to dispose of the contentious Saar question, returning the troublesome little valley to West Germany in a bilateral agreement with Chancellor Adenauer.

West Germany then became the fifteenth member of the Atlantic Alliance on May 5, 1955. At the same time, the residual occupation powers were dissolved, and soon after, the first soldiers of the new Bundeswehr went into uniform.

Two days after West Germany joined NATO, the Soviet Union under Nikita Khrushchev denounced its wartime friendship treaties with France and Great Britain, and followed this by announcing the conclusion of the Warsaw Pact. Five years after SHAPE Headquarters had been established, a Warsaw Pact unified military command for Eastern Europe was quickly formed under a Soviet marshal. These Soviet moves, however, were only the delayed expression of an existing reality.

The doctrine of "massive retaliation" as the basis of Western defense during the Eisenhower-Dulles years depended, of course, on American nuclear superiority over the Soviet Union and America's own invulnerability. Neither could last forever, and there were visible signs of the erosion of both well before the end of the decade. Massive retaliation also carried with it an increased United States hegemony over Europe, which the Europeans somewhat placidly accepted, since it lessened the burden of massive expenditure to build up conventional ground and air forces for Continental defense. In order to work, the threat of massive retaliation had to be made to seem real, and on at least two occasion Dulles had shown himself ready to play brinkmanship with nuclear weapons. The first such threat was conveyed through India to the Red Chinese and North Koreans ostensibly to prod the peace talks to end the Korean War. In 1954 Dulles then literally horrified the French and the British by offering to drop an atomic bomb on North Vietnam to support the beleagured French garrison at Dien Bien Phu, with the idea of forcing the Ho Chi Minh Communists to a quick peace in the Vietnam War. Whether Eisenhower would ever have approved using the bomb in either case is highly doubtful, but certainly both the French and British governments utterly rejected Dulles's idea of atomizing Hanoi.

In any case, however secure Europe might feel under the American nuclear umbrella, this brinksmanship increased the unease that everything depended on America's finger on the trigger. Moreover, American hegemony certainly was bringing with it a loss of Europe's old independence to look after its own affairs – both within its own confines and in the rest of the world. This situation was driven home with brutal clarity in the second great crisis in the Atlantic Alliance – the Suez War.

The secret collusion in November of 1956 by which France and Britain joined the Israelis in mounting an attack on Egypt, ostensibly to restore the Suez Canal to Anglo-French control after it had been nationalized by Egyptian President Gamal Abdel Nasser, was one of the most bizarre episodes of the postwar era. The Suez War broke out, moreover, just as Khrushchev and the Red Army were crushing the Hungarian uprising against Communist rule. President Eisenhower was in the final stages of an election campaign in which a peaceful world had been a major theme. He and Dulles rounded on the British and the French with thundering denunciations and a veto against their Allies in the U.N. Security Council. By the time the crisis blew itself out, Anthony Eden had resigned as prime minister, a shattered man. Anti-American feeling in both Britain and France reached a fever pitch never seen before or since.

But in the aftermath, the British reacted one way and the French another – each reflecting past precepts. When Harold Macmillan took over from Eden at No. 10 Downing Street, he was determined that never again must the British allow themselves, and Europe, to become isolated from the United States, and must never risk such a sundering of the Atlantic Alliance. He therefore set about with almost overweening anxiety and activity to reactivate his old wartime friendship with Eisenhower, and make sure that the whole world knew that the "special relationship" was alive and well and the great central political element within the Atlantic Alliance.

The French, on the other hand, took the view that in light of the American behavior it was more important than ever to build up Europe. At once they stirred into action to negotiate the Treaty of Rome that created the European Common Market on top of the European Coal and Steel Community. Again the British elected to stay out – preoccupied as they were with the "special relationship."

The French government, under Socialist Premier Guy Mollet, also took the momentous decision in the wake of the Suez War that France must have its own nuclear weapons. The French were now well into their Algerian War, and they felt after Suez that there was ample evidence that French interests, European interests, were not always going to be the same as American interests – and to defend one's own interests would require possession of the ultimate weaponry of military power. France was a Gaullist country well before General Charles de Gaulle returned to power.

Then in October of 1957, one year after the Suez War, the Soviet Union launched the first *Sputnik* orbiting satellite into outer space. At a time of declining United States conventional military strength, the beeping signals from *Sputnik* circling the earth were also saying loud and clear that the era of American nuclear and technological superiority on which massive retaliation rested was coming to an end. It also reinforced France's determination to become a nuclear power.

General de Gaulle's return to power in May of 1958 superficially revived an "old comrades" wartime relationship with Eisenhower and Macmillan from the days of the North African campaign in 1943. But there was nothing sentimental about de Gaulle or his view of the Anglo-Saxons. "France will be in NATO less and less," he told Macmillan in their first conversation when he returned, and he meant every word of it. Before the year was out, he addressed letters to his old comrades proposing that since all three had global interests and nuclear weapons they should form a "tripartite directorate" for global strategy and policy going beyond NATO. In effect, de Gaulle was asking for veto power over American nuclear weapons.

"As I expected, the two recipients of my memorandum replied evasively," he later wrote. De Gaulle thus provided himself with one of his excuses eventually to withdraw France from the integrated NATO military command in 1966.

The Eisenhower presidency came to an end, therefore, with a sluggish economy, a visible downturn in American military strength, the Soviet Union increasingly bellicose under Khrushchev and out in front first into space, and General de Gaulle increasingly challenging the picture of a harmonious Atlantic Alliance. From the outset of negotiations for the North Atlantic Treaty, there had always been a Great Dichotomy between the British Atlanticist approach and the French European approach. This was now growing, along with all the other problems that John F. Kennedy inherited when he took office as President of the United States in January 1961, the youngest president in American history.

Under Kennedy, the doctrine of "flexible response" replaced massive retaliation, and an up cycle for America and NATO quickly began. No longer would there be any automatic use of nuclear weapons if NATO was attacked. Conventional attack would be met with conventional response, and any resort to nuclear weapons would be carefully controlled – the American finger on the nuclear trigger, of course. Already under Eisenhower the first deployment of new tactical nuclear weapons in

Europe had begun, and under Kennedy this would increase, along with a new buildup of conventional forces. Europe, in particular West Germany, would be pushed and prodded into greater efforts. Once again the Soviet Union came conveniently to America's assistance in galvanizing this new buildup.

Khrushchev had already broken a moratorium with President Eisenhower on nuclear testing, and now the Soviets followed up their first *Sputnik* by orbiting the first man into space. Flexing this new muscle, Khrushchev was threatening to do what Stalin had failed to do—and liquidate the Western Allied presence in Berlin.

In July 1961, after a brutal confrontation with Khrushchev over Berlin at a summit meeting in Vienna, President Kennedy announced a $3.2 billion increase in American defense spending, an intake of an additional 217,000 men into the U.S. armed forces, and the dispatch of additional combat troops and logistical personnel to Europe. The Soviet response came on August 12, when the East German Volkspolizei sealed off the sector boundary dividing Berlin and began construction of the infamous Berlin wall to halt the hemorrhage of refugees fleeing to the West. This, at least, was a crisis to unite rather than divide the NATO Alliance, with memories still fresh of the days of Stalin's blockade of the city and the Berlin airlift little more than a decade before.

This new Berlin crisis, however, stopped short of another full-scale blockade, and the East-West confrontation was finally resolved not in Berlin but in Cuba. In October of 1962, when the Cuban missile crisis ended in an eyeball-to-eyeball threat of nuclear war and a Soviet climbdown, the Berlin crisis also abruptly fizzled out. Soviet threats and bluster against the city faded like a pop-music radio station going off the air at midnight.

On the rebound from Berlin and Cuba, the United States and the Soviet Union then signed their first bilateral agreement in the field of nuclear arms control – a treaty to end nuclear testing above ground in the earth's atmosphere.

President Kennedy drew one set of political conclusions from these events, but in France, General Charles de Gaulle drew very different conclusions. For Kennedy it had all been a great success for American hegemonic leadership of the Atlantic Alliance, and was a clear demonstration of the importance of nuclear power and the fact that there was only one finger on the nuclear trigger. But de Gaulle saw all this as the end of the Cold War, and a diplomatic opportunity to break out from American hegemony. Above all, it reinforced his own determination to ensure that France would be an independent nuclear power.

General de Gaulle's policy of "being in NATO less and less" had already become quite apparent to the other Allies. He had refused to allow American tactical nuclear bombs to be stationed in France, with the result that the U.S. Air Force had already pulled out of seven French NATO air bases and redeployed to fields in Britain and West Germany. The French Navy had been withdrawn from NATO command in the Mediterranean, ostensibly because of the requirements of the Algerian War, and the French Atlantic Fleet later followed. The semiannual NATO meetings of foreign ministers were increasingly marked by the most petty, contentious wrangling with the French over every word in every final communiqué, as the French fought to expunge any hint or suggestion that their foreign policy was in any way subordinated to the common interests of the alliance. "To cooperate is to lose one's independence," de Gaulle once wrote on a minute prepared by one of the subordinates in the Quai d'Orsay.

In January of 1963, de Gaulle struck decisively against Britain and the United States in a famous press conference. First he pronounced a one-man veto against Great Britain's joining the European Common Market after well over a year of negotiations. Next he contemptuously rejected an offer by President Kennedy to give France the American Polaris nuclear missiles for their submarines if they would place them all under NATO control, and join a proposed NATO multilateral nuclear naval force that was then the favorite project of the State Department integrationists. They apparently had forgotten de Gaulle's fierce opposition to the European army idea ten years earlier.

In November of 1963, President Kennedy was assassinated in Dallas, and despite de Gaulle's attitude, there was a deep and genuine outpouring of French sentiment for America. But the general scarcely paused in his own stride to rid himself and France of the supposed enshacklement of American hegemony – nuclear, economic, political, whether real or imaginary in de Gaulle's mind.

In March of 1966 he was ready for his final blow. Elected to a second seven-year term of office, he was planning a visit to the Soviet Union. He intended it to be a breakthrough for his foreign policy aim of some Pan-European détente with harmony from the Atlantic to the Urals, accompanied by a diminution of the two power blocs, NATO in the West and the Warsaw Pact in the East. But if he was going to move to withdraw from NATO in furtherance of this aim, he clearly had to act before he went to Moscow – not after he had talked with Leonid Brezhnev and the successors to the deposed Khrushchev. He had to show independence between East and West.

On the weekend of March 7, 1966, de Gaulle retired to his country home as was his custom. There at his desk in his study looking out on the farmlands and countryside he wrote out in longhand, in the regal style of a sovereign, personal letters to President Lyndon B. Johnson and government heads of Britain, West Germany and Canada. The Italian government head, in a typical de Gaulle touch, was sent only a typed letter. To each he wrote, "France proposes to recover the entire exercise of her sovereignty over her territory, presently impaired by the permanent presence of Allied military elements, or in the use which is made of her airspace."

There was no offer or suggestion of discussion or negotiation, and certainly with de Gaulle there was no recourse. When he returned to Paris on Monday, the ambassadors of all the NATO countries were summoned to the Quai d'Orsay to be handed a statement of actions being taken by the French government in accordance with de Gaulle's decisions. All French officers were ordered that very day to close up their desks and withdraw from SHAPE and other subordinate military headquarters of the alliance. All French forces in West Germany, all French air and naval units ceased to be under NATO integrated commands.

General de Gaulle gave his Allies one year to get out of France. SHAPE Headquarters was told to move, and the United States was asked to withdraw and close down supply lines, communication facilities and bases in France. Five Franco-American bilateral defense arrangements were abrogated unilaterally by de Gaulle. But, the general wrote to President Johnson, France would remain a member of the alliance "except in the event of developments which might occur in the course of the next three years to change the fundamental factors of East-West relations."

De Gaulle apparently was hoping for big changes from his visit to the Soviet Union. Instead, in August of 1968, Soviet troops moved into Prague to crush the brief Czech efforts at reform to give Communism a human face. On the twentieth anniversary of the NATO treaty in April 1969, there was not the slightest suggestion that France might ever leave the alliance.

So the Americans departed, and NATO decamped without argument or ceremony to new permanent headquarters in Belgium – the political headquarters on the outskirts of Brussels and the military headquarters to the south near the city of Mons. After the shock of de Gaulle's action wore off, it was at least clear that the general had removed his own very large thorn from NATO's side. It was the final analysis of Harlan Cleveland, United States Ambassador to NATO at the time:

> In retrospect the significant thing about the withdrawal of France from the NATO defense system is that it was not very significant. It did not destroy the Alliance – if that was the idea. It did not set France up as the Western European partner best suited to make peace with the Russians – if that was the idea. It did not remove France from dependence on the U.S. nuclear umbrella – if that was the idea. It did not even keep de Gaulle in office. The net effects were to accelerate the reduction of French influence in Europe, in favor of the Germans, and to prod the other Western Allies into changing their strategy and improving their cohesion. These can hardly have been the results consciously desired by a Gaullist France.

By the mid-1960s, the United States was increasingly bogged down militarily, economically and politically in the unhappy quagmire of the Vietnam War. In May of 1968, talks began in Paris to arrange a cease-fire, but it would take four more long and wasteful years before an agreement could be signed. Meanwhile General de Gaulle faded from the French scene when he lost a national referendum vote in April 1969. By this time, a new impetus had taken hold in both Europe and the United States toward East-West détente and diplomatic accommodation with the Soviet Union.

In Europe this was led by West German Chancellor Willy Brandt, who deftly usurped the initiative to the east that de Gaulle had sought to exercise when he pulled France out of the NATO military structure. But when Brandt launched his *ostpolitik* policy of opening up the Bonn government's long freeze on diplomatic relations with Eastern Europe, he had much more to offer the Soviets than de Gaulle had had. On the Soviet side, Leonid Brezhnev was more than ready to try to wipe away the stain and shame of intervention in Czechoslovakia, and find some accommodation with Western Europe.

Lyndon Johnson too began reaching out to the Soviet Union, to help end the Vietnam War and then to lay the groundwork for negotiations to put some cap on the nuclear arms race. In fact, the first Strategic Arms Limitation Talks (SALT) would have begun in the final months of 1968 during Johnson's presidency, had the Red Army not rolled its tanks into Prague. But when President Richard M. Nixon then took office in 1969, he promptly picked up on the Johnson initiative, and the SALT negotiations began in Helsinki in November.

From then on, détente diplomacy began to move forward between East and West. It produced in rapid order in the first half of the 1970s:

A friendship treaty in 1970 between Bonn and Moscow, followed by agreements with Yugoslavia, Poland, Hungary, Romania, Bulgaria and eventually East Germany and Czechoslovakia; in 1971 a Big Four agreement by the U.S., Britain, France and the Soviet Union, ending twenty-five years of postwar conflict and confrontation over the status of Berlin; in 1972, the first superpower SALT agreement, putting a ceiling on strategic nuclear arsenals, along with an antiballistic missile treaty; historic visits by Willy Brandt to East Germany and Richard Nixon to Red China; a cease-fire agreement and withdrawal of American forces at last from South Vietnam, however fragile the temporary peace then turned out to be; the Vladivistok agreement between President Ford and Brezhnev in 1974 to lay the groundwork for a SALT II negotiation; and then as a climax of the détente period, the signing in Helsinki in 1975 by the heads of government of thirty-five states – every state except Albania – of the Agreements on Security and Cooperation in Europe – the closest that Europe is ever likely to get to any formal liquidation of World War II.

By the time the Vietnam cease-fire agreement was signed in 1972, President Nixon was facing much the same domestic economic problems that President Eisenhower had faced in the aftermath of the Korean War – a heavy national debt, inflation, a weakened dollar and a compelling need to rein in national spending. As a culmination of these pressures, the United States had been forced to abandon the Bretton Woods agreement to convert dollars into gold, devalue the dollar and allow the gold price to rise freely. Moreover, with the Vietnam War over, the United States was turning its back on military involvements, and Senator Mike Mansfield was regularly introducing a resolution at the start of each new congressional session to draw down United States forces in Europe and let the Europeans pick up the burden of their own defense.

Thus, the up cycle for America and NATO that began under Kennedy in 1961 now played out on the downside in the final days of Richard Nixon and the presidency of Gerald Ford.

When President Jimmy Carter took office after the brief Ford presidency, in January 1977, there was already an overwhelming accumulation of evidence that political détente with the Soviet Union was not being matched in the least by any military détente or restraint in the Soviet military buildup. The emergence of the Soviet Navy as a global "blue water" force, after its humiliation in the Cuban missile crisis, was clear for all to see. In conventional forces, there had been a vast and steady qualitative improvement in weapons, training, standardization and organization under Soviet supervision and command throughout the entire Warsaw Pact. The first SALT Treaty had provided a rough parity of superpower strategic nuclear forces, but with the heavy throw weight of its intercontinental arsenal, and in sea-launched submarine missiles, the Soviet Union was now able to invade American skies at will.

Finally, most ominously for Europe, deployment had begun of a new class of Soviet medium-range nuclear missiles targeted, eventually, on every capital and every major military installation of the NATO Allies – the SS-20. It was a weapon for which there was then no answer except American strategic retaliation from afar.

Under Nixon and Ford, Secretary of State Henry A. Kissinger sought to shore up the American strategic position with a combination of détente diplomacy and arms-control agreements backed up by a reliance once again on a temporary American technological advantage. The new MIRV multiple warheads for long-range missiles became operational, and this would be followed by the development of land-based and sea-launched low-flying cruise missiles. But as in the days of massive retaliation, it was a given fact that no technological advantage is permanent in the nuclear arms race.

And so, under President Carter a new up cycle for America and the NATO Alliance began – hesitating and confused along with so much else in the Carter presidency, but nevertheless an effort to restore a changing military balance.

At the outset of his presidency in the spring of 1977, Carter held a summit meeting in London with heads of government of the fifteen Allies (Spain was not yet a member) and persuaded the Europeans to fix a common target of a 3 percent annual increase in NATO defense spending. If the target was never consistently met except by a few of the Allies, it nevertheless had some reinvigorating effect on NATO's defense effort in the conventional field in the face of what clearly was happening on the Soviet side. Meanwhile, Carter's new secretary of state, Cyrus R. Vance, sought to pick up where Ford and Kissinger had left off, and press forward with negotiations on a second strategic arms limitation treaty.

But Carter's sense of leadership was muddled and uncertain – particularly his handling of the question of deploying the neutron bomb with the NATO Allies. This weapon, which would kill by radiation rather than destroy by blast, was supposed to counter tank and infantry forces to help restore the conventional tactical balance in Europe. But instead of making up his own mind whether to go ahead with its development, Carter first asked the Allies, in effect, to ask him for its deployment. Perhaps because of the hegemonic nature of American military power in the alliance, it has always been easier for NATO governments simply to *accept* an American decision after consultations rather than take the lead and *ask* for one. President Carter was trying something new – to lead NATO from behind.

Nevertheless, both Helmut Schmidt in West Germany and James Callaghan in Great Britain were willing to stick their necks out to support deployment of the neutron bomb to offset the growing menace of Soviet conventional forces and tactical nuclear weapons. With all this NATO debate going on in public, the Soviet Union of course waded in with a major propaganda campaign against the neutron bomb. Then suddenly, at the last minute, Carter changed his mind, and announced he was dropping the whole project.

Not only did he leave his principal Allies high and dry and fuming. He also provided the Soviet Union with a free propaganda victory. He was seen to have backed down under Soviet pressure.

From this fiasco with NATO, the Carter administration sought to recover on two fronts. First it launched a "two-way street" policy, which was a genuine effort to improve both the balance of transatlantic military procurement and at the same time the standardization of weapons and multilateral production and procurement of military hardware in Europe. Second, and more visibly, the United States began lengthy negotiations within NATO on a major agreement to deploy the new generation of American intermediate-range missiles in Europe to counter the Soviet SS-20s.

The decision to deploy 548 American cruise and Pershing II missiles in Europe was one of the most difficult to negotiate and most divisive, politically, to carry out in the history of the alliance. Not all the Allies were expected or required to accept the weapons on their territory, but a key to the agreement was that all joined in contributing to common infrastructure funds to pay the multibillion-dollar cost of the program.

In May of 1979 President Carter signed the SALT II Treaty for a further cap on the arms race with Brezhnev in Vienna. In December 1979 at a meeting of NATO foreign ministers in Brussels, the agreement to deploy the cruise and Pershing missiles was signed.

Two weeks later, Soviet troops moved into Afghanistan, and the détente era ended with a bang.

Thus a pattern was again repeating itself. The first "NATO cycle" was set off by the Soviet test explosion of the atomic bomb in 1949 followed by the Korean War in 1950, ending on the downside in the Eisenhower presidency. The second cycle was set off by *Sputnik*, Soviet resumption of nuclear testing and the threat to Berlin at the start of the Kennedy presidency, and ended on the downside in détente in the 1970s.

The third cycle began under President Carter, in response to the Soviet conventional buildup and its growing nuclear superiority with massive deployment of the SS-20 under way against Europe – all of this culminating, then, in the Soviet invasion of Afghanistan in 1980. The up cycle was therefore already under way when President Reagan took office in January of 1981 and launched the United States at once into the greatest military spending binge in the peacetime history of the world, coupled with Cold War rhetoric that at times would have made John Foster Dulles sound timid.

Whatever the rhetoric, the United States was committed under the 1979 agreement with its NATO Allies on deployment of the cruise and Pershing missiles to negotiate with the Soviet Union on curbs on nuclear weapons. Under this so-called "two-track NATO decision," negotiation and deployment were to go hand in hand. Therefore talks got under way in Geneva once again in September of 1982, when the American side produced its "zero option" proposal. It called on the Soviet Union to withdraw all of its SS-20s from deployment against Europe, in return for which NATO would cancel its plans to deploy the American missiles as a counterforce.

At the time it was proposed, the zero option looked more like a maneuver by hard-liners in the Reagan administration to ensure that there never would be any agreement with the Soviet Union at all. And indeed, the negotiations did turn into a sterile stalemate while Leonid Brezhnev died, Yuri Andropov died, and finally Konstantin Chernenko died and the last of the Soviet Old Guard leadership was gone.

In the meantime, the NATO countries were racked by anti–nuclear missile demonstrations both peaceful and violent as the date for the start of deployment of the American weapons approached. Dire warnings again were hurled from Moscow – as they had been at every other decisive moment in NATO history from the signing of the treaty. When the first missiles then began arriving secretly and simultaneously in Britain, West Germany and Italy late in November 1983, the Soviets responded with their ultimate diplomatic weapon. They abruptly broke off the nuclear-arms talks in Geneva, and the long-running negotiations that had been going on in Vienna since 1973 between NATO and the Warsaw Pact on reducing conventional forces in Europe. A long freeze of almost total inactivity in East-West relations set in during 1984.

In January of 1985 came the first signs of a thaw. The Soviet boycott of the Geneva arms talks had not halted or impeded the continuous buildup of the new American missiles in Western Europe. The only recourse for the Soviets was a return to the negotiating table. At a Geneva meeting between Secretary of State George P. Shultz and his aging opposite, Andrei Gromyko, it was agreed to reopen the nuclear-arms negotiations. Two months later in March, just as the negotiators arrived in Geneva to get down to work, came the most important and far-reaching break-through of all – the death of Chernenko, which brought Mikhail Gorbachev to power in the Kremlin.

Before the year was out, the outlook for agreement was transformed when Gorbachev suddenly and surprisingly accepted the American proposal of zero option – to eliminate all intermediate-range weapons on both sides. On December 7, 1987, the first superpower agreement to reduce, and not merely limit, nuclear arms was signed in Washington by Reagan and Gorbachev.

The INF treaty has a significance for NATO that goes beyond its military terms. It not only reduces the threat of war. In a broader sense it constitutes Soviet acknowledgment that war is not any realistic "final option" of Soviet policy or political strategy, if indeed it ever was. But it goes without saying that this has only come about as a result of forty years of sustained defense effort in the West, whatever the ups and downs have been, and it is equally obvious and self-evident that this could change without notice unless a healthy East-West military balance continues to be maintained.

Each of the earlier up-and-down cycles of the American effort in NATO also produced useful agreements with the Soviet Union along the way, but this third cycle of the Reagan years produced not merely agreement but fundamental change. The INF treaty is a beginning, but only a beginning, of what now can be and it is hoped will be a long and careful building of East-West trust in place of sterile hostility and confrontation.

The great simple historic truth at the end of the first forty years of the North Atlantic Treaty is that the policy of containment has worked, and the West has prevailed.

"The purpose of containment," wrote George Kennan of his famous 1947 article in *Foreign Affairs Quarterly* that helped give birth to the

NATO Treaty, "was not to perpetuate the status quo to which the military operations and political arrangements of World War II had led; it was to tide us over a difficult time and bring us to a point where we could discuss effectively with the Russians the drawbacks and dangers this status quo involved and to arrange with them for its peaceful replacement by a sounder one."

That "difficult time" lasted far, far longer than even the farsighted Kennan could have predicted, and most of that time it seemed as if the Cold War in some form would be permanent and endure forever. Throughout it all, the North Atlantic Treaty – opposed by Kennan at the time of its negotiation – has been the prime instrument of containment. Indeed, without NATO the Soviet threat to Western Europe, and by extension to the rest of the world, could never have been contained at all.

Soviet power "bears within itself the seeds of its own decay, and the sprouting of these seeds is well advanced," Kennan wrote in his "X" article in 1947.

It would be an exaggeration to say that American behavior unassisted and alone could exercise a power of life and death over the Communist movement and bring about the early fall of Soviet power in Russia. But the United States has it in its power to increase enormously the strains under which Soviet policy must operate, to force upon the Kremlin a far greater degree of moderation than it has had to observe.

It has taken four decades of containment, of unremitting strain in the Soviet economy, of the long slow passing of the direct heirs and apostles of Joseph Stalin, to bring the Soviet Union finally to recognize and acknowledge the "seeds of its own decay" in its economic system and its Marxist-Leninist foreign policy as pursued by Stalin. This acceptance is the great achievement of Mikhail Gorbachev. However long he lasts he has changed history simply by acknowledging reality instead of trying to lead his country into yet another sterile and useless and costly round of political and military cavalry charges against the barricades of containment. His reforms of *glasnost* and *perestroika*, the economic survival of the Soviet empire in its eighth decade and beyond, require peace and stability and equitable relations with the rest of the world and the flourishing economies of Western Europe in particular. He needs to practice moderation to survive.

Gorbachev has brought at last not merely the opportunity but the *necessity*, as Kennan foresaw, "to discuss effectively with the Russians the drawbacks and the dangers that the status quo involved and to arrange with them for its peaceful replacement by a sounder one." To achieve a sounder, more equitable, more open and acceptable status quo than the division of Europe in 1945 – that will be NATO's permanent agenda and its *raison d'être* for the next forty years.

The INF treaty and the withdrawal of these nuclear weapons on both sides is therefore a first step in this adjustment of the status quo. Logically, this should be followed by a carefully negotiated reduction of conventional forces, or even unilateral reductions by each side in some coordinated and parallel understanding that need not require a complicated agreement.

Logically, there should be a reduction in the size of the American contribution to the security of Western Europe, and some shift in the burden to the prosperous and stable NATO European states themselves. If 140,000 American troops kept the peace in Germany during the Berlin blockade, are 385,000 needed, still, forty years later?

Logically, there should be some kind of readjustment in the hegemonic weight of the presence of the superpowers in Europe both East and West. In Eastern Europe this would mean greater ideological and political independence for the countries of the Warsaw Pact to manage their own affairs and develop their own political and economic ties and relations with Western Europe.

On the NATO side, this adjustment would mean the Europeans themselves taking greater responsibilities for their own security in partnership with America, with a much more cohesive and coherent "European identity" in common defense and collective involvement in international diplomacy and world responsibilities. Europe's habit of dependency that grew out of the aftermath of World War II, the Marshall Plan and the nuclear age cannot go on without adjustment forever.

The North Atlantic Treaty has provided Europe with its longest period of peace and its greatest period of economic expansion, stability and well-being in all its history. After forty years, there is no doubt at all anywhere that the cohesion and vitality of the NATO Alliance is as essential to peace, security and world stability as it was in 1949. In this new era of adjustment of the status quo, and of increasing hope for a peaceful and continuous evolution of East-West trust and understanding, NATO is more fundamental than it has ever been to the collective foreign policy and diplomacy and security of its sixteen member states, and so it will remain.

The North Atlantic Treaty

Washington, D.C., April 4, 1949

The Parties to this Treaty reaffirm their faith in the purposes and principles of the Charter of the United Nations and their desire to live in peace with all people and all governments.

They are determined to safeguard the freedom, common heritage and civilisation of their peoples, founded on the principles of democracy, individual liberty and the rule of law.

They seek to promote stability and well-being in the North Atlantic area.

They are resolved to unite their efforts for collective defence and for the preservation of peace and security.

They therefore agree to this North Atlantic Treaty:

Article 1

The Parties undertake, as set forth in the Charter of the United Nations, to settle any international dispute in which they may be involved by peaceful means in such a manner that international peace and security and justice are not endangered, and to refrain in their international relations from the threat or use of force in any manner inconsistent with the purposes of the United Nations.

Article 2

The Parties will contribute toward the further development of peaceful and friendly international relations by strengthening their free institutions, by bringing about a better understanding of the principles upon which these institutions are founded, and by promoting conditions of stability and well-being. They will seek to eliminate conflict in their international economic policies and will encourage economic collaboration between any or all of them.

Article 3

In order more effectively to achieve the objectives of this Treaty, the Parties, separately and jointly, by means of continuous and effective self-help and mutual aid, will maintain and develop their individual and collective capacity to resist armed attack.

Article 4

The Parties will consult together whenever, in the opinion of any of them, the territorial integrity, political independence or security of any of the Parties is threatened.

Article 5

The Parties agree that an armed attack against one or more of them in Europe or North America shall be considered an attack against them all and consequently they agree that, if such an armed attack occurs, each of them, in exercise of the right of individual or collective self-defence recognised by Article 51 of the Charter of the United Nations, will assist the Party or Parties so attacked by taking forthwith, individually and in concert with the other Parties, such action as it deems necessary, including the use of armed force, to restore and maintain the security of the North Atlantic Area.

Any such armed attack and all measures taken as a result thereof shall immediately be reported to the Security Council. Such measures shall be terminated when the Security Council has taken the measures necessary to restore and maintain international peace and security.

Article 6[1]

For the purpose of Article 5 an armed attack on one or more of the Parties is deemed to include an armed attack on the territory of any of the Parties in Europe or North America, on the Algerian Departments of France,[2] on the occupation

[1] The definition of the territories to which Article 5 applies has been revised by Article 2 of the Protocol to the North Atlantic Treaty on the accession of Greece and Turkey.

[2] On January 16, 1963, the North Atlantic Council heard a declaration by the French Representative who recalled that by the vote on self-determination on July 1, 1962, the Algerian people had pronounced itself in favour of the independence of Algeria in co-operation with France. In consequence, the President of the French Republic had on July 3, 1962, formally recognised the independence of Algeria. The result was that the "Algerian departments of France" no longer existed as such, and that at the same time the fact that they were mentioned in the North Atlantic Treaty had no longer any bearing.

Following this statement the Council noted that insofar as the former Algerian Departments of France were concerned, the relevant clauses of this Treaty had become inapplicable as from July 3, 1962.

forces of any Party in Europe, on the islands under the jurisdiction of any Party in the North Atlantic area north of the Tropic of Cancer or on the vessels or aircraft in this area of any of the Parties.

Article 7

This Treaty does not affect, and shall not be interpreted as affecting in any way the rights and obligations under the Charter of the Parties which are members of the United Nations, or the primary responsibility of the Security Council for the maintenance of international peace and security.

Article 8

Each Party declares that none of the international engagements now in force between it and any other of the Parties or any third State is in conflict with the provisions of this Treaty, and undertakes not to enter into any international engagement in conflict with this Treaty.

Article 9

The Parties hereby establish a Council, on which each of them shall be represented, to consider matters concerning the implementation of this Treaty. The Council shall be so organised as to be able to meet promptly at any time. The Council shall set up such subsidiary bodies as may be necessary; in particular it shall establish immediately a defence committee which shall recommend measures for the implementation of Articles 3 and 4.

Article 10

The Parties may, by unanimous agreement, invite any other European State in position to further the principles of this Treaty and to contribute to the security of the North Atlantic area to accede to this Treaty. Any State so invited may become a Party to the Treaty by depositing its instrument of accession with the Government of the United States of America. The Government of the United States of America will inform each of the Parties of the deposit of each such instrument of accession.

Article 11

This Treaty shall be ratified and its provisions carried out by the Parties in accordance with their respective constitutional processes. The instruments of ratification shall be deposited as soon as possible with the Government of the

United States of America, which will notify all the other signatories of each deposit. The Treaty shall enter into force between the States which have ratified it as soon as the ratifications of the majority of the signatories, including the ratifications of Belgium, Canada, France, Luxembourg, the Netherlands, the United Kingdom and the United States, have been deposited and shall come into effect with respect to other States on the date of the deposit of their ratifications.

Article 12

After the Treaty has been in force for ten years, or at any time thereafter, the Parties shall, if any of them so requests, consult together for the purpose of reviewing the Treaty, having regard for the factors then affecting peace and security in the North Atlantic area, including the development of universal as well as regional arrangements under the Charter of the United Nations for the maintenance of international peace and security.

Article 13

After the Treaty has been in force for twenty years, any Party may cease to be a Party one year after its notice of denunciation has been given to the Government of the United States of America, which will inform the Governments of the other Parties of the deposit of each notice of denunciation.

Article 14

This Treaty, of which the English and French texts are equally authentic, shall be deposited in the archives of the Government of the United States of America. Duly certified copies will be transmitted by that Government to the Governments of other signatories.

Done at Washington, the fourth day of April, 1949

For the Kingdom of Belgium:
Pour le Royaume de Belgique:

For Canada:
Pour le Canada:

For the Kingdom of Denmark:
Pour le Royaume du Danemark:

For France:
Pour la France:

For Iceland:
Pour l'Islande:

[signatures]

For Italy:
Pour l'Italie:

[signatures]

For the Grand Duchy of Luxembourg:
Pour le Grand Duché de Luxembourg:

[signatures]

For the Kingdom of the Netherlands:
Pour le Royaume des Pays-Bas:

[signatures]

For the Kingdom of Norway:
Pour le Royaume de Norvège:

[signature: Halvard M. Lange]

[signature: Wilhelm Munthe Morgenstierne]

For Portugal:
Pour le Portugal:

[signatures: José Caeiro da Mata; Pedro Theotonio Pereira]

For the United Kingdom of Great Britain and Northern Ireland:
Pour le Royaume-Uni de Grand-Bretagne et d'Irlande du Nord:

[signatures: Ernest Bevin; Oliver Franks]

For the United States of America:
Pour les Etats-Unis d'Amérique:

[signature: Dean Acheson]

APPENDIX B
The Vandenberg Resolution

U.S. Senate Resolution 239

80th Congress, 2nd Session, 11th June 1948

Whereas peace with justice and the defence of human rights and fundamental freedoms require international co-operation through more effective use of the United Nations: Therefore be it *Resolved*, That the Senate reaffirm the policy of the United States to achieve international peace and security through the United Nations so that armed force shall not be used except in the common interest, and that the President be advised of the sense of The Senate that this Government, by constitutional process, should particularly pursue the following objectives within the United Nations Charter:

1. Voluntary agreement to remove the veto from all questions involving pacific settlements of international disputes and situations, and from the admission of new members.

2. Progressive development of regional and other collective arrangements for individual and collective self-defence in accordance with the purposes, principles, and provisions of the charter.

3. Association of the United States, by constitutional process, with such regional and other collective arrangements as are based on continuous and effective self-help and mutual aid, and as affect its national security.

4. Contributing to the maintenance of peace by making clear its determination to exercise the right of individual or collective self-defence under Article 51 should any armed attack occur affecting its national security.

5. Maximum efforts to obtain agreements to provide the United Nations with armed forces as provided by the Charter, and to obtain agreement among member nations upon universal regulation and reduction of armaments under adequate and dependable guaranty against violation.

6. If necessary, after adequate effort towards strengthening the United Nations, review of the Charter at an appropriate time by a General Conference called under Article 109 or by the General Assembly.

Sources and Selected Bibliography

The official State Department papers relating to the negotiation of the North Atlantic Treaty are contained in *Foreign Relations of the United States* for 1948, Vol. III, *Western Europe*; 1949, Vol. IV, *Western Europe*; 1950, Vol. 1, *National Security Affairs*, and Vol. III, *Western Europe*; and 1951, Vol. 1, *National Security Affairs*.

The British Foreign Office official history of the treaty negotiations, written in 1949 by Nicholas Henderson, was published in 1982 after its release under Britain's thirty-year rule.

The complete war correspondence between President Roosevelt and Prime Minister Winston Churchill was published by Princeton University Press, edited by Warren F. Kemball, in three volumes in 1984.

An unpublished personal memoir written by the late Theodore Achilles, dealing in part with the NATO negotiations, was made available to the author by the Atlantic Institute in Washington, D.C.

The NATO Information Service has published *NATO Basic Documents* and *NATO Facts and Figures*.

Acheson, Dean. *Present at the Creation*. New York: W. W. Norton & Co., 1969.
———. *Sketches from Life of Men I Have Known*. New York: Harper & Brothers, 1959.
Barnet, Richard J. *The Alliance*. New York: Simon & Shuster, 1983.
Bohlen, Charles E. *The Transformation of American Foreign Policy*. New York: W. W. Norton & Co., 1969.
———. *Witness to History*. New York: W. W. Norton & Co., 1973.
Bullock, Alan. *Ernest Bevin, Foreign Secretary*. London: Heinemann, 1983.
Byrnes, James F. *Speaking Frankly*. New York: Harper & Bros., 1947.
Calleo, David P. *Beyond American Hegemony: The Future of the Western Alliance*. New York: Basic Books, for the Twentieth Century Fund, 1987.

Charlton, Michael. *The Eagle and the Small Birds*. London: BBC Press, 1984.
————. *The Price of Victory*. London: BBC Press, 1983.
Clay, Gen. Lucius D. *Decision in Germany*. Garden City, N.Y.: Doubleday, 1950.
Cleveland, Harlan. *NATO: The Transatlantic Bargain*. New York: Harper & Row, 1970.
DePorte, A. W. *Europe Between the Superpowers*. New Haven, Conn.: Yale University Press, 1979.
DeSantis, Hugh. *The American Foreign Service and the Cold War*. Chicago: Chicago University Press, 1980.
Donovan, Robert J. *The Presidency of Harry S Truman*. 2 vols. New York: W. W. Norton & Co., 1977 and 1982.
Feis, Herbert. *Churchill, Roosevelt, Stalin: The War They Waged and the Peace They Sought*. Princeton, N.J.: Princeton University Press, 1957.
Forrestal, James. *The Forrestal Diaries*, edited by Walter Millis and E. S. Duffield. New York: Viking, 1951.
Grosser, Alfred. *The Western Alliance*. London: Macmillan, 1978.
Hamilton, Nigel. *Monty: The Field Marshal, 1944–1976*. London: Hamish Hamilton, 1986.
Harriman, W. Averell, and Elie Abel. *Special Envoy to Churchill and Stalin*. New York: Random House, 1975.
Henderson, Sir Nicholas. *The Birth of NATO*. London: Weidenfeld and Nicolson, 1982.
————. *The Private Office*. London: Weidenfeld and Nicolson, 1984.
Ireland, Timothy P. *Creating the Entangling Alliance*. Westport, Conn.: Aldwych Press, 1981.
Isaacson, Walter, and Evan Thomas. *The Wise Men: Six Friends and the World They Made*. Boston: Faber & Faber, 1986.
Jebb, Gladwyn. *Memoirs of Lord Gladwyn*. London: Weidenfeld & Nicolson, 1977.
Kee, Robert. *1945: The World We Fought For*. London: Hamish Hamilton, 1985.
Kennan, George F. *American Diplomacy, 1900–50*. Chicago: University of Chicago Press, 1951.
————. *Memoirs, 1925–50*. London: Hutchinson, 1968.
Lippmann, Walter. *The Cold War: A Study in U.S. Foreign Policy*. London: Hamish Hamilton, 1947.
Mee, Charles L., Jr. *The Marshall Plan: The Launching of the Pax Americana*. New York: Simon & Shuster, 1984.
Monnet, Jean. *Memoirs*. New York: Doubleday, 1978.
Mowat, R. C. *Ruin and Resurgence: Europe 1939–65*. London: Blandford Press, 1966.
Reid, Escott. *Time of Fear and Hope*. Toronto: McClelland and Stewart, 1977.

Staercke, André de, and others. *NATO's Anxious Birth*, edited by Nicholas Sherwen. London: C. Hurst, 1985.

Steel, Ronald. *Walter Lippmann and the American Century*. Boston: Atlantic Monthly Press, 1980.

Truman, Harry S. *Years of Trial and Hope: Memoirs, 1946–52*. Garden City, N.Y.: Doubleday & Company, 1956.

Vaizey, John. *The Squandered Peace*. London: Hodder & Stoughton, 1983.

Vandenberg, Arthur H., Jr. *The Private Papers of Senator Arthur Vandenberg*. London: Victor Gollancz, 1953.

Weisberg, Bernard A. *Cold War, Cold Peace*. Boston: Houghton Mifflin, 1984.

Wexler, Imanuel. *The Marshall Plan Revisited*. Westport, Conn.: Greenwood Press, 1983.

Index